A Guide

TO

Special Collections

OF THE

John Rylands University Library

OF

Manchester

For books are not absolutely dead things,
but do contain a potency of life in them.
MILTON, *Areopagitica.*

JOHN RYLANDS UNIVERSITY
LIBRARY OF MANCHESTER
1999

First published in Great Britain in 1999 by the
John Rylands University Library of Manchester.

Further copies of this *Guide* may be obtained
from the Audio-Visual Department,
John Rylands University Library of Manchester,
Oxford Road, Manchester, MI3 9PP, tel. 0161 275 3749.

Designed by John Hodgson using Adobe PageMaker.
Set in 11.5/13.5 and 9.5/10.5pt Adobe Garamond and
Garamond Expert, created by Robert Slimbach in 1989.
Covers designed by Neville Stott of Epigram, 3rd Floor,
Barclay House, 35 Whitworth Street West, Manchester,
MI 5NG, tel. 0161 237 9660.

Printed on 115 gsm Mellotex Super White paper by
Linneys Colour Print, Adamsway, Mansfield, Notts,
NGI8 4FL, tel. 01623 450450.

ISBN 0 86373 138 4

Cover illustrations. Top left: detail of the frontage of the
John Rylands Library, Deansgate. Left and bottom left:
details from Edward Young's *The Complaint and the
Consolation; or, Night Thoughts* (London: R. Edwards, 1797),
hand-coloured by William Blake, p. 49. Centre, left to right:
an 18th-century embroidered binding on a vellum copy of
Francesco Petrarch's *Sonetti et Canzoni* (Venice: Aldus, 1501);
miniature showing the dove returning to Noah's ark with an
olive branch, from a 13th-century French Bible picture-
book, or *Bible Historiée,* French MS 5, fo. 14r.; miniature of
Khusraw at Shirin's castle, from *Nizami: Khusraw and
Shirin,* Tabriz, c.1530 AD, Persian MS 6, fo. 43v.; Sumerian
cuneiform clay tablet concerning the conquest of Kish
under Agga, by Gilgamesh, 3rd millennium BC, Sumerian
Tablet 931. Bottom: lettering on the front of the John
Rylands Library, Deansgate, carved and gilded in 1992 by
staff from David Kindersley's workshop. Back cover: the
Main JRULM building off Oxford Road, Manchester.

Frontispiece: 'Archives' by Edwin Morgan, from *Selected
Poems* (Manchester: Carcanet Press, 1985).
Reproduced by courtesy of Edwin Morgan and Carcanet
Press. (*See page 149*)

A GUIDE TO
SPECIAL COLLECTIONS

Archives

generation upon
generation upon
generation upon
generation upon
generation upon
generation upon
generation upon
generation upon
generation upon
generation upon
generation upon
generation upon
generation upon
generation upon
generation upon
generation upon
generation upon
generation upon
generation upon
g neration upon
g neration up n
g nerat on up n
g nerat n up n
g nerat n p n
g   erat n p n
g   era   n p n
g   era   n   n
g   er   n   n
g   r   n   n
g   n   n
g   n
g

CONTENTS

PREFACE

This publication attempts, for the first time, to paint a comprehensive picture of the incredible wealth of primary source materials to be found in the Special Collections Division of the John Rylands University Library of Manchester. It is not intended to replace existing guides to research resources in particular fields, or the numerous catalogues and handlists of individual collections; rather, to serve as an initial entry point into the system of finding aids, enabling researchers to identify collections relevant to their studies.

The need for such a publication has long been felt. While the John Rylands University Library of Manchester is a comparatively young foundation, having been established in 1972, its predecessor institutions had long and distinguished histories: the John Rylands Library opened to the public in 1900, while the origins of the University of Manchester Library go back as far as 1851. Although brief overviews of the collections have been published previously (these are listed in the general bibliography) and many individual catalogues issued, researchers might reasonably argue that they have waited long enough for a comprehensive guide to the major collections.

It is particularly appropriate that such a *Guide* should be published now. Firstly, the compilation of the *Guide* has been facilitated by, and it in turn serves to promote, the major projects which have been underway since 1995 to improve access to the collections through the creation of on-line catalogues of printed books and archives. These projects have been generously supported by non-formula funding from the Higher Education Funding Council for England. Secondly, as the Library and the University of Manchester approach significant anniversaries in the years 2000 and 2001, the *Guide* celebrates the wonderful richness of the Special Collections, which constitute one of the University's greatest research assets, and a resource of international importance.

The *Guide* had modest beginnings, in early 1997, as a summary of the Library's many archive and manuscript collections. It was soon realized that its usefulness would be immeasurably enhanced if printed-book collections were also incorporated. Insect-like, it developed through several stages, in ever-growing computer-generated and photocopied forms, finally metamorphosing into a published edition. In any dynamic and growing library a guide to collections is likely to become out of date almost as soon as it is published. It is anticipated that future editions will take account of new acquisitions and developments in cataloguing, while the parallel, on-line version of this *Guide* will be regularly updated.

As editor I have been charged with putting the *Guide* together, and must accept the concomitant responsibility for all errors and deficiencies. However, the *Guide* is essentially a summation or epitome of the work of countless colleagues over many years, who must share any credit for the value of the publication. Of present colleagues I must thank particularly David Riley and John Canner, whose unrivalled knowledge of the printed-book collections at Deansgate and the Main Library has helped to bridge the many gaps in my own bibliographical expertise; Anne Young, who has answered countless queries concerning the manuscript collections; Stella Halkyard, who has supported the project throughout with her customary enthusiasm; Peter McNiven, who kindly put at my disposal earlier surveys of collections which he had compiled, and who also proof-read the entire text and made many useful comments; and Dorothy Clayton, who not only furnished a great deal of information on sources for North-West history but also greatly assisted in bringing the *Guide* to publication. Other colleagues who have generously offered advice or information, or upon whose earlier work I have drawn, include Fran Baker, Dave Brady, Alistair Cooper, John Gale, John Gandy, Jane Hudson, Caroline Hull, Chris Hunt, John Laidlar, Diana Leitch, Gareth Lloyd, Peter Nockles, the Rev. Ann Peart, Chris Perkins, James Peters, Jocelyn Richardson, Ian Rogerson, Brenda Scragg, Jacquie Sen, Judith Shiel, Katherine Thomas and Janet Wallwork. Jon Agar from the Centre for the History of Science, Technology and Medicine supplied information on the National Archive for the History of Computing. Marcia Pointon, Pilkington Professor of Art History, put forward several suggestions for material to be included in the *Guide*. Of the many former colleagues whose writings in the form of catalogues, handlists, guides, articles, exhibition captions and miscellaneous documents I have freely used, I can thank individually only the following who are known to me personally (others may be identified in citations): J.F. Coakley, Clive Field, Ruth Hobbins, Sarah Lawrance, Evelyn Lord, Glenise Matheson, David Moore, Alison Peacock, Alexander Samely, Jan Schmidt, Sarah Smith, John Tuck, Geoff Tweedale and Jacqueline Yallop.

The design of the Guide was inspired by the writings of two eminent typographers, Robert Bringhurst and the late Jan Tschichold. I have also benefited from the technical advice provided by Neville Stott of Epigram (who also designed the splendid covers), Keith Stubley of Sheffield, and Mike Bowker of Linneys Colour Print, who ensured a trouble-free passage through the press. Finally, my thanks must go to Mike Pollard of the Department of Art History and Archaeology for so expertly taking and developing the photographs.

John R. Hodgson
Co-ordinating Archivist

February 1999

The first advertisement for a book printed in England, William Caxton's *Ordinale Sarum* (Westminster: c.1477). One of only two extant copies, this handbill was annotated by a former owner, Dr Richard Farmer.
(*See page 22*)

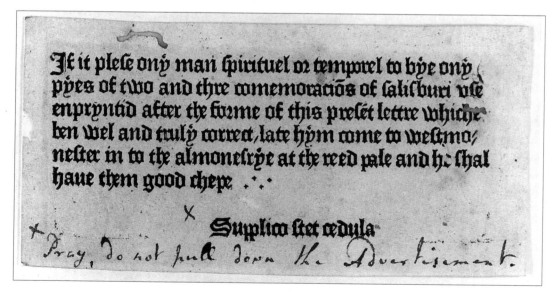

8

INTRODUCTION

The john rylands University Library of Manchester was formed in 1972 by the merger of Manchester University Library and the formerly independent John Rylands Library.

The origins of Manchester University Library may be traced back to 1851, when James Heywood donated some 1,200 volumes to the newly-opened Owens College, which half a century later became the Victoria University of Manchester. The College moved from its original premises on Quay Street to its present site on Oxford Road in 1873. The Library was first accommodated in a suite of rooms in the main building, but was later rehoused in purpose-built premises, erected between 1895 and 1898 to an early English Gothic design by Alfred Waterhouse. The building was constructed by the munificence of Professor Richard Copley Christie, and was named in his honour.

Early benefactors of Owens College Library included Bishop James Prince Lee, Angus Smith, E.A. Freeman, Walter L. Bullock and Christie himself, who bequeathed his fine collection of Renaissance literature from France and Italy. After Owens College became the University of Manchester in 1904, rapid expansion of the stock necessitated two extensions to the Christie Library, in 1914 and 1927, and eventually a completely new arts and social science library was opened in 1936. By 1972 the University Library held approximately one million books, of which 200,000 were deemed to be rare.

The John Rylands Library was founded by Mrs Enriqueta Augustina Rylands, as a memorial to her husband, who died in 1888. John Rylands was one of the most successful entrepreneurs of the 19th century, developing the family firm of Rylands & Sons into the largest cotton-manufacturing enterprise in Britain. He left a fortune of £2.75 million. Mrs Rylands commissioned the architect Basil Champneys to design her Library in the neo-Gothic style. Construction of the building on Deansgate, in the heart of Manchester, began in 1890 and was completed in 1899, the first readers being admitted on January 1st 1900.

Mrs Rylands's original intention had been to create a public reference and lending library with a bias towards Nonconformist theology. However, the purchase of two major collections transformed her foundation into a research library of international importance. In 1892 she purchased from Lord Spencer what was generally regarded as the finest library then in private ownership, comprising over 40,000 volumes, including some 4,000 incunables and many notable Bibles. Nine years later, in 1901, Mrs Rylands bought a collection of over 6,000 manuscripts in some fifty different languages, assembled by the 25th and 26th Earls of Crawford. The John Rylands Library's status as a research library of world-wide standing was thus assured.

Mrs Rylands generously endowed her Library to ensure its long-term viability after her death in 1908. However, the combined effects of inflation triggered by the First World War, and the decline of the Lancashire cotton industry from 1921 onwards, from which most of the Library's investment income was derived, seriously reduced the Library's financial base. Nevertheless, through donations and deposits the stock of the John Rylands Library continued to expand, and several extensions were made to the original Champneys building. By 1972 the John Rylands Library held approximately 570,000 printed books, 17,000 manuscripts and some 250,000 deeds, charters and papers, covering virtually every area of the humanities.

Formal and informal links between Manchester University Library and the John Rylands Library had always been close. Many of the University's academic staff had served on the Rylands Council of Governors, contributed to its lecture series, written for the *Bulletin of the John Rylands Library*, and assisted in cataloguing its collections. From 1949 the University had also provided financial assistance to the John Rylands Library to mitigate the shortfall in its income. This ever-closer co-operation culminated in 1972 in the merger of the two institutions into the John Rylands University Library of Manchester.

The outstanding collections of rare books, manuscripts and archives which both predecessor institutions had built up now constitute the Special Collections Division of the JRULM. The vast majority of these research resources are housed in the Deansgate Building of the former John Rylands Library, in Manchester's city-centre, while the teaching and reference stock and electronic resources are concentrated at the Main University Library.

In the last decade concerted efforts have been made to promote greater awareness of, and access to, the Library's Special Collections. In 1987 the John Rylands Research Institute was established to fund research, cataloguing, conservation and promotion of the collections, and the preservation and maintenance of the Deansgate Building. More recently the Library has been the recipient of generous non-formula funding from the Higher Education Funding Council for England (HEFCE). This has facilitated the retrospective conversion of the numerous manual catalogues of printed books into machine-readable form; for the first time scholars are able to search through a single database of the Library's printed books, not only within the Library itself but, with access to the Internet, from anywhere in the world. Moreover, many hitherto unlisted archive and printed-book collections have been newly catalogued, while significant improvements have been made to the Library's conservation resources and facilities. Hand-in-hand with these developments, there is an active outreach programme to promote the collections within the University of Manchester and among the wider academic community.

It is hoped that this *Guide* will serve further to promote knowledge and use of the outstanding Special Collections of the John Rylands University Library of Manchester.

Manuscripts and Archives

The Library's manuscript collections originated in Mrs Rylands's purchase of the personal collection of the Earl of Crawford in 1901. Holdings of individual manuscript items now cover more than fifty languages, including all the major European and Middle Eastern languages, and numerous Far Eastern scripts. They span five millennia, and are written on virtually every medium ever employed. The subject range is vast, encompassing literary, historical, antiquarian, genealogical, biblical, devotional, ritualistic, medical, scientific, legal and administrative texts.

The Library first acquired archive collections in the 1920s when local landed families were invited to donate or deposit their papers. In addition to family muniment collections, the Library now holds the archives of numerous companies, business associations, trade unions, charities, social organizations and religious institutions. The Methodist Church and other Nonconformist denominations are particularly well represented. The archives of Manchester University and the papers of individual scientists and academics are another important element in the Library's holdings, while the large archive of the *Manchester Guardian* newspaper is a key resource for a wide range of research interests. In another area, the Library is continually adding to its wealth of 20th-century literary and dramatic archives.

Printed Book Collections

The printed book collections of the JRULM are among the finest in the world. The foundation stone of the Library's printed collections was laid in 1892 when Mrs Rylands purchased the Spencer Collection. This was generally acknowledged to be the finest library then in private ownership. The JRULM holds some 4,000 incunables, representing over 500 European presses, including the largest collection of Aldines in the world and the second largest collection of works printed by Caxton. There are some 12,500 books printed between 1475 and 1640, and some 45,000 printed between 1641 and 1700. 18th- and 19th-century holdings comprise 160,000 and 400,000 volumes respectively.

These collections encompass almost all the landmarks of printing through five centuries, including magnificent illustrated books, examples of fine printing, landmark works in typography, key historical texts and exquisite bookbindings. They cover a wide range of subjects: theology and philosophy; economic, social, political and military history; travel and exploration; literature, drama and music; art and archaeology; science and medicine.

Guide to Special Collections

This *Guide* contains summary descriptions of the majority of the outstanding Special Collections held by the JRULM. In almost all cases more detailed finding aids to individual collections are available from the Library: these are cited in the *Guide*. It should also be noted that a subject card catalogue of printed books is available within the Deansgate Building. Some collections which are poorly documented or are of secondary importance have been omitted from the *Guide*. As new collections are acquired, or unlisted collections are catalogued, these will be incorporated into future editions. If the collection or subject you are interested in does not feature, please seek advice from the Library staff (see below).

In the following pages the Library's manuscript, archive and printed collections have been grouped into twelve subject/format categories, which are listed on the Contents page. Each section or chapter commences with a general description and alphabetical listing of the collections it encompasses; the descriptions of individual collections follow, manuscript/archive collections generally preceding printed-book collections. Many collections are diverse in their subject matter and research potential, and consequently feature in more than one category. An on-line version of this *Guide* is available at: http://rylibweb.man. ac.uk/data2/spcoll/.

All collections are housed at the Deansgate Building unless otherwise stated.

Catalogues

There is no single, comprehensive catalogue of all the collections in the Deansgate Building. The various catalogues of printed books are currently being computerized during a major project funded by the Higher Education Funding Council for England (HEFCE). By the time of publication records from the principal Deansgate catalogues will be available on the Library's computer catalogue, and will be accessible via the Internet at http://rylibweb. man.ac.uk/spcollcat. The principal catalogues include: (a) the printed Guardbook Catalogue in seven volumes, listing the John Rylands Library's acquisitions between 1889 and c.1896, most notably the Spencer Collection; (b) the Supplementary Catalogue on slips recording accessions between c.1896 and 1978; (c) the Special Collections card catalogue containing details of rare books transferred from the Main Library to Deansgate since 1972, together with all books added to stock since 1978; (d) the published catalogue of the Christie Collection. In addition to the retrospective conversion programme, original cataloguing is taking place on over twenty discrete printed collections. Readers are advised that, while the majority of Deansgate printed books will be recorded in the 'Special Collections' computer catalogue, some discrete collections and recently-acquired materials are available in the 'Main' catalogue.

There are also numerous published and unpublished finding aids to the Library's manuscript and archival collections. Many archive catalogues have been produced since 1995 as part of another HEFCE-funded project, and it is intended that these will be made available on-line, via the Internet, in the near future. The majority of the manuscript and archive finding aids have also been reproduced on microfiche in the *National Inventory of Documentary Sources in the United Kingdom and Ireland*, copies of which are available in a number of major research libraries across the world.

General Bibliography

The *Bulletin of the John Rylands University Library of Manchester* (first published in 1903 and until 1972 entitled the *Bulletin of the John Rylands Library*) is the most important of the Library's publications. For many years each issue included a 'Notes and News' section containing details of each important collection as soon as it had been acquired. Indexes to the *Bulletin* for volumes 1–25, 26–50 and 51–60 have so far been published. Recent acquisitions are now reported in the *John Rylands Research Institute Newsletter*.

Catalogue of the Printed Books in the John Rylands Library, 3 vols (Manchester, 1899), contains details of the Spencer Collection and other printed collections acquired by c.1896; it was reproduced on microfiche by Chadwyck-Healey (see below).

Chadwyck-Healey, *Catalogue of Printed Books in the Rare Books Division of the John Rylands University Library of Manchester* (Cambridge, 1989). This microfiche edition of the Library's principal research catalogues gives details of holdings up to 1978. It was issued in two parts: the Guardbook Catalogue of 1899 (3,972 pp.), and the Supplementary Slip Catalogue (501,933 slips).

Henry Guppy, *The John Rylands Library, Manchester, 1899–1924: a Record of its History with Brief Descriptions of the Building and its Contents* (Manchester, 1924).

Henry Guppy, *The John Rylands Library, Manchester, 1899–1935: a Brief Record of its History with Descriptions of the Building and its Contents* (Manchester, 1935).

The Riches of the Rylands: Prospectus of the John Rylands Research Institute (Manchester, 1993).

Frank Taylor, *The John Rylands University Library of Manchester* (Manchester, 1982).

Frank Taylor, 'The John Rylands Library, 1936–72', *Bulletin of the John Rylands University Library of Manchester*, vol. 71, no. 2 (1989), pp. 39–66.

Moses Tyson, 'The First Forty Years of the John Rylands Library', *Bulletin of the John Rylands Library*, vol. 25 (1941), pp. 46-66.

Admission to the Deansgate Building for reading purposes is by ticket only, either a valid University of Manchester Library card or a ticket issued from Deansgate itself. In the latter case prior written application is normally required though immediate admission may sometimes be possible on production of a letter of introduction and/or formal proof of identity. In either case additional identification or authorization may be requested where the reader wishes to consult especially rare books or manuscripts, or certain deposited collections. The Library reserves the right to refuse applications for tickets in the interests of the conservation and security of stock. No charge is made for readers' tickets issued from the Deansgate Building. Special access arrangements for external users apply at the Main University Library. In all cases readers are advised to contact the Library in advance of their visit.

DEANSGATE BUILDING
John Rylands University Library,
150 Deansgate, Manchester, M3 3EH
Telephone: +44 (0)161 834 5343
Fax: +44 (0)161 834 5574

General enquiries: Dr Peter McNiven, Head of Special Collections
Archive enquiries: John Hodgson, Co-ordinating Archivist
Modern literary archive enquiries: Stella Halkyard, 20th-Century Literary Archivist
Methodist enquiries: Dr Peter Nockles, Methodist Church Archivist.

MAIN LIBRARY
John Rylands University Library,
Oxford Road, Manchester, M13 9PP
Telephone: +44 (0)161 275 3738
Fax: +44 (0)161 275 7488

General enquiries: Ms Janet Wallwork, Reference and Enquiry Librarian.

De inutilibus libris.

Inter precipuos pars est mihi reddita stultos
  Prima:rego docili fastaꝗ vela manu.
En ego possideo multos/quos raro libellos
  Perlego:tum lectos negligo;nec sapio.

De
bus

Primus inexcelsa teneo ꝗ naue rudentes
Stultiuagosꝗ sequor comites per flumina vasta:
Non ratione vacat certa:sensuꝗ latenti :
Congestis etenim stultus confido libellis   b.iii

HISTORY OF THE BOOK & GENERAL PRINTED COLLECTIONS

FROM the earliest years of its existence, with the acquisition of the Spencer Collection, the John Rylands Library has housed one of the most important collections in the world relating to the birth and development of Western printing and the history of the book. The merger with the University Library in 1972 added the Christie and Bullock collections, particularly rich in Italian and French printing, to the Rylands's holdings.

There are now over 4,000 Incunabula in the Library, most of which date from between 1455 and 1480, representing more than 500 European presses, some being the only known copies. Germany, Italy, France, the Netherlands, Spain and England all feature prominently; the texts printed by Caxton represent the second largest collection in the world. A concise conspectus of early printing is afforded by the Hiero von Holtorp Collection, which contains specimen leaves from virtually all 15th- and 16th-century printers in Germany, Italy, France, Spain, the Netherlands and England.

For the 16th century, the Library's greatest strengths lie in the field of Italian printing. The largest Aldine Collection in the world contains virtually every work produced by Aldus Manutius and his Venetian successors between 1495 and 1598, while the Bullock Collection holds an even wider range of Italian writers.

As a whole the collection of early printed books constitutes one of the world's principal resources for the study of European publication of the classics of Greece and Rome, as well as of the writings of late medieval and early modern authors.

The Library holds some 12,500 books printed between 1475 and 1640, and a further 210,000 printed between 1641 and 1800. They cover a wide range of subjects: theology, history, literature, travel and exploration, science and medicine. The first and finest editions of later authors in the European canon of great writers have been systematically sought. De-luxe editions, extra-illustrated and large-paper copies and fine bindings are plentiful, but there are also substantial collections of working-class literature, such as broadsides and chapbooks.

Notable collections include the Tabley Book Collection, a fine country-house library from Tabley House in Cheshire which incorporates many 17th- and 18th-century works; the library from Sedbergh School in Cumbria, a representative example of a public-school library, ranging in date from the 16th century to the 20th and full of bibliographical interest; the Lloyd Roberts Collection, which contains numerous first editions of major English authors; and the Shackleton Collection, which is especially rich in 18th-century French and English publications. Fine printing in the 18th century is further represented by the Glaswegian Foulis Press Collection, and by the works of the greatest English and Italian printers of the period, John Baskerville and Giambattista Bodoni. The Library also holds comprehensive collections of publications by several exclusive bibliographical societies founded in the 19th century, such as the Roxburghe Club and the Scottish Bannatyne and Maitland Clubs.

An outstanding Private Press Collection (including complete or near-complete collections of books from the Kelmscott, Doves, Ashendene and Essex House Presses), is complemented by the Casdagli Collection of first editions and books from the Gregynog and Golden Cockerel Presses.

There are countless fine bindings among the Library's collections, ranging from original bindings of the 15th century through to contemporary design bindings. Bindings of the 16th to 18th centuries may be found among the Spencer, Christie, Bullock and Aldine collections, while the Lloyd Roberts Collection includes a large number of fine bindings from the 15th and 16th centuries, such as those produced for Grolier and Grimaldi, as well as the work of 19th-century trade binders such as Zaehnsdorf and Bedford. The Library holds the largest extant collection of bindings by Roger Payne, the greatest English binder of the 18th century, as well as a collection of his bills (English MSS 440 and 944). The reinvigoration of bookbinding in the late 19th century, as part of the Arts and Crafts re vival, is shown in examples of the output of the Doves Bindery and the work of individual craft binders such as Douglas Cockerell and Katherine Adams within the Private Press Collection. Finally the two Tregaskis Collections constitute an unique synopsis of the state of fine bookbinding throughout the world in 1894 and 1994.

Other collections relating to the history of the book include the Viner Collection of bookplates designed by Charles William Sherborn and John Paul Rylands; the Cassedy Collection of Irish texts, including works on local history, topography, genealogy, the Protestant and Catholic faiths and the Gaelic language; the Strachan Collection of works on Celtic and Scandinavian language, literature, history, archaeology, art and folklore; the Deaf Education Collection of books from the 16th to 19th centuries on the education of the deaf; and the Neil Salvesen Collection which contains many scarce works in and about Esperanto.

It should also be noted that the John Rylands Library Archive (p. 192) contains much information on the acquisition of printed books by Mrs Rylands and her Library.

Bibliography

Catalogue of the Owens College Library, 5 vols (Manchester, 1894–99).

Thomas Frognall Dibdin, *Bibliotheca Spenceriana*, 7 vols (London, 1814–23).

Campbell Dodgson, *Woodcuts of the Fifteenth Century in the John Rylands Library* (Manchester, 1915).

E. Gordon Duff, *Catalogue of Books in the John Rylands Library, Manchester, Printed in England, Scotland and Ireland and of Books in English Printed Abroad to the End of the Year 1640* (Manchester, 1895).

English Incunabula in the John Rylands Library: a Catalogue of Books Printed in England and of English Books Printed Abroad, 1475–1500 (Manchester, 1930).

'Exhibition of Library Bindings', *Bulletin of the John Rylands Library*, vol. 54 (1972), pp. 241–5.

Nigel Griffin, 'Spanish Incunabula in the John Rylands University Library of Manchester', *Bulletin of the John Rylands University Library of Manchester*, vol. 70, no. 2 (1988), pp. 3–141.

Charles W.E. Leigh, *Catalogue of the Christie Collection Bequeathed to the Library of the University of Manchester* (Manchester, 1915).

Anthony Lister, 'The Althorp Library of Second Earl Spencer, now in the John Rylands University Library of Manchester: its Formation and Growth', *Bulletin of the John Rylands University Library of Manchester*, vol. 71, no. 2 (1989), pp. 67–86.

Select alphabetical list of resources:

Aldine Collection

1,500 items.

Both Lord Spencer and Richard Copley Christie assiduously collected Aldines, and therefore the Library has many duplicate and variant copies. Of the 127 authenticated editions printed by Aldus Manutius from 1495 to 1515, the Library lacks only seven very rare and minor items. There is also a virtually complete collection of all the publications of the Aldine Press from 1515 to 1598. The Rylands collection of Aldines includes a substantial number of vellum copies. These are almost all ornately illuminated and form valuable source material for the study of book decoration. The Library has nineteen Aldine editions and variants of Baldassare Castiglione's *Il Libro del Cortegiano* (*The Book of Courtesy*) printed between 1528 and 1553. The collection also contains over 150 counterfeit Aldines, mainly printed at Lyon.

Finding aids: recorded in general printed-book catalogue; the collection is also recorded in a marked-up copy of Renouard's *Annales de l'imprimerie des Aldes*.

Bannatyne and Maitland Collection

250 items (dispersed).

The Bannatyne Club, the exclusive Edinburgh bibliographical society, was limited to 31 members at its institution in 1817. They included the Scottish judge, Sir William McLeod

Bannatyne. A complete set is available of the 176 volumes published by the Club up to 1867. These are a major source for Scottish literature and history, as are the publications of the Glaswegian Maitland Club, founded in March 1828 to honour the Scottish poet and lawyer, Sir Richard Maitland, Lord Lethington. Again, a complete set of the publications of this society up to 1859 is available.

Finding aids: recorded in general printed-book catalogue.

Baskerville Collection

30 items (dispersed).

The Library holds over half of the entire output of John Baskerville (1706–75) of Birmingham, England's greatest 18th-century printer. Baskerville's first and arguably finest work, the 1757 Virgil, is available in two different states, one with the extra illustrations supplied by the plates from Ogilby's translation printed in 1654. Among other classical authors are Horace (1762), Lucretius (1772) and Terence (1772), while English works include Milton (1758 and 1759), Addison (1761), and Lord Shaftesbury (1773), together with the *Book of Common Prayer* of 1760–62, and the Bibles of 1763 and 1769–72.

Finding aids: recorded in general printed-book catalogue. See also David W. Riley, 'English Books of the Seventeenth to Nineteenth Centuries in the John Rylands University Library of Manchester, with Particular Reference to History and Literature', *Bulletin of the John Rylands University Library of Manchester*, vol. 71, no. 2 (1989), pp. 95–6.

Bodoni Collection

200 items (dispersed).

The Library's collection of books printed by Giambattista Bodoni (1740–1813), the greatest Italian printer of the period, includes eight duplicates and twenty items not recorded by Giani or Renouard. The total consists solely of books, with no examples of the ephemeral material, lottery tickets, passports and inscriptions issued at Parma. The Library has 127 of the titles listed by Giani together with fourteen of the items from the Royal Press and one of the typographic works, the famous *Manuale Tipografico* of 1818. Of almost equal importance is the 1806 folio edition of the *Oratio Dominica*. Authors printed by Bodoni include Longus, Torquato Tasso, Lodovico Ariosto, Francesco Petrarch, Giovanni Battista Guarini, Giovanni Fantoni, Luigi Cerretti, Prospero Manara and Maria Luisa Cicci. Available in Manchester are both the 1795 and 1796 editions of Dante, the earlier being copy number 42 presented by Bodoni to Lord Spencer.

Finding aids: recorded in general printed-book catalogue.

Bullock Collection

The collection now contains only 16th- and 17th-century items; most post-1640 works were integrated into the main stock of the University Library, from which pre-1801 material was subsequently removed to the general Special Collections stock.

5,000 items.

The collection was formed by Walter Llewellyn Bullock, first in Chicago and later in Manchester, where he was Professor of Italian Studies from 1935 until his death in 1944. It illustrates the literature and social life of Italy, with over 2,600 items dating from the 16th century. The major Italian authors are, of course, represented, but the greatest strength of the collection lies in the large number of works by minor and obscure authors which it contains. Authors like Lodovico Dolce, Lodovico Domenichi, Giovanni Battista Gelli,

Giovanni Battista Giraldi, Girolamo Muzio and Francesco Sansovino are represented by between five and 50 items each. There are over 100 16th-century comedies and 50 tragedies together with over 200 works of literary theory. Other subjects for which a substantial number of items is available in the collection are medicine, religion, education, law, letter writing, travel and the art of war.

Finding aids: recorded in general printed-book catalogue. See also Walter L. Bullock, 'A Collection of *Cinquecento* Books', *Italica*, vol. 8, no. 4 (1931), pp. 1–6.

History of the Book & General Printed Collections

Casdagli Collection

200 items.

Part of the library of Olga X. Casdagli of Southport, Lancashire, bequeathed on her death in 1988. The collection comprises Private Press books of the 1920s and 1930s, particularly from the Golden Cockerel and Gregynog Presses, as well as works, many in signed first editions, of George Meredith, Lewis Carroll, Oscar Wilde, T.S. Eliot, David Jones, Charles Morgan and Norman Douglas.

Finding aids: recorded in general printed-book catalogue.

See also the Private Press Collection (p. 22).

Cassedy Collection

1,200 items (dispersed).

The collection was formed by James Cassedy (Seamus O Casaide), the Celtologist and bibliographer. There are some 200 periodicals, Dublin and provincial newspapers, directories, almanacs and chapbooks. The books, which include some exceedingly rare titles, date mainly from the late 18th and early 19th centuries. Subjects covered include genealogy, local history, both the Protestant and Roman Catholic faiths, Gaelic dictionaries, grammars and texts, Anglo-Irish verse and prose, natural history and topography. There is a special section devoted to the publications of Patrick Lynch (1754–1818), the Secretary of the Gaelic Union of Dublin.

Finding aids: recorded in general printed-book catalogue; see also bookseller's catalogue.

Christie Collection

8,000 items.

Professor Richard Copley Christie bequeathed his collection to the University of Manchester in 1901. Christie formed his collection "with a view of illustrating and enabling its owner to study the Renaissance, and especially the classical Renaissance of Italy and France,… and the lives, labours and works of a certain limited number of scholars upon whose lives and labours I had at one time hoped to write something. Etienne Dolet, Aldus, Pomponatius, Clenardus, Giulio Camillo, Ramus, Sturm, Postel, J.C. Scaliger, Paul Scaliger, Giordano Bruno, Vanini, Scioppius, Hortensio Lando are some of these."

The Christie Collection includes an unrivalled set of virtually all the Greek texts published in the 15th and 16th centuries, together with a very substantial collection of Aldines (see p. 17). Christie acquired over 50 counterfeit Aldines printed at Lyon between 1502 and 1527, some of which are rarer than genuine editions. While the collection is not remarkable for its holdings of major Italian authors such as Ariosto, Boccaccio and Dante, it does contain a very representative collection of Italian printers up to 1550 with nearly 190 houses being included. As an indication of the quality of 16th-century French printing to be found in the collection, there are 55 works produced by the Parisian press of Simon de Colines and 40 works printed by his successor, Robert Estienne, 44 books issued by Étienne Dolet of Lyon, and no less than 550 titles from the *atelier* of Sebastian Gryphius in Lyon.

Christie specialized in collecting editions of the work of authors about whom he hoped to write at a future date including Pietro Pomponazzi (eighteen items), Giulio Camillo (nineteen items), Giordano Bruno (45 items), Ortensio Lando (73 items), Étienne Dolet (113 items, including seven unique titles), Guillaume Postel (72 items), and Caspar Schoppe (216 items). Christie believed that it would be difficult, if not impossible, for others to match, let alone surpass, such comprehensive collections. Another indication of the strength of the Christie Collection is that it includes over 800 editions of Horace.

Among the many fine bindings in the Christie Collection are examples of the work of Francis Bedford, Roger de Coverly, Christian Kalthoeber, Charles Lewis, Roger Payne, Robert Rivière and Joseph Zaehnsdorf in England; and of Bauzonnet, Chambolle-Duru, Derome, Duseuil, Padeloup, Simier and Trautz in France.

Finding aids: recorded in general printed-book catalogue. See also Charles W.E. Leigh, *Catalogue of the Christie Collection bequeathed to the Library of the University of Manchester* (Manchester, 1915).

Deaf Education Collection

11,000 items.

The Library for Deaf Education, or Deaf Education Collection, is probably the most important collection on surdo-mutism in the British Isles. It was established in Manchester University Library in 1919 with the aid of a grant from the Carnegie United Kingdom Trust, and out of this grant the Arnold Library was purchased from the National College of Teachers of the Deaf in 1922. Abraham Farrar donated to the Library his valuable collection of books relating to deafness, many of them rare, in 1932.

See also the Henry Baker Papers (p. 175).

The collection as a whole comprises over 11,000 items, and includes works dealing with the various systems of teaching the deaf, lip-reading, speech therapy, the psychology of speech and hearing, phonetics, acoustics, and the anatomy, physiology and diseases of the ear, as well as sociological, historical and other works concerning the deaf. The bulk of the collection, comprising modern monographs and periodicals, is held at the Main University Library. The Farrar Collection is located at Deansgate, together with other rare material removed from the rest of the Library for Deaf Education or acquired since 1932.

There are approximately 1,000 items dating from the 16th century to the 19th century. Authors include Jan Conraad Amman, Thomas Arnold, Charles and Henry Baker, Alexander Graham Bell, Franz Hermann Czech, Daniel Defoe, Charles-Michel de l'Épée, Manuel Ramirez de Carrion, John Wallis and Paulo Zacchia, together with many early editions of classical authors who mentioned deafness in their works.

Finding aids: recorded in general printed-book catalogue. See also published catalogues, Abraham Farrar, *An Annotated Catalogue of Books on the Education of the Deaf and Cognate Subjects* (Stoke-on-Trent, 1932); Charles W.E. Leigh, *Catalogue of the Library for Deaf Education* (Manchester, 1932).

Location: JRULM (Deansgate and Main Library).

Foulis Press Collection

150 items (dispersed).

The brothers Robert and Andrew Foulis printed some 600 titles in Glasgow from 1740 to 1776, and the press was carried on rather less actively until 1806 by Andrew Foulis the younger. The Library's collection of 150 titles, which derive from the Spencer Collection (p. 25), is not large by international standards, but it includes a high proportion of the editions of Greek and Latin texts for which the press was noted. These include the only recorded vellum copy of the 1748 Epictetus; the silk copies of the 1751 Anacreon and the 1754 Pindar; and four works with bindings bearing the coat of arms of Louis XV: the 1761 Herodotus and the 1762, 1764 and 1767 editions of Xenophon.

Finding aids: recorded in general printed-book catalogue. See also David W. Riley, 'English Books of the Seventeenth to Nineteenth Centuries in the John Rylands University Library of Manchester, with Particular Reference to History and Literature', *Bulletin of the John Rylands University Library of Manchester*, vol. 71, no. 2 (1989), p. 95.

Hiero von Holtorp Collection

The collection consists of specimen 15th- and 16th-century leaves from virtually all printers of Germany, Italy, France, Spain, the Netherlands and England. Holtorp, who spent over 50 years accumulating and arranging the items, attached notes of identification to each specimen, thus tracing the progress of printing in each town represented. In addition, there are five portfolios of borders and alphabets, two of engravings and etchings, three portfolios of titles and printers' devices, and no less than eight portfolios of woodcuts, four German, two French and two miscellaneous. The woodcuts include major works of Dürer and other early masters. The original twenty lots, sold at Sotheby's on 29 March 1906, are now stored in ten large boxes.

Finding aids: auctioneer's catalogue, Sotheby, Wilkinson and Hodge, *Catalogue of valuable books including H von Holtorp's typographical and xylographic collections sold by auction on 27 March 1906 and four following days* (London, 1906).

Incunabula Collection

4,500 items.

The Library has fifteen block-books and a number of block-prints, including the *St Christopher Woodcut*, the only surviving example of the first piece of European printing bearing a date, 1423. Of the collection of incunables, 3,000 come from the Spencer Collection (p. 25), 215 were bequeathed by Richard Copley Christie (p. 19), and the remainder have been acquired from other sources. Approximately 1,000 are of German origin, about 2,000 were printed in Italy and the remainder represent the presses of other European countries and of England.

Of the earliest type-printed documents to which a place or date can be assigned there are the Letters of Indulgence of Pope Nicholas V, the 36- and 42-line Bibles, the first three Mainz Psalters and in all about 50 productions of the Mainz press associated with Gutenberg, Fust and Schöffer, several being the only recorded copies. The Library has the only complete examples in Britain of books printed by Albrecht Pfister in Bamberg. The work of over 100 German presses is represented in the Collection.

In Manchester there are 66 volumes printed by Sweynheym and Pannartz, the first printers in Italy working in Subiaco and Rome between 1465 and 1473. It is the most complete collection in the country, lacking only the Aristotle and Perottus of 1473. 253 printers working in nearly 50 different Italian towns are represented on the Library's shelves. There are 349 volumes printed in Rome (329 separate editions) and these include 39 items printed by Ulrich Han. Of particular importance is Han's 1467 edition of the *Meditationes* of Cardinal Turrecremata, the only copy in the country of the first Italian illustrated book. Venetian incunables total 576 volumes (485 separate editions), with 42 printed by Vindelinus de Spira and 43 by Nicholas Jenson. Other Italian towns for which significant numbers of incunables are available include Milan (125 volumes, 111 separate editions of which 30 were printed by Zarotus), Florence (110 volumes, 93 separate editions), and Naples (100 volumes, 96 separate editions). The 49 volumes of 44 separate editions printed in Brescia are of particular importance as ten are not available elsewhere in Britain, and five items, the work of Thomas Ferrandus, are unique.

There are some 30 examples of the first Parisian printers, Gering, Friburger and Crantz, and about 100 other examples of the work of other printers in the French capital. French provincial printers are also well represented, particularly those of Lyon and Toulouse, a unique item from the latter town being the 1488 edition of Aesop with Spanish text.

Some twenty Spanish incunables are in the Library, together with a significant number of items originating in the Low Countries including William Caxton's first book (and the first book ever printed in English), *The Recuyell of the Histories of Troye* (Brugge, ?1473).

The English incunables include over 60 Caxtons of which 36 are complete and unsophisticated, and four are unique, constituting the second largest such collection in the world. Other English printers well represented include John Lettou, William de Machlinia, Richard Pynson, Julian Notary, the Schoolmaster printer of St Albans, and Wynkyn de Worde, the copy of whose 1498 edition of *Morte Darthur* is unique; the Library also has one of the only two surviving copies of the Caxton edition of *Morte Darthur*.

Approaching three-quarters of the incunables date from before 1480. "Ephemera" include advertisements (Strasbourg, Mentelin, c.1471; Westminster, Caxton, c.1477), and the only surviving wood block used to print a block-book, an as yet unidentified variant edition of the *Apocalypse*.

Finding aids: recorded in general printed-book catalogue and on the Incunabula Short Title Catalogue (ISTC) database. See also the Bibliography above.

Private Press Collection

600 items (dispersed).

See also the Casdagli Collection (p. 19), the Tregaskis Collections (p. 26) and the Peter Huchel Collection (p. 152).

This comprises all 53 publications of William Morris's Kelmscott Press, including a vellum copy of the press's masterpiece, the 1896 edition of Chaucer's *Works*; all but one of the works of T.J. Cobden-Sanderson's Doves Press; and most of the publications of C.H. St John Hornby's Ashendene Press and the Essex House Press of C.R. Ashbee. The Library also possesses a volume of original drawings and designs for the masterpiece of the Essex House Press, *The Prayer Book of King Edward VIII* (1903). In addition there are smaller numbers of publications from the Daniel, Dun Emer/Cuala, Eragny, Golden Cockerel, Gregynog, Nonesuch, Shakespeare Head and Vale Presses, and a selection of works from contemporary presses such as Gwasg Gregynog, the Fleece Press, the Rampant Lions Press and the Whittington Press. There is also much ephemeral material such as announcements, prospectuses, catalogues and specimen pages. Altogether the collection provides a complete conspectus of 20th-century British wood-engraving.

Finding aids: recorded in general printed-book catalogue. See also David W. Riley, '"A Definite Claim to Beauty": Some Treasures from the Rylands Private Press Collection', *Bulletin of the John Rylands University Library of Manchester*, vol. 72, no. 2 (1990), pp. 73–88.

Lloyd Roberts Collection

5,000 items.

David Lloyd Roberts, the distinguished Manchester doctor and bibliophile, bequeathed his books to the Library, and the items were accessioned in the 1920s. A substantial portion of the collection is devoted to first editions of major English authors ranging from Thomas Browne to Lord Byron and John Ruskin. However, the bequest added significantly to the Library's holdings of early editions of Ariosto and Dante Alighieri, and the collection also contains some mid 18th-century costume books by Tommaso Maria Mamachi. Also included are a large number of fine bindings dating from the 15th and 16th centuries, such as those produced for Jean Grolier and for Giovanni Battista Grimaldi, with the characteristic Apollo and Pegasus cameo stamp. There are also numerous examples of the work of 19th-century binders such as Zaehnsdorf, Bedford and Chambolle-Duru.

Finding aids: recorded in general printed-book catalogue. See also David W. Riley, 'English Books of the Seventeenth to Nineteenth Centuries in the John Rylands University Library of Manchester, with Particular Reference to History and Literature', *Bulletin of the John Rylands University Library of Manchester*, vol. 71, no. 2 (1989), pp. 98–9.

Roxburghe Club Collection

300 items (dispersed).

The Library has the copy of the 1471 Valdarfer edition of Boccaccio, sold by the Duke of Roxburghe in 1812 for the then record price of £2,200, after which event the Roxburghe Club was founded. The Library also holds a complete set of the publications of the Club, many of the volumes being the personal copies of members. Worthy of special notice is Lord Spencer's own copy, uniquely printed on vellum and handsomely illuminated, of *The First Three Books of Ovid De Tristibus*, translated into English by Thomas Churchyarde (1816). This was the third publication of the Club, and the first to be presented to its members by the President, Lord Spencer.

Finding aids: recorded in general printed-book catalogue.

Neil Salvesen Esperanto Collection

710 items.

This important collection of books published in and about Esperanto once formed part of the extensive library of Neil Salvesen (1944–90). For most of his adult life Salvesen held administrative posts in the textile industry. He was introduced to Esperanto by a friend and quickly became an enthusiastic Esperantist and active member of the Manchester Esperanto Society. A little over two years before his early death in 1990 he was appointed an official of the Universal Esperanto Association (Universala Esperanto-Asocio) and was based in Rotterdam. The collection is arranged according to broad subject groups: encyclopaedias and dictionaries; original and translated poetry; original works; translated works; works in other languages about Esperanto; and journals and yearbooks. The significance of the collection is indicated by the fact that, of the 710 volumes present, only 246 are to be found in the Library of Congress, and a mere 66 are held by the British Library.

Finding aids: recorded in general printed-book catalogue; see also unpublished handlist. Location: JRULM (Main Library).

Sedbergh School Library

900 items.

The historic library of Sedbergh School in Cumbria (formerly the North Riding of Yorkshire) was deposited on permanent loan in 1972–73. The school was founded in 1525 by Dr Roger Lupton, Provost of Eton and a native of Sedbergh, and endowed by him with lands associated with a chantry. The constitution of the school was revised by the Endowed Schools Commissioners in 1874, when the buildings were greatly enlarged. Today Sedbergh is an independent boarding school for boys with 350 pupils.

The collection is a good representative example of an English public-school library. Of the 900 volumes, approximately 300 date from the 16th to 18th centuries. Prominent among these are works of Classical literature, including an edition of Horace (Paris, 1519); historical works such as Matthew Parker's *De Antiquitate Ecclesiae et Privilegiis Ecclesiae Cantuariensis*, revised by Samuel Drake (London, 1729); and also religious texts, for example the works of Peter the Martyr (Zurich, 1567), and Benedictus Aretius's *Commentarii in Quatuor Evangelistas* (Morges, 1580). The remainder of the collection, dating from the 19th and 20th centuries, covers a broad subject range, and includes works in Spanish, German and French. More popular series include *The Story of the Nations*, a French ten-volume *Histoire Générale*, and *Stanford's Compendium of Geography*. There are several presentation volumes from eminent old-boys.

Finding aids: cataloguing in progress.

Shackleton Collection

3,300 items.

The collecting activities of Robert Shackleton (1919–86), one-time Marshal Foch Professor of French Literature at the University of Oxford and Bodley's Librarian, were particularly associated with the publications of the Age of Enlightenment, and therefore the collection has made possible substantial additions to the Library's holdings of 18th-century publications in French and English. The collection's strength is in 18th- and 19th-century French studies, especially literature, philosophy and civilization, with some 3,000 works published before 1850. However, the collection also contains some 200 16th-century Italian books. There are a significant number of counterfeit editions, encyclopaedic dictionaries and reference works.

Finding aids: recorded in general printed-book catalogue. See also John P. Tuck, 'French Studies: a Guide to Research Resources in the John Rylands University Library of Manchester', *Bulletin of the John Rylands University Library of Manchester*, vol. 72, no. 2 (1990), pp. 12–14.

Spencer Collection

History of the Book & General Printed Collections

43,000 items.

In 1892 Mrs Rylands purchased from John Poyntz Spencer (1835–1910), 5th Earl Spencer, what was acknowledged to be the finest library in private ownership, notable for its outstanding collection of Bibles (see p. 66). The majority of the items were acquired at the end of the 18th century and the beginning of the 19th century by George John (1758–1834), 2nd Earl Spencer, although both earlier and later acquisitions were made by other members of the Spencer family.

Lord Spencer's prime concern in building his collection was to acquire first editions of the Greek and Latin classics and to establish a complete collection of Aldines (see p. 17). He visited Italy to accomplish his aims, purchasing, for example, a large portion of the Neapolitan library of the Duke of Cassano-Serra. However, Spencer did not neglect other aspects of collecting both by language and by date: it is estimated that the Collection contains 10,000 Italian books of all periods, one quarter of the total. Spencer subscribed to many 18th- and early 19th-century publications, and his wide interests can be illustrated by the large number of editions of the works of Vitruvius, Andrea Palladio and Leon Battista Alberti which he possessed.

Today the Spencer Collection, including the libraries of Count Reviczky, Stanesby Alchorne and the Duke of Cassano-Serra, is of fundamental importance for the history of printing in Europe in the era of the hand-press, with all the important presses represented.

Finding aids: recorded in general printed-book catalogue. See also *Catalogue of the Printed Books in the John Rylands Library*, 3 vols (Manchester, 1899), which contains details of the Spencer Collection, reproduced on microfiche by Chadwyck-Healey, 1989; Thomas Frognall Dibdin, *Bibliotheca Spenceriana*, 7 vols (London, 1814–23); Anthony Lister, 'The Althorp Library of Second Earl Spencer, now in the John Rylands University Library of Manchester: its formation and growth', *Bulletin of the John Rylands University Library of Manchester*, vol. 71, no. 2 (1989), pp. 67–86.

Strachan Book Collection

See also the John Strachan Papers (p. 189).

600 items.

The personal library of John Strachan (1862–1907), one of the greatest Celtologists of the 19th century. Strachan was Hulme Professor of Greek, 1885–1907, and Professor of Sanskrit and Comparative Religion, 1890–1907, in Owens College and later the University of Manchester. In 1904, in recognition of his outstanding contribution to Celtic scholarship, he was appointed lecturer in Celtic. After Strachan's death his personal library was purchased by friends and colleagues and presented to the University Library. It contains a number of rare printed works from the 16th, 17th and 18th centuries. Among those of most interest to Celtic studies are Bedell's translation of the Old Testament into Irish (London, 1685), Connor Begly's *English-Irish Dictionary* (Paris, 1732), John Davies's *Antiquae Linguae Britannicae Dictionarium Duplex* (London, 1632), James Johnstone's *Antiquitates Celto-Scandicae* (Copenhagen, 1786), Edward Lhuyd's *Archaeologica Britannica* (Oxford, 1707), Francis Molloy's *Lucerna Fidelium* (Rome, 1676), John O'Brien's *Focalóir Gaoidhilge-SaxBhéarla* (Paris, 1768), John David Rhys's Welsh grammar (London, 1592), and John Smith's *Gaelic Antiquities* (Edinburgh, 1780).

However, a very wide range of languages, many esoteric, is represented in the collection: Albanian, Armenian, Avestic, Breton, Cornish, Early English, French, Greek, Irish, Latin, Lithuanian, Manx, Old Prussian, Oscan, Persian, Sanskrit, Telugu, Thai and Umbrian.

Finding aids: recorded in general printed-book catalogue; see also separate duplicated handlist.

Location: JRULM (Deansgate); only a small proportion of Strachan's original collection is at Deansgate: most of it was integrated into the stock of the Main Library.

Tabley Book Collection

*See also the Tabley
Muniments (p. 85).*

5,000 items.

The personal library of the Leycester/Leicester/Warren family and Barons de Tabley from Tabley House near Knutsford, Cheshire, includes the books of the 17th-century antiquary and Royalist, Sir Peter Leycester, and those of the great patron of British artists, Sir John Fleming Leicester (1762–1827), 1st Baron de Tabley.

The collection contains items ranging from the early 16th to the early 20th centuries, with the majority dating from the 17th and 18th centuries. They cover a wide variety of subjects: art, English and foreign literature, the classics, history, law, politics, religion, natural history and travel. Miscellaneous material includes scrapbooks and sketch-books. Many works are finely illustrated and some have attractive bindings. Items of note include an incunable, Jacobus Philippus de Bergamo's *Supplementum chronicarum* (Venice, 1486); a First Folio of Shakespeare (1623); and a full 24-volume set of the *Naturalist's Miscellany* with colour engravings.

Of the 5,000 items in the collection, approximately 460 are located at the JRULM (Deansgate) and have been fully catalogued. The rest of the collection remains at Tabley House and will be catalogued in the future.

Finding aids: partially recorded in general printed-book catalogue.

Location: JRULM (Deansgate) and Tabley House.

Tregaskis Collections

*See also the Private
Press Collection (p. 22).*

150 items.

The original Tregaskis Collection contains 73 copies of the Kelmscott Press's *Tale of King Florus and the Fair Jehane* (1893) in unique bindings from 27 different countries, commissioned for exhibition in 1894 by James and Mary Lee Tregaskis. The Library also owns the Tregaskis Centenary Collection, which comprises over 80 copies of the Folio Society edition of Andrew Marvell's *The Garden & Other Poems* in contemporary design bindings from around the world. The collection was commissioned for exhibition in 1994 by Designer Bookbinders and was purchased by the Library with support from the Museums and Galleries Commission and the Victoria & Albert Museum Purchase Grant Fund.

Finding aids: published catalogue, *Tregaskis Centenary Exhibition: a Catalogue of the Tregaskis Centenary Exhibition 1994, together with a facsimile of the Tregaskis Exhibition catalogue of 1894 and colour plates of the bindings in both exhibitions* (London, 1994).

The collection of over 1,500 bookplates, donated by George H. Viner, consists largely of those designed by Charles William Sherborn between 1860 and 1912, but the designs of John Paul Rylands are also represented.

Another important collection of bookplates is to be found among the Tabley Muniments (p. 85).

Finding aids: published catalogue of Sherborn bookplates, Charles Davies Sherborn, *A Sketch of the Life and Work of Charles William Sherborn, Painter-Etcher… with a catalogue of his bookplates* (London, 1912). See also note in *Bulletin of the John Rylands Library*, vol. 33 (1950–51), p. 199.

History of the Book & General Printed Collections

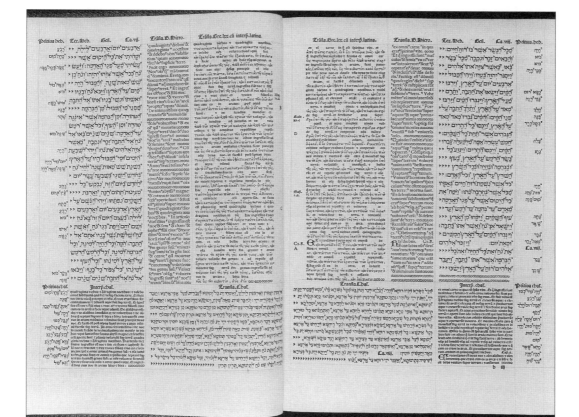

Biblia Sacra Polyglotta, or Complutensian Polyglot Bible, sponsored by Cardinal Ximenes (Alcalá: Arnão Guillén de Brocar, 1514-17), fos b2v. and b3r. (*see page 66*)

WESTERN (EUROPEAN) MANUSCRIPTS

AMONG the Western manuscripts are over 500 medieval codices, including outstanding examples of calligraphy and illumination in books of hours, psalters and other devotional works. Most are in Latin, but fine illuminations also appear in English, French, Greek and Italian texts. Manuscripts from important monastic and other centres are numerous, among them Bremen, Erfurt, Essen, Luxeuil, Murbach, Trier and Weissenau, and there are also many secular works including cartularies, royal wardrobe books and chronicles. Post-medieval material has a strong emphasis on literary papers, as well as antiquarian collections, socio-historical material, and personal correspondence and papers. There are many original bindings, medieval jewelled book covers, and ivory carvings.

There are major collections of manuscripts in English (p. 28), French (p. 29), German (p. 30), Greek (p. 30), Irish (p. 31), Italian (p. 31), Latin (p. 31) and Spanish (p. 32), with smaller collections or individual items in Bulgarian, Dutch (p. 28), Hungarian, Icelandic (p. 30), Mexican, Portuguese, Romanian, the Slavonic languages and Welsh.

Dutch Manuscripts

Date range: 15th–20th centuries.

16 items, mainly devotional and genealogical texts and armorials. These include two 15th-century *Horae* (Dutch MSS 8 and 12); a martyrology of 1472 (Dutch MS 10); and an armorial of c.1600 containing 160 emblazoned coats of arms of knights of the Golden Fleece (Dutch MS 6).

Finding aids: F. Taylor, *Supplementary Handlist of Western Manuscripts in the John Rylands Library* (Manchester, 1937), pp. 31–4; N.R. Ker, *Medieval Manuscripts in British Libraries, III, Lampeter – Oxford* (Oxford, 1983), pp. 394–8.

English Manuscripts

Date range: 14th–20th centuries.

Over 1,300 collections or individual items, comprising historical, biblical, devotional, literary and genealogical texts, and collections of letters and papers relating to military, political, industrial, social and local history, literature, art, and the history of Dissent.

Among the earliest items are: two 15th-century manuscripts of Chaucer's *Canterbury Tales* (English MSS 63, 113); a richly-illuminated copy of John Lydgate's *Seige of Troy*, and a copy of his translation of Boccaccio's *Falle of Pryncys*, from the first half of the 15th century (English MSS 1–2); three manuscripts of *The Pricke of Conscience*, traditionally attributed to the mystic Richard Rolle de Hampole, from the late 14th and early 15th centuries (English MSS 50, 51, 90); fifteen manuscripts of the Wycliffite Bible, or of parts of the Bible, written in the 14th and early 15th centuries; six copies of the *Brut* chronicle, 14th and 15th centuries (English MSS 102–105, 206, 207); a *Form of Cury*, or recipe book, compiled by the master cook to Richard II in its original vellum binding, of the early 15th century (English MS 7); medieval chronicles and devotional works; and several fine armorials with coats of arms beautifully emblazoned, some by leading members of the College of Heralds.

The most significant collections are described individually elsewhere in this *Guide*. They include: an important Moravian Church collection, 18th–20th centuries, p. 59; the Thomas Raffles Collection (theological, autograph collection), p. 61; the Tealdi Correspondence (textile trade), p. 97; the Wedgwood Correspondence (ceramic industry and 18th-century society), p. 97; the Heald Family Papers (trade, military and physical medicine), p. 106; the Hibbert-Ware Papers (military, medical, antiquarian), p. 107; the Pink Papers (political biographies), p. 108; the Wadsworth Manuscripts (social and economic history), p. 109; the Spring Rice Collection (19th-century court, social, political and diplomatic affairs), p. 84; the Bowring Papers (Hong Kong and China), p. 121; the Melville Papers (East India Company), p. 123; the Mount-Stewart Collection (consular correspondence), p. 123; the Thrale-Piozzi Manuscripts (18th-century literature, Johnson circle), p. 144; the Dorothy Richardson Papers (travel in 18th-century England), p. 167; the Elizabeth Gaskell Manuscript Collection and Walter Savage Landor Papers (19th-century literature), pp. 135 & 139; the John Ruskin Papers (19th-century literature and art), p. 142; the Walt Whitman Manuscript Collections (19th-century American literature), p. 145; the Holman Hunt Papers, the Fairfax Murray Papers and the Spielmann Collection (19th-century art, Pre-Raphaelites), pp. 165–6 & 168; and the Henry Roscoe Papers (19th-century science), p. 180.

There are also several miscellaneous autograph collections containing many hundreds of holograph letters from (primarily 19th-century) statesmen, theologians and churchmen, artists, literary figures, men of letters and members of the nobility.

Finding aids: M. Tyson, *Handlist of English Manuscripts in the John Rylands Library* (Manchester, 1929), and additional volumes by M. Tyson (1935), F. Taylor (1951), and G.A. Matheson and F. Taylor (1977); F. Taylor, *Supplementary Handlist of Western Manuscripts in the John Rylands Library* (Manchester, 1937), pp. 21–31; card index of autograph collections.

French Manuscripts

Date range: 13th–19th centuries.

Over 130 items, comprising biblical, devotional, literary, historical, legal and genealogical works. These include a 13th-century *Bible Historiée*, or Bible picture book (French MS 5); a 14th-century *Passion de Nostre Seigneur de Jésus Christ*, with miniatures executed *en grisaille* (French MS 3); a copy of the Arthurian text *Lancelot del Lac*, from the early 14th century (French MS 1); the works of Guillaume de Deguilleville, with many fine illustrations, from the early 15th century (French MS 2); a 15th-century illustrated copy of the *Grandes Chroniques de France* (French MS 62); a 14th-century manuscript of the *Roman de la Rose* (French MS 66); 15th-century *coutumiers* of Brittany (French MSS 58 and 74) and Normandy (French MS 73); a *Mappemonde* (world map) made by Pierre Desceliers in 1546 (French MS 1*); several medieval chronicles (13th–15th centuries); armorials of French, English, Irish and Scottish nobility; and 17th- and 18th-century correspondence, including letters of Marie le Bailleul, Marquise d'Huxelles, which shed light on the social and political history of France in the reign of Louis XIV, and newsletters, or *gazettes manuscrites*, and other records relating to the French Revolution.

Finding aids: M. Tyson, 'Handlist of the Collections of French and Italian Manuscripts in the John Rylands Library', *Bulletin of the John Rylands Library*, vol. 14 (1930), pp. 563–628; F. Taylor, *Supplementary Handlist of Western Manuscripts in the John Rylands Library* (Manchester, 1937), pp. 34–7. See also John P. Tuck, 'French Studies: a Guide to Research Resources in the John Rylands University Library of Manchester', *Bulletin of the John Rylands University Library of Manchester*, vol. 72, no. 2 (1990), pp. 3–25; Caroline S. Hull, 'Rylands MS French 5: the form and function of a medieval Bible picture book', *Bulletin of the John Rylands University Library of Manchester*, vol. 77, no. 2 (1995), pp. 3–24.

German Manuscripts

Date range: 14th–19th centuries.

29 items, mainly devotional, historical, alchemical and genealogical works, including an illustrated 15th-century *Alchemica* (German MS 1); *Deutsches Stammbuch*, with over 1,800 emblazoned coats of arms of nobilities and dignities of the Empire, 1565 (German MS 2); and a mystic miscellany, *Büchlein von der Liebe Gottes*, written in southern Germany in the second half of the 15th century (German MS 11).

Finding aids: F. Taylor, *Supplementary Handlist of Western Manuscripts in the John Rylands Library* (Manchester, 1937), pp. 37–43; N.R. Ker, *Medieval Manuscripts in British Libraries, III, Lampeter – Oxford* (Oxford, 1983), pp. 452–4. See also F.P. Pickering, 'A German Mystic Miscellany of the Late Fifteenth Century in the John Rylands Library', *Bulletin of the John Rylands Library*, vol. 22 (1938), pp. 455–92.

Greek Manuscripts

Date range: 3rd century BC–19th century AD.

These comprise 31 ostraca, 54 codices and over 700 papyri. The codices, ranging from the 10th to the 19th century, are mostly biblical and devotional volumes, including some notable early *Evangelia* (10th–13th century). The papyri collection (3rd century BC–7th century AD) consists of classical, biblical, liturgical and medical texts, and important documentary papyri, including business papers, public records, files of local government offices, taxation documents and financial memoranda. Undoubtedly the most famous papyrus is the fragment of St John's Gospel, probably the earliest extant piece of the New Testament (from the first half of the 2nd century AD). Papyri from Hermopolis (1st–7th centuries AD) comprise conveyances, receipts, and official and private legal documents.

Finding aids: Arthur S. Hunt [and others], *Catalogue of the Greek and Latin Papyri in the John Rylands Library Manchester*, 4 vols (Manchester, 1911–52); Alan K. Bowman and J.D. Thomas, 'Some Additional Greek Papyri in the John Rylands University Library', *Bulletin of the John Rylands University Library of Manchester*, vol. 61 (1978–79), pp. 290–313.

Icelandic Manuscripts

Date range: 15th and 17th centuries.

There are five Icelandic manuscripts, of which Icelandic MSS 1–4 were acquired with the Crawford collection in 1901, the fifth being acquired later from another source. They comprise a 15th-century pocket-book containing the text of the computational treatise *Rímbegla*, a calendar in Latin and several devotional works (Icelandic MS 1); a set of three 17th-century copies of the medieval law text *Jónsbók*, (Icelandic MSS 2–4), one of which (Icelandic MS 2) is beautifully decorated; and another *Jónsbók* from the mid-15th century (Icelandic MS 5).

Finding aids: B.S. Benedikz, 'Notes on Some Medieval Icelandic Manuscripts', *Bulletin of the John Rylands University Library of Manchester*, vol. 60 (1977–78), pp. 289–302; N.R. Ker, *Medieval Manuscripts in British Libraries, III, Lampeter – Oxford* (Oxford, 1983), pp. 454–6; Olai Skulerud, *Catalogue of Norse Manuscripts in Edinburgh, Dublin and Manchester* (Kristiania, 1918), pp. 57–60.

Irish Manuscripts

Date range: 15th, 18th and 19th centuries.

Over 130 items, in English and Irish. The sole 15th-century manuscript is a valuable *Materia Medica* (Irish MS 35). The remainder of the collection consists primarily of literary (Fenian and Ossianic tales and poems), historical, genealogical and grammatical works. There are numerous transcripts by well-known 19th-century scholars of important manuscripts, which were formerly in the Royal Irish Academy but are now lost.

Finding aids: unpublished list; the *Materia Medica* is described in N.R. Ker, *Medieval Manuscripts in British Libraries, III, Lampeter – Oxford* (Oxford, 1983), pp. 456–8.

Italian Manuscripts

Date range: 14th–19th centuries.

75 items, mostly literary, historical, genealogical and musical works. Notable are a rare text of the poems of Dante and Petrarch, written in the second half of the 14th century for the son of Carlo degli Strozzi, a member of one of the leading noble families of Florence (Italian MS 1); four manuscripts of Dante's *Divina Commedia*, including one written in 1416 by Bartholomew Landi de Landis (Italian MS 49), and another fine 15th-century example (Italian MS 2); a late 14th-century copy of the *Fioretti* of S. Francis and of the Legend of S. Clare (Italian MS 51); a 15th-century illuminated manuscript of the *Scala del Paradiso* of S. John Climacus (Italian MS 4); a 15th-century manuscript of *Somma sopra e sette peccati mortali* by S. Antoninus, Archbishop of Florence (Italian MS 53); and a group of manuscripts relating to the great Florentine reformer Fra Girolamo Savonarola (Italian MSS 7–11, 13, 30 etc.). There are also documents concerning Florence, Venice, Bologna and other cities, and records relating to the Medici, Strozzi and Orsini families.

Finding aids: M. Tyson, 'Handlist of the Collections of French and Italian Manuscripts in the John Rylands Library', *Bulletin of the John Rylands Library*, vol. 14 (1930), pp. 563–628; N.R. Ker, *Medieval Manuscripts in British Libraries, III, Lampeter – Oxford* (Oxford, 1983), pp. 458–64.

Latin Manuscripts

Date range: 7th–19th centuries.

Over 500 items, containing a wide range of texts: biblical, liturgical, patristic, theological, historical, legal and philosophical. There are manuscripts of outstanding importance both textually and for their illumination. M.R. James stated that the illuminated codices contain 'examples of first-class quality of the art and calligraphy of all the great schools of Europe'. Among the outstanding items are the Ravenna papyrus of the early 7th century (Latin MS 1); an Exultet Roll of the early 11th century (Latin MS 2); an illuminated Lectionary, Gospel Books and Bibles from Germany, France and Flanders, 9th–12th centuries (Latin MSS 4–5, 7, 9–11); the magnificent 12th-century *Beatus super Apocalypsim* from Spain (Latin MS 8); the beautiful Missal of Henry of Chichester from the mid-13th century (Latin MS 24); the 14th-century French Apocalypse (Latin MS 19); numerous *Horae* from the French and Flemish schools, including a fine example of the work of the master illuminator Pierre Remiet (Latin MS 136); and the illuminated missal of Cardinal Pompeio Colonna, a superlative example of Italian Renaissance art in six volumes (Latin MSS 32–37).

Western (European) Manuscripts

See also the Medici Records (p. 81).

Secular works include medieval chronicles, cartularies, armorials, royal wardrobe books of the reign of Edward I and from the household of Philippa of Hainault, Queen of Edward III, household accounts and rentals (13th–16th centuries), and manuscripts of Scipio Le Squyer, Vice-Chamberlain of the Treasury of the Exchequer under James I and Charles I.

Finding aids: M.R. James, *A Descriptive Catalogue of the Latin Manuscripts in the John Rylands Library at Manchester* (Manchester, 1921), reprinted with an introduction and additional notes and corrections by F. Taylor (München, 1980); M. Tyson, 'Handlist of Additions to the Collection of Latin Manuscripts in the John Rylands Library, 1908–28', *Bulletin of the John Rylands Library*, vol. 12 (1928), pp. 581–609; F. Taylor, *Supplementary Handlist of Western Manuscripts in the John Rylands Library* (Manchester, 1937), pp. 7–21; N.R. Ker, *Medieval Manuscripts in British Libraries, III, Lampeter – Oxford* (Oxford, 1983), pp. 464–8.

Spanish Manuscripts

Date range: 16th–19th centuries.

29 items, comprising historical, genealogical and philological works. They include an important 16th-century collection of texts of well-known Spanish chronicles (Spanish MS 1); a collection of the historical writings of Esteban de Garibay, royal historiographer to Philip II (Spanish MSS 9–25); and a richly-decorated early 17th-century record of a lawsuit to prove gentlemanly rank (Spanish MS 27).

Finding aids: M. Tyson, *The Spanish Manuscripts in the John Rylands Library* (Manchester, 1932).

JEWISH, NEAR EASTERN & ORIENTAL STUDIES

Manuscript Resources

The Library's near eastern and oriental manuscript collections come in large measure from the famous libraries formed by Pierre Leopold van Alstein, H.C. Millies, Nathaniel Bland, G.W. Hamilton and others, which had been assimilated in whole or in part into the Bibliotheca Lindesiana of Lord Crawford. The 20,000 items are in some forty different languages and range in date from the third millennium BC to the present day. They are written on most of the materials ever used by men and women for their records, including clay tablets, papyrus, linen, parchment, paper, wood, palm-leaf, bone, bamboo and bark.

The Library has one of the most important NEAR EASTERN manuscript collections in Britain. By far the earliest items are the Sumerian and Akkadian cuneiform clay tablets from the 3rd and 2nd millennia BC, while Arabic, Persian, Coptic, Hebrew, Samaritan and Turkish manuscripts are especially well represented. The Arabic manuscripts, which cover a period of roughly 1,000 years, comprise almost 900 codices, some 800 papyri and approximately 1,500 paper fragments. The Persian collection comprises almost 950 codices of the early 13th to 19th centuries AD, many superbly illuminated. There are well over a thousand Coptic items from the 4th century onwards. The Hebrew manuscripts comprise 10,600 fragments from the Genizah of the Synagogue of Elijah in Old Cairo, together with 400 codices. The Samaritan manuscripts consist of 377 codices, including some notable texts of the Pentateuch. Many of the Samaritan, Hebrew and Arabic manuscripts derive from the collection of Dr Moses Gaster, the noted Hebrew scholar, and in addition the Library holds over 500 letters exchanged between Gaster and the Samaritan community in Nablus. There are also 195 Turkish manuscripts from the 15th century through to the 19th, chiefly written in Ottoman Turkish.

There are smaller collections of Armenian manuscripts, including early Gospel books; Egyptian papyri, in hieroglyphic, hieratic and demotic; Ethiopian manuscripts, among them rare Christian texts; and Syriac manuscripts.

The FAR EASTERN manuscript collections are extraordinarily rich in their diversity. There are South-East Asian Manuscripts in ten languages: Burmese, Siamese, Malay, Batak, Buginese, Balinese, Madurese, Javanese, Kawi and Makasarese. Eleven Modern Indian Languages are represented, including Hindustani, Punjabi, Pashto, Sinhalese and Tamil. The Hindustani grouping contains the *Laur-Chanda*, an almost complete text of a work known elsewhere only from a few leaves preserved in various Indian libraries. There are 83 Pali manuscripts, written on paper and palm-leaf in Sinhalese, Burmese and Cambodian. The Library holds the second largest Mo-So collection in Europe, while smaller collections comprise Chinese manuscripts and watercolour drawings, and manuscripts in Japanese, Parsi, Sanskrit and Tibetan.

In addition to 'native' manuscripts, the Library holds several collections of papers which provide a European perspective on the Orient, and reveal the colonial, trading and missionary activities of Europeans in the East. The Bowring Papers contain correspondence of Sir John Bowring (1792–1872), mainly concerning political and commercial affairs in the Far East at the time when Sir John was Consul at Canton, Plenipotentiary to China and, from 1854, Governor of Hong Kong. These are an important source for studies of Anglo-Chinese relations and the opening of Japan. Within the Methodist Archives, the Lewis Court Bible Christian Collection contains material relating to missionary activities in

China during the 19th century. The papers of the Methodist missionary Harold Burgoyne Rattenbury, who worked in China from 1902 to 1934, contain a great deal of information on Chinese life and affairs during a momentous period in the country's history. The Carrington Papers include a small quantity of letters and papers relating to Sir Codrington Edmund Carrington's term as Chief Justice of Ceylon (Sri Lanka), 1800–06.

In addition to the Hebrew manuscripts, modern Jewish history and the foundation of Israel are represented in several archive collections. The massive *Guardian* Archive includes correspondence with the Zionist pioneer Chaim Weizmann, and it documents through despatches and published articles the history of the Second World War, the founding of Israel and the later Middle East conflicts. Correspondence with Weizmann is also to be found among the papers of Samuel Alexander (1859–1938), a supporter of the campaign for a Jewish homeland in Palestine, while the W.P. Crozier Papers incorporate interviews with Weizmann and other statesmen over the issue of the Jewish National Home. The Military Papers of Major-General Eric Edward Dorman O'Gowan include material relating to the Arab-Israeli conflict.

It should also be noted that the Library holds the papers of the Egyptologist Dr Eve Reymond, and the archive of the Manchester Egyptian and Oriental Society.

Printed Resources

The Chinese and Japanese collections comprise substantial numbers of printed books, and smaller quantities of manuscript material. Both were acquired in 1901 with Mrs Rylands's purchase of the Crawford Collection. The Chinese Collection contains books reflecting almost every aspect of Chinese life and culture, including histories, biographies, ceremonials, dictionaries, grammar books, and works on calligraphy. The smaller Japanese Collection contains a number of manuscripts and printed books of great interest and rarity, among them works of history, biography, poetry, drama, anthropology and topography.

The Library has some twenty Hebrew incunabula, approximately one fifth of the total number of extant titles. The collection includes examples of the work of six different Italian printers. Attention can be drawn to a vellum copy of the *Yosippon* or *Historia Judaica* of Joseph ben Gorion, printed in Mantua by Abraham Conat in 1476. The Library also holds 36 of the 40 Hebrew editions of the Bible printed before 1600 as listed in Darlow and Moule. The collection includes a copy of the Psalter, the first portion of the Hebrew Bible to be printed, probably in Bologna, in 1477, and a handsome copy of the second Hebrew Bible printed in 1491 or 1492.

The Haskalah Collection relates to the Jewish Enlightenment, and contains 19th-century works of Hebrew literature and general literary texts in Hebrew translation. The Marmorstein Collection of Judaic literature is especially rich in classical rabbinic texts and in East European responsa printed in Hebrew, English, Hungarian and other languages.

The Dame Mabel Tylecote Printed Collection contains printed material relating to the Anglo-Israel Association, the foundation of Israel and the Middle East conflict.

See also the section Military, Colonial and Diplomatic History and Travel (p. 119).

Bibliography

Philip Alexander, *The Jewish Heritage: Catalogue of an Exhibition held in the John Rylands University Library of Manchester* (Manchester, 1988).

E.M. Herzig (ed.), *Gilded Word and Radiant Image*, catalogue of an exhibition of Islamic manuscripts (Manchester, 1992).

F. Taylor, 'The Oriental Manuscript Collections in the John Rylands Library', *Bulletin of the John Rylands Library*, vol. 54 (1971–72), pp. 449–78.

Jewish, Near Eastern & Oriental Studies

Select alphabetical list of resources: (MS: Manuscript/Archive; PR: Printed)

saint-monk (Ethiopian MS 37). Ethiopian MSS 29–34 are magical scrolls, mainly 19th century. Ethiopian MS 11, an 18th-century Homilies in honour of St Michael, contains 32 miniatures in the Gondar style of illumination. Ten codices can be dated precisely (1590–1742).

Finding aids: Stefan Strelcyn, *Catalogue of Ethiopic Manuscripts in the John Rylands University Library of Manchester* (Manchester, 1974).

Moses Gaster Collection

In 1954, with the aid of the Pilgrim Trust, the Friends of National Libraries and private donations, the Library purchased the collection of manuscripts in Hebrew, Samaritan and other scripts assembled by Dr Moses Gaster (1856–1939).

Gaster, Romanian by birth, was forced to leave his native country in 1885 as a result of persecution, and took refuge in England. He became Chief Rabbi (Hakham) of the Sephardic Communities of British Jews in 1886, and held the office until his retirement in 1919. A distinguished scholar with a long list of publications to his name, his interests ranged from the Hebrew prayer-book, the minutiae of Hebrew text study and apocryphal Hebrew literature to Jewish amulets and Romanian folklore. He made a special study of the Samaritans and became a recognized authority on their language and literature. He visited Nablus, the headquarters of the Samaritan community, and induced them to part with manuscripts covering the whole range of their literature. Where he could not secure the originals he had copies made for him by Samaritan priests.

*For further information
see under Arabic
Manuscripts (p. 36),
Hebrew Manuscripts
(p. 39) and Samaritan
Manuscripts (p. 42).*

The collection comprised over 10,000 fragments in Hebrew and Judaeo-Arabic from the Genizah of the Synagogue of Ben Ezra in Old Cairo; some 350 Hebrew codices and scrolls including prayer-books of many Jewish communities, apocryphal writings, commentaries, treatises, letters, marriage contracts, *piyyûtîm*, and thirteen scrolls of the Law; some 350 Samaritan manuscripts, among them manuscripts of the Pentateuch, commentaries and treatises, and liturgical, historical, chronological and astronomical codices, detailed census lists of the Samaritans and lists of manuscripts in their possession; and almost 1,500 uncatalogued Arabic fragments on paper from the Synagogue of Ben Ezra.

A further 123 codices were donated to the Library by the family of Dr Gaster, including manuscripts in Arabic, Greek, English, Latin, German, Flemish, Italian, Spanish, Portuguese, Romanian, Bulgarian, Persian, Turkish and Ethiopic. Many of the items relate to Jewish history. The Library also holds the substantial, but uncatalogued, correspondence of Dr Gaster with the Samaritan community in Nablus, in Hebrew but written in the Samaritan script; there are English translations of most of these letters.

In addition there are 115 printed items, of which 25 are monographs, the remainder comprising a mixture of periodicals (*Quest, Jewish Review* etc.), offprints of single articles, and bound volumes containing a miscellany of small monographs, articles, reviews and newspaper cuttings. The items date mainly from the 1870s to the 1930s, and the vast majority were written by Gaster, contain an article by him, or refer to his writings. Much of the material is heavily annotated by Gaster and some ephemera is enclosed. The collection is exclusively about Jewish history, folklore and religion, with special reference to eastern Europe and specifically to Romania. Most of the collection is written in Romanian, with smaller quantities in English, Hebrew, German and French.

Finding aids: unpublished handlists of manuscripts in Hebrew and miscellaneous languages; see under individual languages. Printed material recorded in general printed-book catalogue. See also note in *Bulletin of the John Rylands Library*, vol. 37 (1954–55), pp. 2–6; M. Gaster, 'The Story of My Library', *The British Library Journal*, vol. 21, no. 1 (1995), pp. 16–22.

Hebrew Manuscripts

There are about 400 codices, Torah scrolls and marriage contracts, dating from the 14th to the 19th century AD. Hebrew MSS 1–34 were purchased by Mrs Rylands from Lord Crawford in 1901. They include a lavishly illuminated early 14th-century Sephardi Haggadah (Hebrew MS 6); a text of Nachmanides' *Commentary on the Pentateuch*, containing illuminations by the Florentine artist Francesco Antonio del Cherico (Hebrew MS 8); a collection of 19th-century benedictions from Honan (Hebrew MS 24); a 14th-century text of the '*Ammude ha-Golah* of Isaac ben Joseph of Corbeil (Hebrew MS 31); and, among the Scrolls of Esther, the earliest known Italian illuminated *Megillah*, 1618 (Hebrew MS 22). Hebrew MSS 34–49 are miscellaneous manuscripts acquired between 1909 and 1952.

Most of the remaining manuscripts were acquired in 1954 when the Library bought the collection of Dr Moses Gaster. The collection includes prayer-books of many Jewish communities, apocryphal writings, commentaries, treatises, letters, marriage contracts, *piyyûtîm*, and thirteen scrolls of the Law. Among countries represented are Spain, France, Belgium, Germany, Poland, Romania, Italy, Morocco, and, particularly, Yemen.

In addition there are almost 10,600 fragments in Hebrew and Judaeo-Arabic from the Genizah of the Synagogue of Ben Ezra in Old Cairo, purchased from Dr Moses Gaster in 1954. About 90% of the items are on paper, the remainder on parchment. The vast majority are very small fragments. They date from the 10th to the 19th century AD and include religious and literary texts, and material relating to grammar, philosophy, medicine, astrology and astronomy. Many parts of the Mediterranean world are represented in the collection, and there are numerous fragments written in Ashkenazi hands. There are several autograph fragments of Maimonides, including portions of his *Guide of the Perplexed* and *Commentary on the Mishna*.

Finding aids: catalogue of Hebrew MSS in course of preparation. See also Alexander Samely, 'The Interpreted Text: Among the Hebrew Manuscripts of the John Rylands University Library', *Bulletin of the John Rylands University Library of Manchester*, vol. 73, no. 2 (1991), pp. 1–20. Genizah fragments uncatalogued: see S.D. Goitein, 'An Eleventh-Century Letter from Tyre in the John Rylands Library', *Bulletin of the John Rylands Library*, vol. 54 (1971–72), pp. 94–102; Malachi Beit-Arié, 'A Maimonides Autograph in the Rylands Genizah Collection', *Bulletin of the John Rylands University Library of Manchester*, vol. 57 (1974–75), pp. 1–6; Simon Hopkins, 'Two New Maimonidean Autographs in the John Rylands University Library', *Bulletin of the John Rylands University Library of Manchester*, vol. 67 (1984–85), pp. 710–35.

Manchester Egyptian and Oriental Society Archive

Date range: c.1906–65.

The society, which was closely associated with the University of Manchester, was formed in 1912 by the merger of the Manchester Egyptian Association and the Manchester Oriental Society. The archive contains minutes of the MEA, 1906–12, the MOS, 1910–12, and the MEOS, 1912–61; a membership book; financial papers; journals of the Manchester Branch

Qur'an, works on Sufism, and the lives of saints and prophets; literary and poetic texts, romances, chronicles and fables; writing manuals, books on grammar, dictionaries and encyclopedias; volumes on the history of India, the Mogul Empire and Indian local history; and works on law, philosophy, medicine, natural history, geography, cosmography, occult science, astronomy and astrology. There are numerous calligraphic and lavishly illustrated texts and decorated bindings.

Finding aids: unpublished handlist of Crawford items, Michael Kerney, *Catalogue of Persian Manuscripts belonging to the Earl of Crawford* (n.d., ?1890s); see also B.W. Robinson, *Persian Paintings in the John Rylands Library: a Descriptive Catalogue* (London, 1980).

Eve Reymond Papers

Date range: 1945–85.

The personal and professional papers of the former Manchester University Egyptologist, Dr Eve Reymond, include professional and personal correspondence; diaries; manuscript and proof copies of *Introduction to the Study of Temple Inscriptions* and *The Mythical Origin of the Temple*; notes on hieroglyphic, hieratic and demotic texts; photographs of demotic texts; notes on Egyptian language, literature, religion, funerary rites, history and culture; and an abundance of printed matter.

Finding aids: outline list.

Samaritan Manuscripts

377 items on parchment and paper. Samaritan MSS 1–27 were acquired in 1901 with the Crawford collection and include what is apparently the earliest dated manuscript (1211 AD) of the whole Samaritan Pentateuch to be found outside Nablus, six other Pentateuchs in whole or in part (two bilingual), three noteworthy theological codices, and interesting liturgical and astronomical texts. Samaritan MSS 28–375 are from the collection of Dr Moses Gaster, acquired by the Library in 1954 (see p. 38). Among them are manuscripts of the Pentateuch (including bilingual and trilingual texts), commentaries and treatises, and liturgical, historical, chronological and astronomical codices. There are detailed census lists of the Samaritans and lists of manuscripts in their possession. The Library also holds the substantial, but uncatalogued, correspondence of Dr Gaster with the Samaritan community in Nablus, in Hebrew but written in the Samaritan script.

Finding aids: Edward Robertson, *Catalogue of the Samaritan Manuscripts in the John Rylands Library*, 2 vols (Manchester, 1938 & 1962); Gaster Samaritan MSS 374 (Book of Joshua) and 375 (Chronicle, with the Book of Joshua) were omitted from the catalogue.

Sanskrit Manuscripts

29 items on paper and palm-leaf, dating between the 17th century and the 19th. Sanskrit MSS 1–17 were acquired in 1901 with the Crawford collection. Sanskrit MSS 3, 7, 9, 18 and 28 are illuminated. Included are items in Hindi and Punjabi.

Finding aids: unpublished 19th-century handlist of Crawford items by Professor Geldner and others.

123 items, on palm-leaf, copper plate, paper, bark, bamboo and bone, mainly acquired with the Crawford Collection in 1901. Ten languages are represented:

Burmese: 21 items, partially catalogued, from the 18th and 19th centuries, including various Buddhist works and grammatical, magical and astrological treatises. Burmese MSS 2, 4 & 17 are illustrated.

Siamese (Thai): 15 items, dating between the 17th and 19th centuries, comprising eleven literary works, two concerning divination, one medical text and one concerning charms. Most significant are Siamese MS 1, a 17th-century collection of invocations, sayings and Buddhist terms, and Siamese MS 2, a copy of a text of c.1340 AD dealing with *The Three Worlds*.

Malay: 11 items, from the 18th and 19th centuries, comprising romantic tales; various histories, including the *Sejarah Melayu* (Malay MS 1) and a history of Johore (Malay MS 10); a law-book of Minangkabau (Malay MS 2); a valuable text of *Hikayat Banjar* (Malay MS 4); and an 18th-century text of *Hikayat Hang Tuah* (Malay MS 11).

Batak: 33 items, on tree-bark, bamboo and paper, written in the dialects of Toba, South Toba, Mandailing and South Mandailing from the island of Sumatra. The texts are largely concerned with protective magic (*pagar*) and divination and were used by medicine-men (*datu*) in performing ceremonies.

Buginese: 5 items, from the 18th and 19th centuries, comprising a collection of didactic poems (Buginese MS 1); a letter of 1845 from Majoor Kalang Kangang to the Governor of Makayar (Buginese MS 2); parts of the Galigo epic (Buginese MSS 3, 3a); and a collection of Muslim prayers with a Buginese translation, c.1800 (Buginese MS 4).

Balinese: 7 items, dating between the 16th century and the 19th, including an Old Javanese law code (Balinese MS 2); a chronicle of the relation between the royal families of Bali and Lombok (Balinese MS 5); and medical and mystical works.

Madurese: 1 item, *Tanda Angrek*, 1848, acquired with the Crawford collection.

Javanese: 26 items, dating from the 18th and 19th centuries, comprising histories, chronicles, legends, romances and stories, and religious, legal and poetical works. Many items are illustrated, Javanese MSS 7 (*Legends of Damar Wulan*) and 16 (*Radèn Pañji Semara Bangun*) profusely.

Kawi: 2 items, *Bharata Yuddha*, 18th-century (Kawi MS 1), and a portion of the Kawi version of the *Mahabharata*, 19th-century (Kawi MS 2).

Makasarese: 2 items, collections of four moral tales (Makasarese MS 1) and six miscellaneous historical treatises (Makasarese MS 2), both 19th-century.

Finding aids: unpublished handlists by Henri-Léon Feer, H. Juynboll and others of Burmese, Siamese, Batak and Indonesian (Malay, Buginese, Balinese, Madurese, Javanese, Kawi and Makasarese) MSS in the Crawford collection; P. Voorhoeve, 'Batak Bark Books', *Bulletin of the John Rylands Library*, vol. 33 (1950–51), pp. 283–98.

Sumerian and Akkadian Clay Tablets

Over 1,000 items in Sumerian and Akkadian cuneiform scripts. Most of the Rylands tablets come from the great temples of Drehem and Umma and date from the Ur III dynasty (22nd–21st centuries BC), but there are also First Babylonian Dynasty fragments (20th–17th centuries BC) and later Babylonian and Assyrian pieces. Texts comprise royal inscriptions, letters, economic, administrative and agricultural documents and literary texts.

Jewish, Near Eastern & Oriental Studies

Finding aids: T. Fish, *Catalogue of the Sumerian Tablets in the John Rylands Library* (Manchester, 1932); C.L. Bedale, *Sumerian Tablets from Umma in the John Rylands Library* (Manchester, 1915); Tohru Gomi, 'Ur III Texts in the John Rylands University Library of Manchester', *Bulletin of the John Rylands University Library of Manchester*, vol. 64 (1981–82), pp. 87–116; Benjamin R. Foster, 'Sargonic and Pre-Sargonic Tablets in the John Rylands University Library', *Bulletin of the John Rylands University Library of Manchester*, vol. 64 (1981–82), pp. 457–80.

Syriac Manuscripts

70 items (some composite), ranging from the 6th century to the 20th, were acquired from Lord Crawford, James Rendel Harris and Alphonse Mingana. They are mainly theological and liturgical codices, and include a 6th-century Gospel Book (Syriac MS 1), parts of the Old and New Testaments, lectionaries, commentaries, psalters, collections of hymns, and prayers, amulets or charms, and liturgical books. Secular texts include dictionaries, grammatical treatises, and works on astrology and divination. 48 items are West Syrian, the remainder East Syrian and Melkite.

Finding aids: J.F. Coakley, 'A Catalogue of the Syriac Manuscripts in the John Rylands Library', *Bulletin of the John Rylands University Library of Manchester*, vol. 75, no. 2 (1993), pp. 105–207.

Tibetan Manuscripts

15 items on paper, of which Tibetan MSS 1–6 were purchased in 1901 with the Crawford collection, the remainder being acquired subsequently from various sources. Tibetan MS 6 comprises two sandalwood book covers, with inscriptions in Chinese, Mongolian and Sanskrit and six coloured miniatures. Tibetan MS 14 consists of ritual texts of the *bon.po* sect, the pre-Buddhist religion of Tibet, with sheets of drawings of ritual objects and human figures. The collection includes other ritual texts and prayer-wheels.

Finding aids: unpublished 19th-century handlist of Crawford items; unpublished typescript catalogue of Tibetan MSS 1–12 and notes on Tibetan MSS 13–15 by Geoffrey B. Samuel.

Turkish Manuscripts

195 items on paper, mainly acquired in the Crawford purchase of 1901. Most are written in Ottoman Turkish, but there are twelve items with texts in Çagatay, the literary eastern variant of the language. There is also one manuscript with Turkish and Armenian texts in Latin transcription. They range in date from the 15th century through to the 19th, the majority of dated examples being from the 17th and 18th centuries. The subject range is wide, including anthologies (*divans*) of poetry, narrative poetry (*mesnevis*), fables and stories, commentaries, books on grammar, letters, including documents issued by Ottoman institutions, guides for dervish novices, biographies and biographical dictionaries, travelogues, library catalogues, dictionaries and vocabularies, and texts on religious ethics,

jurisprudence, history, geography, cosmography, mathematics, astronomy, medicine, physiognomy, music and genealogy.

Finding aids: forthcoming catalogue, Jan Schmidt, 'A Catalogue of the Turkish Manuscripts in the John Rylands University Library of Manchester', *Bulletin of the John Rylands University Library of Manchester*, vol. 80 (1998); see also an unpublished handlist of Crawford items, Michael Kerney, *Catalogue of Turkish Manuscripts belonging to the Earl of Crawford* (1892).

Jewish, Near Eastern & Oriental Studies

PRINTED RESOURCES

Chinese Collection

500 items.

The bulk of the collection of Chinese printed books and manuscripts was acquired in 1901 with the purchase of the Crawford collection. The foundation of Lord Crawford's collection was laid by his purchase *en bloc* of the library of Pierre Leopold van Alstein in 1863. Crawford made further acquisitions, from booksellers in Britain and Continental Europe and via agents in Beijing. The collection is noteworthy for the comparatively small number of imperfect works. The books date mostly from the 18th and 19th centuries, although 28 items are dated before 1600. They include histories, biographies, ceremonials, dictionaries, grammar books, and works on calligraphy in Chinese, English, French and Latin. With the omission of science and technology, almost every aspect of Chinese life and culture is represented. Some are associated with the distinguished French sinologist, Jean Pierre Abel Rémusat (d. 1832).

See also the Mo-So Manuscripts (p. 41) and Tibetan Manuscripts (p. 44).

31 manuscripts were included in the Crawford purchase. With the Crawford collection also came 57 volumes and folders containing approximately 1,000 watercolour paintings, mostly 18th- and 19th-century, depicting many aspects of China and Chinese life. Eight similar volumes were acquired in 1957. Another 56 printed books derive from the former University Library Chinese collection, while six books were donated in 1992 by Han Suyin.

Finding aids: published outline catalogue of the Crawford collection (including some items not received by the Library), J.P. Edmond, *Catalogue of Chinese Books and Manuscripts* (privately printed, 1895); manuscript catalogue of Chinese books compiled by John Williams between 1863 and 1875; manuscript catalogue of Chinese paintings; unpublished handlist of University collection; unpublished typescript list by John Deane and Professor Zheng Yaying, 1991.

Haskalah Collection

900 items.

Acquired in 1970 from Professor Chimen Abramsky, the collection relates to the Jewish Enlightenment, and consists of 700 titles in 900 volumes of 19th-century Hebrew literature and general literary works in Hebrew translation. There are some very scarce serial runs.

Finding aids: card catalogues.

230 items.

The collection of Japanese books and manuscripts, assembled by the 25th Earl of Crawford in the 1860s and '70s and purchased by the John Rylands Library in 1901, is not large by international standards, but it contains a number of manuscripts and printed books of great interest and rarity. Many of the books derived from the collections of some of the most famous japanologists of the 19th century, and a few can be traced back to the collection of Isaac Titsingh, who lived in Japan in the 18th century and who is considered by many to be the founder of modern japanology.

The collection includes 22 manuscripts, as well as over 200 printed books. They mostly date from the 18th and 19th centuries and include works on history, biography, poetry, drama, anthropology and topography, with dictionaries, directories of samurai, encyclopedias and maps, in Japanese, Dutch and English. Among them are four volumes of annotated drawings of plants and insects.

Finding aids: published catalogue, P.F. Kornicki, 'The Japanese Collection in the Bibliotheca Lindesiana', *Bulletin of the John Rylands University Library of Manchester*, vol. 75, no. 2 (1993), pp. 209–300.

Marmorstein Collection

6,600 items.

A collection of Judaic literature, formerly the working library of Arthur Marmorstein (1882–1946), a noted rabbinic scholar of Hungarian origin who taught at Jews' College, London, from 1912 to 1946. The collection, purchased by the Library in 1973, contains Hebraica and Talmudic literature from the 16th century onwards, but mainly from the 19th century. It is especially rich in classical rabbinic texts and in East European responsa. Some 40 per cent of the collection is in Hebrew, 25 per cent in English, 10 per cent in Hungarian and the remainder in other languages, principally German.

Finding aids: partially catalogued.

CHRISTIAN THEOLOGY & ECCLESIASTICAL HISTORY

Manuscript Resources

Christian theology and ecclesiastical history have always been of paramount importance to the Library. Modern archival holdings are strongest in the field of Nonconformity. The Methodist Archives and Research Centre holds the largest collection in the world of manuscripts relating to the founders of Methodism, John and Charles Wesley, and other members of the Wesley family. Other notable Methodist figures who are represented include Thomas Coke, Joseph Benson, Adam Clarke, William Clowes, Hugh Bourne, John Rattenbury, John Ernest Rattenbury, Harold Burgoyne Rattenbury, and Dr Rupert Davies. The institutional records of Methodism are also well-represented. These include the records of the Methodist Conference and its several committees and large collections deposited by the administrative Divisions of the Church. There is material relating to all the major pre-union Methodist denominations, including the Lewis Court Bible Christian Collection. The Methodist theological college, Hartley Victoria College, and Hunmanby Hall, the Methodist girls' boarding school, are also represented.

Most other major Nonconformist denominations are represented, including archives of Baptists, Christian Brethren, Congregationalists, Moravians and Unitarians (mostly linked with printed collections). There are also records from associated religious organizations and pressure groups, such as the Audenshaw Foundation, the Industrial Mission Association, the William Temple Foundation, the League of the Good Samaritan and the Women in Theology Group.

The Library also holds a collection of medieval charters relating to Pluscarden Priory, Morayshire; the archives of the Canonesses of the Holy Sepulchre, who took over the House of the Frères Coquins in Liège, Belgium; the medieval Beaumont Charters relating to abbeys in Normandy; and a small quantity of archives from Manchester Cathedral.

Papers of individual churchmen and theologians include those of John Graham (Quaker), Jack Keiser (lay ministry), Thomas Manson (Presbyterian, biblical scholar), Arthur Samuel Peake (Primitive Methodist, biblical scholar), Thomas Raffles (Congregationalist, church historian), dom silvester houédard (Benedictine monk, leading figure in the ecumenical movement), and Edward Freeman (church historian). The Bagshawe Muniments contain papers of the Rev. William Bagshawe (1628–1702), the 'Apostle of the Peak', and other early Nonconformist ministers.

Printed Resources

Outstanding among the printed theological and ecclesiastical resources is the Bible Collection which numbers some 10,000 items, including first editions in about 400 languages and dialects published over five centuries. The Protestant Reformation of the 16th century is well documented, with tracts and other publications associated with Luther, Erasmus, Melanchthon and others to be found within the Reformation Collection. The politico-theological controversies of the 17th century are fully rehearsed in the English Tract Collection and the Sutherland Collection.

John Rylands was himself a devout Nonconformist; his Hymn Collection consists of 60,000 English and other hymns in 34 volumes.

The Library is a world centre for the study of Nonconformist theology and history. The transfer of the Methodist Archives Printed Book Collections (comprising some 60,000 items) to the Library in 1977 greatly supplemented the already excellent holdings in this area, such as the Rylands Wesley Collection and the Hobill Collection, to make the Rylands's collections the prime resource for Methodist history.

There are nationally important printed collections illustrating the history of the Baptists (Northern Baptist College Printed Collection), Unitarians (Unitarian College Printed Collection), Congregationalists (Congregational College Printed Collection), Quakers (Midgley Reference Library) and Christian Brethren (Christian Brethren Printed Collection). The Urwick Library from Hatherlow Congregational Church in Romiley, Cheshire, is one of the few 19th-century chapel libraries to have survived.

Other noteworthy collections include the Clogher Diocesan Library from Ireland; the G.L. Brook Theology Collection which contains 17th- and 18th-century theological works; the Dr Bray Clerical Lending Library from Poulton-le-Fylde in Lancashire; a collection of early 19th-century tracts published by the American Sunday School Union; and a collection of biblical and theological literature presented by James Prince Lee (1804–69), Bishop of Manchester. The Cassedy Collection of Irish publications contains works relating to the Protestant and Roman Catholic churches in Ireland.

Bibliography

Clive D. Field and Judith B. Shiel, *Theology and Church History: a Guide to Research Resources in the John Rylands University Library of Manchester* (Manchester, 1990).

Clive D. Field, 'Sources for the Study of Protestant Nonconformity in the John Rylands University Library of Manchester', *Bulletin of the John Rylands University Library of Manchester*, vol. 71, no. 2 (1989), pp. 103–39.

Clive D. Field, 'Anti-Methodist Publications in the Eighteenth Century: A Revised Bibliography', *Bulletin of the John Rylands University Library of Manchester*, vol. 73, no. 2 (1991), pp. 159–280.

Select alphabetical list of resources: (MS: Manuscript/Archive; PR: Printed)

Audenshaw Foundation Archive

Date range: 1945–87.

Archive assembled by Mark Gibbs, a lifelong advocate of the ministry of the laity and co-author with T.R. Morton of *God's Frozen People: A Book for and about Ordinary Christians* (1964) and *God's Lively People: Christians in Tomorrow's World* (1971). Gibbs was the director of the Audenshaw Foundation, which was established first at Audenshaw, east of Manchester, then at neighbouring Denton and finally at Muker in Swaledale, North Yorkshire.

In addition to Gibbs's personal papers the archive contains records of the Foundation, and other lay movements with which he was associated, such as the Christian Frontier Council, the Vesper Society of San Leandro in California, and the International Committee of the German Kirchentag. Material comprises correspondence, financial and administrative papers, reports, typescript and printed articles, and newspaper cuttings concerning the role of the laity in the Churches. There are also runs of periodicals such as *The Christian News-Letter* and *Frontier*.

Finding aids: unpublished outline list.

Northern Baptist College Archive

Date range: 1838–1971.

There is a separate collection of records from Aenon Baptist Church, Burnley. See also the Northern Baptist College Printed Collection (p. 65).

There are 88 manuscript volumes in the Northern Baptist College Archive. There are two items by John Fawcett (1740–1817), but the bulk comprises minute books, account books and other records of various Baptist organizations in North-West England. The largest number relate to Longsight Baptist Church in Manchester, 1887–1970, with smaller archives for churches in Manchester, Padiham, Carlisle and Llangollen. Local associations and organizations represented include the Baptist Building Fund Liverpool Auxiliary, Lancashire and Cheshire Association of Baptist Churches, Lancashire and Cheshire Baptist Women's League, Bury and Rossendale District Baptist Lay Preachers' Association, Manchester District Baptist Union, and Lancashire and Cheshire Baptist Women's Federation.

Finding aids: provisional outline list.

Joseph Benson Papers (Methodist Archives)

Date range: 1766–1820.

Joseph Benson (1748–1821) was born in the parish of Kirkoswald in Cumberland, the son of John and Isabella Benson. He was educated locally until the age of sixteen, when he was introduced to John Wesley in Newcastle. Shortly after this first meeting Wesley appointed him classics master at Kingswood School near Bristol. In 1769 Benson was entered at St Edmund Hall, Oxford, but left in the following year to take up the post of headmaster of Trevocca College. He resigned after less than a year, following a dispute with the College's founder, the Countess of Huntingdon. Benson became a Methodist itinerant after being refused Anglican Orders in 1771. He was soon regarded as one of Wesley's foremost preachers. He served as President of the Conference in 1798 and 1810, and from 1803 until his death held the post of editor of the *Methodist Magazine*.

The collection comprises some 150 items, the majority being letters written by Benson concerning Methodist affairs. Correspondents include John Wesley, John and Mary Fletcher, Thomas Coke, Jabez Bunting and Adam Clarke. There are also engravings of Benson, biographical notes, fragments of letters and other papers.

Finding aids: unpublished detailed catalogue.

Hugh Bourne Collection (Methodist Archives)

Date range: 1803–52.

Papers of Hugh Bourne (1772–1852), co-founder of the Primitive Methodists. Bourne was born near Stoke-on-Trent, Staffordshire, and became a member of the Wesleyan Methodist Connection at Bemersley. Inspired by the preaching of the American evangelist Lorenzo Dow, he was prominent in organizing the first camp meeting held on Mow Cop in May 1807. Following criticism of his role in the camp meeting movement, he was expelled from the Wesleyan Connexion in 1808. The followers of Bourne joined with those of another Staffordshire preacher, William Clowes (*q.v.*), to form the Primitive Methodist Connexion in 1811. Bourne played a leading role in establishing Primitive Methodism as one of the country's leading free churches, and by the time of his superannuation in 1842 it had a membership of almost 80,000.

After Bourne's death his papers passed to his nephew John Walford and were purchased by the Primitive Methodist Conference in 1858, when those items deemed sensitive were destroyed. The collection comprises letters from Bourne to William Garner and others; an engraving of Bourne; manuscripts of Bourne's autobiography; and Hugh Bourne's journals.

Finding aids: unpublished detailed catalogue.

Archive of the Canonesses of the Holy Sepulchre

Date range: 13th–18th centuries.

The English Canonesses of the Holy Sepulchre were founded by Susan Hawley (1622–1706), who was professed at the convent of Tongres in Belgium. In 1642 she and four others went to Liège to establish a community there, of which she became the first Prioress in 1652. Two years later the Canonesses took over the property of a house of Frères Coquins, who had in fact been expelled to make room for them. The Frères Coquins were a lay order following the Rule of St Augustine, and were originally known as the Brothers of the Hospital of St Christopher. The Canonesses remained in Liège until the French Revolution, when they took refuge in England, in 1798 settling near Chelmsford, Essex.

The documents relate to the temporal possessions of the Frères, and subsequently the Canonesses, at Liège. They comprise estate records, consisting of more than 120 volumes of registers, manuals and accounts, and over 650 deeds relating to the property and finances of the two religious communities. Records of the Brothers date from the 13th century to 1655; those associated with the Canonesses from the second half of the 17th century to the 18th century. They include a brief of Pope Innocent X, dated 13 June 1654, suppressing the Coquins and authorising the transfer of their property to the nuns; a list of lands sold by the Sepulchrines in 1699; and an 18th-century map of the property belonging to the Canonesses. The archive constitutes a valuable source for study of the land ownership and administration of religious houses.

Finding aids: unpublished handlist. See also note in *Bulletin of the John Rylands Library*, vol. 34 (1951–52), pp. 244–5.

Christian Theology & Ecclesiastical History

Christian Brethren Archive

Date range: 1815–1983.

The archive contains some 6,000 manuscript items, in addition to printed materials, relating to individual Brethren and Brethren assemblies. The former include papers of John Nelson Darby (1800–82), Benjamin Wills Newton (1807–99) and his circle, Piero Guicciardini (1808–86), Teodorico Pietrocola Rossetti (1825–83), James Harvey McNairn, George Henry Lang (1874–1958), Harold St John (1876–1957), Ransome Wallace Cooper (1881–1979), Joseph Barnes Watson (1884–1955), and Dorothy Isaac, concerning missionary work in the Belgian Congo, 1921–24.

See also the Christian Brethren Printed Collection (p. 67).

Institutional records relate to Brethren assemblies in Bramhall, Carlisle, Eccles, Grosmont, Hereford, Leominster, Ludlow, Ross-on-Wye, Stafford and Stretford, as well as the Devonshire Conferences of 1906 and 1907 (which discussed the terms of fellowship between gatherings of Open and Exclusive Brethren), and the Christian Brethren Research Fellowship for 1962–81.

Finding aids: partial unpublished handlist and card catalogue. See also David Brady, 'The Christian Brethren Archive in the John Rylands University Library of Manchester', in Lorenza Giorgi and Massimo Rubboli (eds), *Piero Guicciardini, 1808–1886: un riformatore religioso nell' Europa dell' ottocento* (Firenza, 1988).

Location: JRULM (Main Library).

Adam Clarke Papers (Methodist Archives)

Date range: 1785–1832.

Papers of Dr Adam Clarke (1762–1832), theologian and biblical scholar. Adam Clarke was born at Moybeg in the parish of Kilcronaghan, co. Londonderry, the son of a school-master, and was educated at Kingswood School near Bristol. He was appointed to his first Methodist circuit at Bradford, Wiltshire, in 1782, and served as a Methodist minister in several areas of the country. He was President of the Wesleyan Conference in 1806, 1814 and 1822.

Clarke enjoyed a very high reputation as a scholar, and produced works on a wide range of subjects, including theology, oriental languages and biblical studies. His most important work was his Bible Commentary, published in eight volumes between 1810 and 1826.

The bulk of the collection consists of correspondence and associated papers, which were gathered together by Clarke's family after his death. Correspondents include Joseph Benson, Jabez Bunting, Samuel Harpur, George Marsden, Richard Tabraham, Ruth Thurston and Catherine Whitacre. The letters concern Clarke's personal life, his academic pursuits and Church affairs. The collection also contains biographical materials, fragments of letters, literary fragments, and engravings of Adam Clarke.

Finding aids: unpublished detailed catalogue.

William Clowes Collection (Methodist Archives)

Date range: 1836–38.

Papers of William Clowes (1780–1852), evangelist and co-founder of the Primitive Methodists. Clowes was born at Burslem, Staffordshire, and trained as a potter. He was converted under the influence of the local Wesleyan Methodist Society and began preaching locally. He was expelled from the Connexion in 1810 as a result of his involvement in the camp meeting movement. His followers, who were known as Clowesites, subsequently merged with the group led by Hugh Bourne (*q.v.*) to form the Primitive Methodist Connexion. Clowes was an outstanding evangelist and played a major role in the expansion of the movement, leading important missions to several parts of the country.

Very few manuscripts of William Clowes have survived. The collection comprises seven notebooks of Clowes covering topics such as his relationship with Hugh Bourne, Primitive Methodism in Hull, and his early life within the Methodist Church. The notebooks were formerly in the possession of Hartley Victoria College and represent much the most important source of information concerning Clowes's life.

Finding aids: unpublished detailed catalogue.

Thomas Coke Papers (Methodist Archives)

Date range: 1775–1814.

Papers of Dr Thomas Coke (1747–1814), Methodist missionary. Coke was born in Brecon, the son of a medical practitioner. He was educated at Brecon Grammar School and Jesus College, Oxford, and was elected mayor of Brecon shortly after graduating in 1768. Coke took Holy Orders in August 1772 but was ejected from his curacy in Somerset for trying to run the parish on Methodist principles. He moved to London and placed himself under the direction of John Wesley, swiftly reaching a position of prominence.

Coke has been described as being "in some respects the most important of John Wesley's recruits to Methodism from the ranks of the Anglican clergy. He was certainly the most dedicated of Wesley's clerical supporters" (Vickers: see below). His greatest achievement was in the field of foreign missions. He made a total of eighteen trans-atlantic trips, and is regarded as one of the founders of the Methodist Church in the United States and West Indies. Coke also made repeated visits to Ireland and the Continent of Europe, and served as President of the British Conference in 1797 and 1805.

In December 1813 Coke set sail from England to establish a mission in India but died at sea on 3 May 1814.

Coke maintained an extensive correspondence throughout his life on a wide range of subjects, and the collection consists largely of these letters and associated papers. Many of the letters are copies of originals held elsewhere.

Finding aids: published catalogue, Gareth Lloyd, 'The Papers of Dr Thomas Coke: A Catalogue', with an introduction by Dr John A. Vickers, *Bulletin of the John Rylands University Library of Manchester*, vol. 76, no. 2 (1994), pp. 205–320.

Congregational College Archives

Christian Theology & Ecclesiastical History

Date range: 1783–1980.

Archives of the Northern Congregational College, formerly the Lancashire Independent College, and of its predecessor and constituent institutions. There are academic and financial records of twelve other training institutions which have been absorbed or become affiliated over the years: Rotherham College (1795–1889), Idle Independent Academy (1800–31), Leaf Square Academy, Pendleton (1809–16), Blackburn Academy (1815–43), Airedale Independent College (1831–89), Western College, Bristol (1845–1969), Cavendish Theological College, Manchester (1860–64), Congregational Institute, Nottingham (1864–1920), Yorkshire United Independent College, Bradford (1887–1958), Paton College, Nottingham (1899–1968), Bradford Student House (1909–58), and Edinburgh Student House (1919–40). There are minutes and other records from four Congregational churches in Bradford (1783–1953), and the correspondence, diaries and papers of the Manchester minister William Roby (1766–1830).

See also the Congregational College Printed Collection (p. 67) and the Thomas Raffles Collection (p. 61).

Finding aids: unpublished outline list.

Lewis Court Bible Christian Collection (Methodist Archives)

Date range: 1815–1932.

Lewis Henry Court (1871–1960) was born into a Bible Christian family in Kingsbrompton, Somerset. He became a local preacher at the age of seventeen, and entered the full-time ministry four years later. He served in home circuits for 42 years, mainly in the south-west of England, before he was forced into retirement by ill-health in 1934. Court was a gifted writer and artist, who produced several books on Methodist history and related subjects. He also published several collections of poetry.

The Bible Christian Church was founded by a dissident Wesleyan Methodist preacher, William O'Bryan (1778–1868), who began a plan of independent evangelism on 18 October 1815 in North Cornwall. The first society of 22 members was established at Lake Farm in the small Devon village of Shebbear. They were termed Bible Christians because of their practice of regularly consulting the scriptures for guidance. Bible Christians were noted for their evangelical zeal and extensive use of female preachers.

The movement spread rapidly in south-west England and by 1820 missions had been established in the Channel Islands and Kent, although the heartland of the Bible Christian Connexion remained in the south-west. Overseas missions were established in Canada (1845), Australia (1850), New Zealand (1878) and China (1885). The Bible Christians joined with the United Methodist Free Churches and the Methodist New Connexion in 1907 to form the United Methodist Church. At the time of the union they had 220 ministers, 1,500 local preachers and 34,640 members.

The collection, amassed by Lewis Henry Court over a period of about 50 years, consists of the correspondence of the O'Bryan family, 1815–65; letters of prominent 19th-century preachers; material concerning missionary activities in Australia, New Zealand, Canada and China; material relating to the Methodist Church in Australia, New Zealand and Canada; photographs and portrait engravings of several hundred Bible Christian and United Methodist ministers, 1840–1932; and correspondence concerning the preservation of the collection.

Finding aids: unpublished detailed catalogue.

Rupert Davies Collection (Methodist Archives)

Date range: 1964–94.

Dr Rupert Eric Davies (1909–94) was educated at St Paul's School and Balliol College, Oxford, before training for the Methodist ministry at Wesley House, Cambridge. He was ordained in 1937. After five years in the circuit ministry in Bristol he was appointed tutor in church history at Didsbury College, Bristol, and from 1967 until 1973 he served as Principal of Wesley College. Davies later returned to circuit work and in 1976 he took up an appointment as Warden of the New Room, Bristol. He served as President of the Methodist Conference in 1970, sat on numerous committees and councils, and was a prolific writer in the fields of Church history, theology and ecumenicity.

The collection contains material relating to Dr Davies as an ecumenicist, educationalist, minister, writer, Church historian and advocate of Church unity. Material includes diaries; a typescript autobiography; lecture and sermon notes; correspondence; photographs; newspaper cuttings; papers relating to the presidential year 1970–71; draft and published copies of Davies's books, articles and reviews; papers of the Harborne Group; papers relating to the Church overseas, especially in Hong Kong, Sri Lanka, Sierra Leone, Korea, the United States, Canada, Portugal and Burma; papers relating to Anglican/Methodist conversations, ecumenism, the World Council of Churches and the British Council of Churches.

Finding aids: unpublished detailed catalogue.

Early Preachers Collection (Methodist Archives)

Date range: 1737–1831.

The Early Preachers Collection, which is part of the Methodist Archives, comprises two folio volumes or scrapbooks containing approximately 160 letters and associated papers. The first volume consists of over 100 letters written mainly to Charles Wesley (*q.v.*), while the second is more general in nature.

A wide range of correspondents is represented in the collection. There are papers of important Anglican evangelicals such as George Whitefield and William Grimshaw, as well as letters from preachers and lay people of every social class. The letters illuminate the lives and activities of John and Charles Wesley, and the development of the Methodist Church. There are also some items relating to early American Methodism and the Episcopalian Church. The subject range of the collection is extremely wide, as the correspondents write of official as well as personal matters. Researchers from several different historical disciplines will find the collection valuable.

Finding aids: unpublished detailed catalogue.

John Graham Papers

Date range: c.1844–1964.

Papers of John William Graham (1859–1932), Tutor in Mathematics, 1886–97, and Principal, 1897–1924, of Dalton Hall, the Quaker hall of residence at Owens College and later the University of Manchester. He played a prominent part nationally and internationally in the Society of Friends, through membership of its Meeting for Sufferings and its Peace, Education and Literature Committees, through his astonishing output of articles and books, through his involvement in secular campaigns against vivisection, smoke nuisance and militarism (he advocated conscientious objection in the First World War), and through his participation in Liberal party politics.

Graham's papers comprise correspondence (mainly with his family), lecture notes, three volumes of his articles and letters in newspapers, copies of other published papers and pamphlets, reviews of his books, obituaries, a family photograph album, other family papers, and reminiscences by those who knew Graham, collected after his death by his son Michael for an intended biography.

Finding aids: unlisted. See Clive D. Field, 'Sources for the Study of Protestant Nonconformity in the John Rylands University Library of Manchester', *Bulletin of the John Rylands University Library of Manchester*, vol. 71, no. 2 (1989), pp. 117–20.

Location: JRULM (Main Library).

For other Quaker-related material see the John Dalton Papers (p. 176), the Elfrida Vipont Collection (p. 145), and the Midgley Reference Library (p. 69).

Hartley Victoria College Collection (Methodist Archives)

Date range: c.1782–1966.

The Manchester Theological College admitted its first students in July 1881. The College's early years were marred by severe financial difficulties, but by the beginning of the 20th century, under the direction of the Principal, Dr Arthur Samuel Peake, 105 students were being trained at the College for the Primitive Methodist Ministry.

In 1906 the College was renamed after the industrialist Sir William Hartley, and in 1934 Hartley College amalgamated with the nearby Victoria Park College to form the Hartley Victoria College. In 1972 the decision was taken to close Hartley Victoria, but the College survived and continues to operate on a smaller scale in premises shared with the Baptist Church.

See also the papers of Arthur Samuel Peake (p. 60).

The collection consists of the records of the College itself, spanning the years 1876 to 1966, and of those establishments which it replaced, such as the Sunderland Theological Institute. College records comprise photographs of the college buildings, staff and students; income and expenditure account books; cash books; and committee minute books. The collection also contains materials collected by the College relating to the Primitive Methodist Church and other Methodist denominations, including circuit plans, chapel records, school records, connexional archives, illustrations, papers relating to foreign missions, sermons, and Wesley family illustrations and memorabilia.

Finding aids: unpublished handlist.

Hunmanby Hall School Records (Methodist Archives)

Date range: 1928–92.

Hunmanby Hall School, near Filey in East Yorkshire, was opened in 1928 by the Board of Management for Wesleyan Secondary Schools, as a boarding school for girls. It was administered as an independent trust by a board of governors, and provided education for up to 250 junior and secondary pupils. The school closed in 1991 and the buildings were sold for development in 1996.

Records comprise personal files on pupils and staff; minutes of the school council; financial records; group photographs of the school; school magazines; headmistresses' reports; minutes of the board of governors; class registers; cuttings books; architectural plans; files concerning open days and speech days; papers relating to Hunmanby Methodist

Church, the Old Girls Association, and external education bodies; printed matter such as prospectuses; and miscellaneous material. Certain classes are subject to a fifty-year closure from the date of their creation.

Finding aids: unpublished handlist.

Industrial Mission Association Archive

Date range: 1942–90.

Substantial archive of the Industrial Mission Association of Great Britain, relating to the history of the Association and to the work of industrial mission teams in more than twenty areas in Britain and, to a lesser extent, industrial missions overseas. Papers include minutes, reports and papers, correspondence, press cuttings and ephemera of the Association and other Christian organizations such as the World Council of Churches and the British Council of Churches. The collection is useful for studies of the lay ministries, industrial missions and the ecumenical movement, and for wider social studies of unemployment, the impact of industrial decline and economic change on the labour-force and communities, the Church's response to these problems, and Church-State relations.

See also the Jack Keiser Papers (below) and the William Temple Foundation Archive (p. 64).

Finding aids: unpublished handlist.

Jack Keiser Papers

Date range: 1931–93.

Jack Keiser (b. 1915) has combined a career in the engineering industry with active participation in the lay ministry. He has been involved in the Student Christian Movement and the Industrial Mission Association. He was licensed as a lay reader in the Church of England in 1951 and he joined the staff of the William Temple College and Foundation in 1969. The collection contains Keiser's personal papers, which comprise diaries, travel notes, correspondence, texts of sermons and talks, and a typescript autobiography.

There are also papers relating to the Student Christian Movement, the Industrial Mission Association, the William Temple College and Foundation, the World Council of Churches, the British Council of Churches and the Fabian Society. These include newsletters, annual reports, publications and publicity materials, and runs of periodicals such as *Student World, Ecumenical Review* and *Frontier*. The collection is of interest to students of social history, the lay ministry, industrial missions and the Christian socialist movement.

Finding aids: unpublished handlist.

League of the Good Samaritan Archive

Date range: 1910–87.

The League of the Good Samaritan was founded in 1910 by Herbert Buckley (d. 1924) at the Oxford Road Wesleyan Methodist Church in Manchester. The League was intended for men aged seventeen and over who were 'prepared to follow the example of the Good Samaritan by showing brotherly kindness and neighbourliness to those in trouble and in need'. From 1925 lodges affiliated to the League were established throughout England (but particularly in the North and Midlands). Most lodges were attached to Methodist churches but some were connected with Anglican, Baptist and Congregational places of worship. In 1986 there were 30 lodges grouped into five regions, plus a country lodge for members unable to attend a local lodge. In 1969 it was stated that the aim of the League was "to encourage the practical application of good neighbourliness and promote and expand a fellowship of Christian men and women dedicated to further the objects of the League".

The archive contains minute books, accounts and attendance registers for the Foundation Lodge from 1910 onwards, as well as minutes of the National Executive Committee and correspondence, typescripts and printed ephemera relating to the Lodge at a national level.

Finding aids: unpublished handlist; additional material unlisted.

Manchester Cathedral Archives

Date range: 16th–18th centuries.

A small quantity of archives were deposited by the Dean and Canons of Manchester Cathedral in 1962. The documents comprise 8 mortality report books recording causes of death, and burial and sexton's fees, 1731–1830; court rolls for the manor of Newton in Manchester, 1572–1695; 21 muniments of title relating to the property of the Cathedral College chiefly in the Deansgate area of Manchester and in Newton [Newton Heath], 1558–1750; a survey and rental of the manor of Newton, 1649; an enclosure and valuation book for College property in Deansgate and other parts of Manchester, 1649; and a boundaries book of Newton containing plans, 1798.

In 1980 additional deeds relating to properties in Bolton were deposited, and at the same time deeds and documents concerning land in Pendlebury were donated to the Library, 19th–20th centuries.

Finding aids: unpublished outline lists.

Thomas Manson Papers

Date range: 1910–67.

Papers of the Rev. Thomas Walter Manson (1893–1958), a distinguished New Testament scholar and minister of the Presbyterian Church of England. Manson trained for the ministry at Westminster College, Cambridge, and was ordained in 1925. In 1932 he was appointed Yates Professor of New Testament Greek and Exegesis at Mansfield College, Oxford, resigning in 1936 to take up the post of Rylands Professor of Biblical Criticism and Exegesis in the University of Manchester, a position which he held until his death in 1958. In 1953 he was elected Moderator of the General Assembly of the Presbyterian Church of England, which united with the Congregational Church in 1972 to form the United Reformed Church. Most of Manson's writings are in the field of New Testament studies (he served on the New Testament and Apocrypha panels for the *New English Bible*), but he was also an authority on Hebrew, Aramaic, Syriac, Coptic and Ethiopic texts.

The collection consists mainly of memorabilia of Manson's army service, academic career and foreign visits; notes and manuscripts of his articles and lectures; offprints of his articles; notes for, and texts of, sermons, addresses and broadcasts; correspondence; newspaper cuttings; and 2 files relating to his Moderatorship of the General Assembly of the Presbyterian Church of England in 1953. There is also material relating to the Manson Memorial Lectures, 1962–67.

Finding aids: unpublished catalogue.

Date range: 18th–20th centuries.

The Methodist Archives and Research Centre (MARC) was established by the Methodist Church of Great Britain in 1961 to house the Connexional records of the Church. The Centre was originally located at John Wesley's Chapel, City Road, London, but in 1977 it was transferred on deposit to the Library. MARC holds the world's largest collection of manuscripts relating to the founders of Methodism, John and Charles Wesley (p. 63), and other members of the Wesley family (p. 64). In all, the collection comprises approximately 5,000 letters, notebooks and associated papers of the period 1700–1865.

Prominent 18th-century Evangelicals, other than the Wesleys, whose personal papers are represented in the collections include George Whitefield (1714–70), the Countess of Huntingdon (1707–91), Howel Harris (1714–73) and Benjamin Ingham (1712–72). In addition, there is a very large collection (44 boxes) of manuscript material relating to John Fletcher (1729–85) of Madeley and his wife Mary Bosanquet (1739–1815).

The Methodist Archives also include extensive small collections of personal papers of approximately 4,000 ministers and lay-Methodists from the 18th century to the present. These include Thomas Coke (1747–1814), Joseph Benson (1748–1821), Adam Clarke (1760–1832), William Clowes (1780–1852), Hugh Bourne (1772–1852), Jabez Bunting (1779–1858), John Rattenbury (1806–79), John Ernest Rattenbury (1870–1963), Harold Burgoyne Rattenbury (1878–1962), and Dr Rupert Davies (1909–94).

The institutional records of Methodism are also well-represented. These include the records of the Methodist Conference and its several committees, and large collections deposited by the administrative Divisions of the Church, such as the Property Division, the Home Mission Department, the Divisions of Social Responsibility, Ministries, and Education and Youth, and the Armed Forces Board. There is material relating to all the major pre-union Methodist denominations, including the Lewis Court Bible Christian Collection (p. 54). The Methodist theological college, Hartley Victoria College, and Hunmanby Hall, the Methodist girls' boarding school, are also represented (p. 56).

Finding aids: several catalogues and handlists are available or are in preparation.

Moravian Church Manuscripts

Date range: 18th–20th centuries.

The majority of Moravian manuscripts were bequeathed by John Norman Libbey, Principal of the Moravian College at Fairfield. There are original documents from the period 1746–1861, transcripts made by Libbey from the archives of the British Province in London and from those of Herrnhut in Germany, and papers and reference tools illustrating Libbey's work as an historian of the Moravians. These records shed light both on the European background of the Church and on its development in Britain and Ireland. Most notable is an almost complete set of the Moravian headquarters diary, consisting of an 18th-century English translation for 1747–53 and 1755–64, and a German version for 1747–54. Libbey's working papers include a History of Unitas Fratrum in four notebooks, lists of English ministers and other Moravian 'labourers' up to 1900, analyses of the contents and authors of Moravian hymn-books from 1741 to 1940, and correspondence with English, American and German Moravian scholars, 1900–41.

Christian Theology & Ecclesiastical History

See also the following printed collections relating to Methodism: the Rylands Wesley Collection (p. 70), the Hobill Collection (p. 68) and the Methodist Archives Printed Book Collections (p. 69).

Other items include 14 original letters of James Hutton (1715–95), founder of the Moravian Church in England, 1774–84, and the journal of Christian Ignatius Latrobe (1758–1836) for 1788–89 and 1792. The latter provides valuable insights into the state of the continental Brethren, Moravian missionary work, and the anti-slavery movement.

There are also several hundred printed volumes, including a number of rare periodicals on Moravian subjects or by Moravian authors, from Libbey's collection and other sources, 17th–19th centuries.

Finding aids: recorded in published handlists of English Manuscripts (English MSS 110, 706, 871, 905, 910, 945–950, 965, 1054–1087, 1244, 1276). See also Frank Taylor, 'The John Rylands Library, 1936–72', *Bulletin of the John Rylands University Library of Manchester*, vol. 71, no. 2 (1989), p. 42.

Arthur Samuel Peake Papers

Date range: 1884–1929.

Papers of Arthur Samuel Peake (1865–1929), biblical scholar and Primitive Methodist layman. Peake was the first holder of the Rylands Chair of Biblical Criticism and Exegesis in the University of Manchester, from its establishment as an independent institution in 1904. He was thus the first non-Anglican to become a professor of divinity in an English university. From 1892 he had been tutor at the Primitive Methodist Theological Institute in Manchester, which was renamed Hartley College in 1906 (p. 56). He was largely responsible for broadening the curriculum which intending Primitive Methodist ministers were required to follow, and for raising the standards of the training. Peake was also active as a layman in wider Methodist circles, and did a great deal to further the reunion of Methodism which took effect in 1932, three years after his death. In the wider ecumenical sphere Peake worked for the National Council of Evangelical Free Churches, serving as president in 1928, and was a member of the Conference on Faith and Order held in Lausanne in 1927. He published and lectured extensively, but is best remembered for his one-volume commentary on the Bible (1919), which, in its revised form, is still in use.

The collection comprises extensive family, academic and church correspondence; correspondence on the Methodist Church and church unity; correspondence relating to his publications; press cuttings containing biographical information about Peake, articles and reviews by him, reviews of his own books, and obituaries and tributes; manuscripts, typescripts and offprints of articles by Peake; material on Hartley College; notebooks and diaries; and miscellaneous notes.

The Library also has a small collection of books from the library of A.S. Peake.

Finding aids: unpublished catalogue. See also Leslie S. Peake, *Arthur Samuel Peake: a Memoir* (London, 1930).

J. Arthur Pearson Papers

Date range: 1884–1955.

See also the Unitarian College Archives (p. 62).

Papers of the Rev. J. Arthur Pearson (1870–1947), Unitarian minister. Pearson was a student of what is now the Unitarian College, Manchester, from 1889 to 1896. The collection includes letters from fellow students at the College and from Alexander Gordon (1841–1931), who is also represented in the Unitarian College Archives. The material details the activities of the Presbyterian College, Carmarthen, and its relationship to the Presbyterian

Fund, and the affairs of Dr Williams's Trust, of which Pearson was a trustee for some years. There are also papers relating to the British and Foreign Unitarian Association (Incorporated), the Nonconformist Students Fraternal, Manchester, and Unitarian Sunday Schools, and a selection of Unitarian printed matter.

Finding aids: unpublished catalogue.

Christian Theology & Ecclesiastical History

Thomas Raffles Collection

Date range: 17th–19th century.

Collection of Thomas Raffles (1788–1863), eminent Congregationalist, one of the chief founders and, from 1842 to 1863, chairman of the Lancashire Independent College, and autograph collector. The collection falls into two sections which were separately acquired by the Library. The first comprises many thousands of letters and portraits of eminent Englishmen, chiefly of the 19th century, which were collected by Raffles. Those who are represented include authors, poets, artists, members of the nobility, and ecclesiastics, among them 133 Nonconformist divines from 1658 to 1821 (English MSS 369–371) and 135 missionaries (English MS 387).

See also the Congregational College Archives (p. 54).

The second section consists of Raffles's own papers, including 28 boxes of sermons delivered between 1807 and 1861; a three-volume holograph of 1819–21 entitled 'Collections for a History of the Nonconformist Churches of Lancashire'; and five volumes of letters chiefly written to him by Nonconformist ministers.

Finding aids: first part recorded in published handlist of English Manuscripts (English MSS 343–387), with card index of correspondents; unpublished handlist of second part.

Harold Burgoyne Rattenbury Papers (Methodist Archives)

Date range: 1927–47.

Harold Burgoyne Rattenbury (1878–1962), grandson of John Rattenbury and brother of John Ernest Rattenbury (*q.v.*), was born at Witney in Oxfordshire. He trained for the Wesleyan ministry at Headingley and in 1902 was appointed to the China Mission. He remained in China for 32 years, the last thirteen of which were spent as Chairman of the Wuchang District. His residence in China ended in 1934 when he was appointed to a secretaryship at the Mission House in London, but he returned to China and other parts of the Far East on several tours. He was elected President of the Methodist Conference in 1949. Rattenbury wrote extensively about China and made regular radio broadcasts on Chinese affairs.

The collection consists of several hundred letters written between 1927 and 1947, the majority from Rattenbury to his wife Emily during their extended periods of separation. There is also a typescript journal compiled between April and June 1934. The collection is a valuable source for China's affairs at a momentous time in its history. Rattenbury witnessed the end of the period of the War Lords and the beginning of the civil war between the Nationalists and the Communists. In addition to his commentary on political and social conditions, he provides a valuable insight into the daily life and work of the Methodist Mission at a time of widespread persecution.

Finding aids: unpublished detailed catalogue.

Date range: 1827–79.

John Rattenbury (1806–79) joined the Wesleyan Methodist Society in Manchester at the age of sixteen, and began to preach three years later. He trained for the ministry under the Rev. Joseph Roberts and was appointed to his first circuit in 1828. He was highly regarded as a minister and was an effective evangelist who was well-known for inspiring revivals such as the one that occurred during his ministry in Leeds in 1837. He was elected President of the Conference in 1851. He withdrew from circuit work in 1873 and spent the last six years of his life raising money for the Worn out Ministers' and Ministers' Widows' Auxiliary Fund.

The collection consists of 86 letters and associated documents relating to John Rattenbury's personal life and ministry. Several of the letters contain eye-witness accounts of the proceedings of the Wesleyan Conferences of 1833, 1834, 1836 and 1839, and are particularly informative about the struggles between the supporters of Jabez Bunting and the Wesleyan reformers.

Finding aids: unpublished detailed catalogue.

John Ernest Rattenbury Papers (Methodist Archives)

Date range: 1918–20.

John Ernest Rattenbury (1870–1963), grandson of John Rattenbury and brother of Harold Burgoyne Rattenbury (*q.v.*), was born in Stanningley near Leeds and trained for the Wesleyan ministry at Didsbury College in Manchester. Much of Rattenbury's ministry was spent in city missions, including eighteen years from 1907 in the West London Mission where he established himself as one of the outstanding Nonconformist ministers in the capital. He was one of the leading evangelists and preachers of his day. From 1918 to 1922 he was on the editorial board of the *Methodist Times* and in 1936 he served as President of the National Free Church Council. His popularity and status within the Connexion made him a formidable opponent of Methodist union in 1932. His opposition was grounded on his fear that union would damage the prospects for wider Christian unity.

The collection consists of correspondence, newspaper cuttings and printed tracts relating to anti-Catholic agitation organized by groups such as the Protestant Truth Society immediately after the First World War. Rattenbury came into conflict with the leaders of the Protestant extremists because of his alleged Catholic tendencies.

Finding aids: unpublished detailed catalogue.

Unitarian College Archives

Date range: c.1720–1953.

The Unitarian College, Manchester, was founded in c.1855 as the Unitarian Home Missionary Board, in order to train men for ministry among the poor, following the departure of Manchester College to London. In 1889 it changed its name to the Unitarian Home Missionary College, and assumed its present title in 1925. It has gradually achieved parity of status with Harris Manchester College which is now situated in Oxford.

The Unitarian College Archive encompasses the institutional records of the Unitarian College in Manchester, the records of other Unitarian bodies, and the papers of numerous individuals who were prominent in the Unitarian movement. It is of major importance not only to the history of the College but also to the history of Unitarianism, Puritanism and Dissent in general. The College's own records include applications for admission; reports of the principal, tutors and visitors on students and applicants; correspondence providing information on admissions, examinations and finance; library records; and various minute books and record books, 1854–1953.

Other institutional records concern the history of Dissenting and Presbyterian/Unitarian colleges and academies, particularly those at Warrington, Rathmell, Hoxton, Homerton, Daventry and Hackney, 1754–96; lectures delivered at Manchester College during its Manchester, York and London phases, 1787–1856; minutes of the meetings of Presbyterian and Unitarian ministers in Lancashire and Cheshire, 1820–75; minutes of the Manchester District Sunday School Association, 1845–1934; records of the Manchester Unitarian Sunday School Union, 1864–1914; minutes of the Monthly Conference of Ministers, 1882–1943; minutes of 'The Brotherhood', the Manchester and district ministerial society, 1889–1917; and records of several Unitarian churches and chapels.

Personal papers comprise letters, diaries, texts of sermons and tracts, lecture notes, accounts and autobiographical material, c.1720–1943. Among those represented are George Benson (1699–1762), Joseph Ryder (1693–1768), Nicholas Clayton (1733?–97), Theophilus Lindsey (1723–1808), William Shepherd (1768–1847), James Hews Bransby (1783–1847), John Relly Beard (1800–76), John Gordon (1807–80), James Martineau (1805–1900), George Fox (1834–1916), Alexander Gordon (1841–1931) and Walter Herbert Burgess (1867–1943). Alexander Gordon contributed biographies of some seven hundred Nonconformist figures to the *Dictionary of National Biography*; his papers include a substantial collection of research notes on approximately six hundred and fifty of these.

Finding aids: selective card index and unpublished handlist; detailed cataloguing in progress.

Christian Theology & Ecclesiastical History

See also the papers of Thomas Manson (p. 58), Rev. J. Arthur Pearson (p. 60), W.E.A. Axon (p. 103), and the Fielden Brothers (p. 104), the papers of C.P. Scott within the Guardian Archive (p. 104), and the Unitarian College Printed Collection (p. 70).

Charles Wesley Papers (Methodist Archives)

Date range: 1726–87.

Charles Wesley (1707–88) was born at Epworth in Lincolnshire, the son of a poverty-stricken clergyman. He was educated at Westminster School and Christ Church, Oxford, where he was one of the founder members of the Holy Club or Oxford Methodists, a small Christian group which included the Wesley brothers, and their fellow Evangelists George Whitefield and Benjamin Ingham. After his ordination and a brief period spent as a missionary in Georgia, Charles Wesley underwent a conversion experience in London in May 1738, a few days before John Wesley's famous Aldersgate experience.

For seventeen years after his conversion Charles Wesley was one of the central figures in the great Evangelical revival which saw the birth of the Methodist Church. He travelled constantly in England, Wales and Ireland, suffering frequent harassment, which was often instigated by fellow clergymen. While his brother John was without doubt the leader of the Methodist movement, Charles was his most trusted colleague, and often exercised a restraining influence on those Methodists who wished to break away from the Church of England.

Charles Wesley's greatest legacy to Methodism is his hymns which are regarded as among the finest ever written. The Methodists gave hymn-singing a central place in worship, contrary to contemporary Anglican practice. Wesley's hymns formed the basis of the

Methodist hymn-books of the 18th and 19th centuries, and are still sung all over the world by Christians of every denomination.

The collection is of major importance for studies of the history of Methodism. It comprises approximately 100 letters written by Wesley from 1728 until shortly before his death, dealing with personal and official matters, and 14 in-letters; loose literary manuscripts and notebooks, containing autograph poems or hymns in Wesley's hand; three folio scrapbooks containing correspondence, journal letters, poems, financial papers and copies of original documents which are now lost; and several notebooks containing very detailed household and other accounts covering the years which the Wesley family spent in London. A draft manuscript journal covers the years 1736–56.

Finding aids: unpublished detailed catalogue. See also Gareth Lloyd, 'Charles Wesley and Methodist Religious Life, 1750–1775: the manuscript sources', *Proceedings of the Charles Wesley Society*, vol. 1 (1994), pp. 33–45.

Wesley Family Papers (Methodist Archives)

Date range: 1701–1883.

The Wesleys were one of the most remarkable families of 18th-century England, producing the two brothers, John and Charles, who founded the Methodist movement. The collection relates mainly to members of the Wesley family (other than John and Charles Wesley), but there is also a substantial archive relating to the Gwynne family of Garth, Brecknockshire, and its connection with early Welsh Calvinistic Methodism, and to the Waller family of London. Among those represented are: Samuel Wesley (1662–1735) and his wife Susanna (1670–1742); their children Samuel (1690–1739), Emily (Mrs Robert Harper) (1691–1770), Mary (Mrs John Whitelamb) (1696–1734), Mehtabel (Mrs William Wright) (1697–1751), Anne (Mrs John Lambert) (b. 1702), Martha (Mrs Westley Hall) (1707?–91) and Kezia (1710–41); the children of Charles Wesley (1707–88), Sally (1759–1828) and Samuel (1766–1837); and Samuel's children Charles (1793–1859), John (d. 1862), Samuel Sebastian (1810–76) and Eliza (1819–95).

The Wesley family papers consist of original letters, with some manuscript verse, notebooks and other miscellaneous items. Among the subjects covered are the musical careers of the two sons of the Rev. Charles Wesley and the development of the Methodist Church up to the death of John Wesley. In general the collection gives an invaluable insight into Church and society in the 18th and early 19th centuries. The collection is divided into two parts, loose manuscripts and folio bound volumes, which have been separately catalogued, although the material in each is identical in form. The loose papers of John and Charles Wesley were separated many years ago, but the collection does contain many letters written to John and Charles, and the volumes hold some material written by both men.

Finding aids: unpublished detailed catalogue.

William Temple Foundation Archives

Date range: 1942–90.

Archives of the William Temple Foundation, formerly the William Temple College. The College was founded at Hawarden, Flintshire, in 1947, moved to Rugby in 1954, and thence to Manchester in 1971, whereupon it changed its named to the William Temple Foundation. It is now a resource centre for those developing discipleship and ministry in an urban/

Christian Theology & Ecclesiastical History

See also the Wesley Family Papers (below) and the Early Preachers Collection (p. 55).

See also the Charles Wesley Papers (p. 63), the Early Preachers Collection (p. 55) and the Hartley Victoria College Collection (p. 56).

industrial society. It is particularly involved in industry, employment, community work and the issue of poverty, and it provides training for church-related community work.

Material in the archive reflects these concerns and activities, and includes minutes and memoranda, financial accounts, official letters, course programmes, articles and newspaper cuttings, and printed ephemera, documenting the history of the college and its involvement in courses and conferences.

Finding aids: unpublished handlist.

See also the Industrial Mission Association Archive (p. 57) and the Jack Keiser Papers (p. 57).

Women in Theology Group Archive

Date range: c.1980 to present.

The Women in Theology Group was established in the early 1980s as a pressure group to campaign for the full ordination of women in the Church of England. This goal was of course achieved in 1994, but the Group continues to promote the role of women within all churches and acts as a forum for feminist theology.

The archive comprises administrative papers, correspondence files, Executive Committee minutes, membership lists, newsletters and publicity materials. There are also newsletters and publications from many other Christian evangelical and feminist organizations in Britain, the United States and continental Europe. These will be of enormous interest to feminist historians and students of contemporary theology, and they augment the Library's existing rich holdings of theological archives, which are particularly strong in the Nonconformist and evangelical fields.

Access: access to membership lists and correspondence is closed for 50 years from the date of creation. Finding aids: unpublished accession list.

PRINTED RESOURCES

American Sunday School Union Collection

240 items.

The religious and moral tracts published by the Union in Philadelphia between 1825 and 1840 are bound in 50 volumes, housed in their own miniature pedimented bookcase. All the tracts appear to be scarce even so far as the main American library collections are concerned.

Finding aids: card catalogue. See also B.J. Scragg, 'A Collection of American Chapbooks in the John Rylands University Library of Manchester', *American Studies Library Newsletter*, vol. 22 (1986), pp. 4–7.

Northern Baptist College Printed Collection

4,700 items.

The collection contains items printed between 1558 and 1977, the most important for primary source material being issued in the 18th and 19th centuries. 657 volumes represent 47 periodical titles, together with 1,878 pamphlets, 765 monographs, 143 biographies, 462 sermons, 372 hymn-books and related works, and 406 local histories. The vast majority of the items were written by Baptist authors. The collection is of particular significance for the history of the Baptist Church in Britain in the 18th and 19th centuries, with an impressive

See also the Northern Baptist College Archive (p. 50).

number of English provincial and Scottish imprints, but there is some coverage of North America and of Baptist overseas missions.

Finding aids: cataloguing in progress. See also Clive D. Field, 'Sources for the Study of Protestant Nonconformity in the John Rylands University Library of Manchester', *Bulletin of the John Rylands University Library of Manchester*, vol. 71, no. 2 (1989), pp. 106–8.

Christian Theology & Ecclesiastical History

Bible Collection

10,000 items.

The Bible Collection, which originated with the purchase by Mrs Rylands of the Spencer Collection in 1892, is of major importance for biblical scholarship, bibliography and the history of printing. It includes Bibles in more than 400 different languages and dialects, published over almost five centuries. The earliest editions are the 42-line or Gutenberg Bible, printed at Mainz in c.1455, and the even rarer 36-line Bible printed at Bamberg in 1458–60. Nearly 100 editions of the Latin Vulgate printed before 1500 are available, together with first editions in virtually every language, the four great Polyglots of the 16th and 17th centuries, including the Complutensian sponsored by Cardinal Ximenes, six editions of the Erasmian New Testament, and a complete conspectus of the history of the English text from Tyndale to the present day.

Mrs Ernest Hartland of Chepstow donated in the 1930s 2,000 Bibles and 1,500 miscellaneous volumes, including 32 incunabula, in memory of her late husband who had, in his turn, absorbed the library of Walter A. Copinger, Professor of Law at Owens College from 1892 until his death in 1910.

Finding aids: recorded in general printed-book catalogue. See also Richard Lovett, *The English Bible in the John Rylands Library* (Manchester, 1899); John Rylands Library, *Catalogue of an exhibition illustrating the history of the transmission of the Bible* (Manchester, 1935); for the Hartland collection see note in *Bulletin of the John Rylands Library*, vol. 20 (1935), pp. 176–8.

Dr Bray Clerical Lending Library

135 items.

During the 1690s the Rev. Dr Thomas Bray (1656–1730) devised a scheme for establishing parochial libraries in every deanery in England and Wales. By the time of his death some eighty had been set up. The library project soon developed into the larger scheme by which the SPCK was founded. Two thirds of this collection, from Poulton-le-Fylde in Lancashire, comprise works of Anglican theology and church history published between 1690 and 1720. The remainder are general theological books of the 19th century.

Finding aids: uncatalogued.

G.L. Brook Theology Collection

See also the G.L. Brook Drama Collection (p. 147).

1,050 items.

The collection of George Leslie Brook (1910–87), the famous historian of English drama and Professor of English Language and Medieval English Literature at Manchester University, 1945–77, is devoted to the theology and literature of the 17th and early 18th centuries. It contains 70 titles by Gilbert Burnet and 25 by Thomas Fuller.

Finding aids: recorded in general printed-book catalogue.

Christian Theology & Ecclesiastical History

Christian Brethren Printed Collection

15,000 items.

The collection was acquired in 1979 and has subsequently received several substantial additional collections including the Bristol Library for Biblical Research, the library in the offices of *Echoes of Service* in Bath and the collection of G.C.D. Howley, editor of *The Witness* from 1955 to 1977. Over 400 publishers of Brethren works world-wide are represented. The collection is one of the best in Britain for the study of Brethren texts, and the biography of notable personalities and missionaries. There are 280 periodical titles, 5,300 books and 7,500 pamphlets and tracts. There is some bias towards British material but other languages represented include Arabic, Chinese, Dutch, French, German, Italian, Polish, Portuguese and some African tongues. However, coverage of the most recent Exclusive division, the Taylor-Symington faction, is relatively poor.

See also the Christian Brethren Archive (p. 52).

Finding aids: card catalogues. See also Clive D. Field, 'Sources for the Study of Protestant Nonconformity in the John Rylands University Library of Manchester', *Bulletin of the John Rylands University Library of Manchester*, vol. 71, no. 2 (1989), pp. 135–9.

Location: JRULM (Main Library).

Clogher Diocesan Library

1,100 items in 115 volumes.

The collection was acquired in September 1953, when the Church of Ireland diocesan library was dispersed. The items date from 1531 to 1884, with 176 pre-1700 titles and nearly all the remainder dating from the 18th century. They are chiefly sermons and other theological works, with a high proportion printed in Dublin or otherwise of Irish interest.

See also the Cassedy Collection of Irish literature (p. 19).

Finding aids: recorded in general printed-book catalogue.

Congregational College Printed Collection

2,300 items.

The Library holds a substantial collection of printed books from the Northern Congregational College, formerly the Lancashire Independent College. The collection, purchased in 1974–75, comprises 1,878 volumes containing 2,300 items. 390 volumes were published in England or on the Continent before 1640. Among these are eleven incunables (the earliest of 1480), but most date from 1550 onwards. They cover a wide range of subjects, although inevitably there is a bias towards theology. The remaining 1,488 volumes were printed between 1641 and 1928, but mainly before 1800. They comprise Bibles and religious works by Anglican, Nonconformist and foreign authors. The Dissenting element is a large one and is particularly strong for the 1640s to the 1690s, including 95 volumes by the Presbyterian Richard Baxter (1615–91), many of them first editions, as well as writings by John Owen (1616–83) and other early apologists for Independency.

See also the Congregational College Archives (p. 54).

Finding aids: uncatalogued; however, incunabula are recorded in the general printed-book catalogue. See Clive D. Field, 'Sources for the Study of Protestant Nonconformity in the John Rylands University Library of Manchester', *Bulletin of the John Rylands University Library of Manchester*, vol. 71, no. 2 (1989), pp. 108–11.

Hobill Collection

4,600 items.

See also the Rylands Wesley Collection (p. 70) and the Methodist Archives Printed Book Collections (p. 69).

Formed by G.A.K. Hobill, a leading layman of the Methodist New Connexion, the collection passed into official Church ownership in 1894, and from 1934 was housed at Hartley Victoria College (*q.v.*) where it was augmented by works on Primitive Methodism and by part of the personal library of James Everett. When transferred to the Library in 1973 it consisted of 475 periodical volumes, 1,000 books and 3,100 pamphlets, embracing all aspects and all periods of Methodist history but with particularly strong coverage of Wesleyan Methodism, Primitive Methodism and the Methodist New Connexion as well as a significant element of local and ephemeral material.

Finding aids: unpublished handlist. Pamphlets recorded on Eighteenth-Century Short Title Catalogue (ESTC) and Nineteenth-Century Short Title Catalogue (NSTC).

Hymn Collection of John Rylands

60,000 items.

The collection comes from the personal library of John Rylands at Longford Hall in Stretford and it consists of 60,000 English and other hymns of varying theological origin, pasted in to 34 large folio volumes in preparation for the 1885 publication of *Hymns for the Church Universal*.

Finding aids: there is a manuscript index of first lines and authors in nine volumes.

Prince Lee Collection

7,000 items (dispersed).

The collection was bequeathed in 1870 by James Prince Lee (1804–69), Bishop of Manchester. It is mainly devoted to biblical literature, theology and history. Prince Lee collected a large number of works relating to the Manchester diocese, and there are several large folio volumes containing engravings and plans illustrating the history and architecture of the diocese, interleaved with the portion of Bishop Gastrell's *Notitia Cestriensis* which relates to it. The collection was, however, a general one and includes books on mathematics, physics, chemistry, natural history and medicine.

Finding aids: recorded in general printed-book catalogue. See also *A Catalogue of the MSS. and Printed Books, bequeathed to Owens College, Manchester by the late Right Rev. James Prince Lee* (Manchester, [1870]).

Location: JRULM (Deansgate: dispersed within Special Collections).

Methodist Archives Printed Book Collections

60,000 items.

Deposited in the Library in 1977, the Methodist Archives Printed Books Collections are unrivalled for the study of the Wesleys and Methodism. They comprise 5,200 bound and boxed volumes of periodicals; 2,900 publications of John and Charles Wesley, including every edition of John Wesley's works listed in Green's bibliography; 400 works published in opposition to Methodism in the 18th century; the personal libraries of Charles Wesley and his family and of John Fletcher of Madeley, Wesley's designated successor; 2,000 biographies; 3,500 hymn-books; 15,000 pamphlets; 10,000 miscellaneous monographs; 4,400 local histories; more than 10,000 circuit plans; and several thousand ephemeral items, such as class tickets and newspaper cuttings.

Finding aids: various published and unpublished guides and catalogues. Pamphlets recorded on Eighteenth-Century Short Title Catalogue (ESTC) and Nineteenth-Century Short Title Catalogue (NSTC). See also Clive D. Field, 'Sources for the Study of Protestant Nonconformity in the John Rylands University Library of Manchester', *Bulletin of the John Rylands University Library of Manchester*, vol. 71, no. 2 (1989), pp. 131–5.

Midgley Reference Library

1,200 items in 221 volumes.

A substantial collection of Quaker literature, formed by James Midgley (1786–1852) of Rochdale and presented by his children to the Lancashire and Cheshire Quarterly Meeting of the Society of Friends in 1863. The collection was eventually transferred to the Library on permanent loan in 1955. 1,036 of the titles are tracts ranging in date from 1648 to 1841, but nearly 90 per cent of the works were published in the late 17th century, these representing about one sixth of all known Quaker publications of the period. Many of the tracts are extremely rare and a few are unique. The collection contains works by all the outstanding Quaker writers of the 17th century. George Fox is represented by over 100 works, William Penn by 38 and Isaac Penington by 45 out of 78 titles recorded in Wing. Among a group of Commonwealth tracts are several rare anti-Quaker items, such as George Emmot's *Northern Blast, or the spiritual Quaker converted* (1655).

Finding aids: recorded in general printed-book catalogue. See also published catalogue, *Midgley Reference Library: Catalogue of Books relating to the Society of Friends, the gift of the surviving children of James Midgley of Rochdale to Lancashire and Cheshire Quarterly Meeting* (Manchester, 1866); also note in *Bulletin of the John Rylands Library*, vol. 37 (1954–55), p. 361.

Reformation Collection

600 items (dispersed).

The Library holds a fine collection of 16th-century tracts and other publications associated with Martin Luther, Desiderius Erasmus, Ulrich von Hutten, Philipp Melanchthon and Huldrych Zwingli. The collection contains a copy of Luther's *Disputatio* or *Ninety-five Theses* printed at Wittenberg in 1517. Erasmian texts include a copy of his *Encomium Moriae*, printed at Basel by Johannes Froben in 1515, an Aldine edition from the same year,

Christian Theology & Ecclesiastical History

See also the Rylands Wesley Collection (p. 70), the Hobill Collection (p. 68) and the manuscript components of the Methodist Archives (p. 59).

and a copy of the first English edition of *The Praise of Folly*, translated by Thomas Chaloner in 1549.

Finding aids: recorded in general printed-book catalogue.

Christian Theology & Ecclesiastical History

Rylands Wesley Collection

2,000 items.

The collection was founded in 1903 with the purchase by Mrs Rylands from R. Thursfield-Smith of 858 volumes published between 1735 and 1898. The content is primarily British Wesleyan Methodist, with works by the founders of Methodism, John and Charles Wesley, together with 18th-century works in opposition to or defence of Methodism, hymn-books and liturgies, biographies and local histories.

See also the Hobill Collection (p. 68) and the Methodist Archives Printed Book Collections (p. 69).

Finding aids: recorded in general printed-book catalogue.

Unitarian College Printed Collection

25,500 items.

The collection consists of 12,000 books, 11,100 pamphlets and 2,400 periodical volumes. Only the pre-1801 items (approximately 13 per cent of the total) are shelved at the Special Collections Division on Deansgate. Although the earliest books and pamphlets derive from the 1520s, the vast majority were printed between the 1640s and the early 1970s. There is good coverage of Puritanism and of all the Old Dissenting denominations, including the Quakers, but the real strength of the collection lies in material for the study of Presbyterianism and Unitarianism in England, Scotland, Ireland and America. Writers represented by 100 or so editions and critical works include Theophilus Lindsey (1723–1808), Joseph Priestley (1733–1804), Thomas Belsham (1750–1829), William Ellery Channing (1780–1842), James Martineau (1805–1900) and Alexander Gordon (1841–1931). Unitarian hymn-books, liturgies and local histories also abound. However, as it was built up as the working library of a theological college, many non-religious works are also represented.

See also the Unitarian College Archives (p. 62).

Finding aids: card catalogues. See also Clive D. Field, 'Sources for the Study of Protestant Nonconformity in the John Rylands University Library of Manchester', *Bulletin of the John Rylands University Library of Manchester*, vol. 71, no. 2 (1989), pp. 111–17.

Location: JRULM (Deansgate and Main Library).

Urwick Library

1,500 items.

The Urwick Library was formed in 1885 by Thomas Greenwood (1851–1908), the famous bibliographer-librarian, in honour of William Urwick (1826–1905), historian of Nonconformity and minister of Hatherlow Congregational Church in Romiley, Cheshire. Although the Library was primarily intended for the congregation of Hatherlow Church, and for scholars attending its day or Sunday schools, other local residents were admitted as borrowers.

The historical value of the collection lies not so much in its wide-ranging content, as in the fact that it is one of the few 19th-century chapel libraries to have survived intact.

Finding aids: published catalogue, *The Urwick Library, Founded on May 9th, 1885, by Thomas Greenwood, in Honour of the Rev. W. Urwick, MA, who was Pastor of Hatherlow Chapel for 23 Years: Catalogue and Rules* (Bredbury, 1902). See also Clive D. Field, 'Sources for the Study of Protestant Nonconformity in the John Rylands University Library of Manchester', *Bulletin of the John Rylands University Library of Manchester*, vol. 71, no. 2 (1989), pp. 110–11.

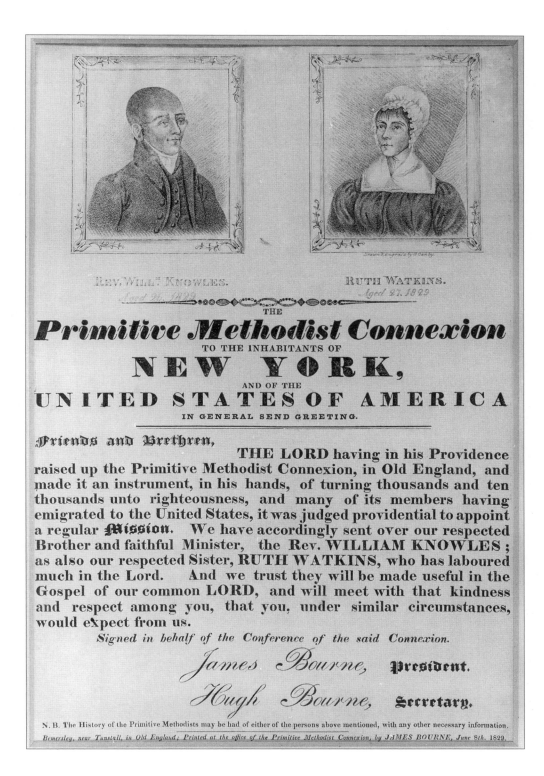

Notice issued by the Methodist New Connexion to the inhabitants of New York and the United States of America, announcing the mission of the Rev. William Knowles and Ruth Watkins, 8 June 1829. (*See page 69*)

Grant of property in
Weston, Cheshire,
from Hugh de Dutton
to his son Adam etc.,
c.1170. Arley Charters,
box 1, no. 47.
(*See page 86*)

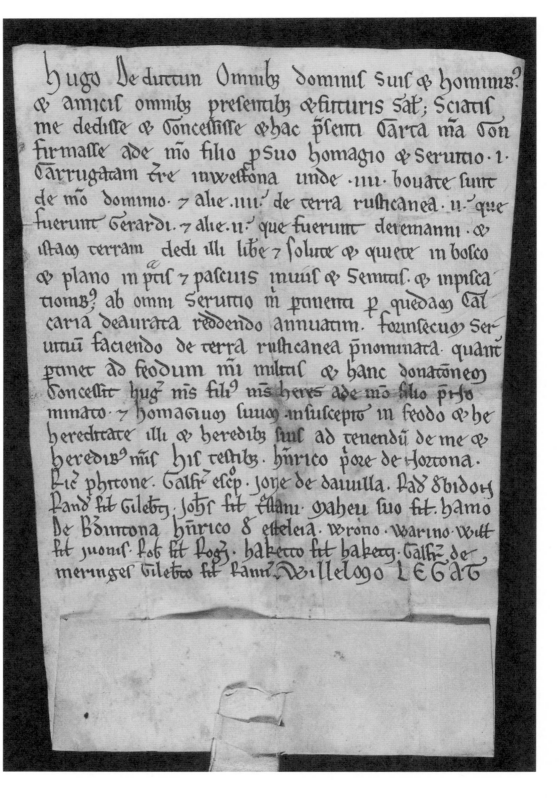

MUNIMENT & CHARTER COLLECTIONS

THE LIBRARY holds many notable muniment collections, principally from north-west England. The majority hail from Cheshire, including the Bromley-Davenport, Brooke of Mere, Cornwall-Legh, Grey (Stamford) of Dunham Massey, Jodrell, Legh of Lyme, Leycester of Toft, Mainwaring, Roundell, Stanley of Alderley, Tatton of Wythenshawe and Warburton of Arley collections. Lancashire is represented by the Clowes Deeds, Ducie Muniments and Legh of Lyme Muniments, Derbyshire by the Bagshawe and Crutchley collections. Among the Beaumont Charters and Phillipps Charters are many important medieval documents, including papal bulls, relating to religious houses in France and Belgium. The latter collection also houses several hundred English secular charters. In addition to discrete collections, the miscellaneous Rylands Charters sequence contains several thousand deeds and charters, acquired from various sources, with wide geographical coverage.

The muniment and charter collections range from the 12th to the 20th century. They are major sources not merely for local affairs but also for the study of national political history and of English economic and social development in general. They are significant for studies of land-ownership, agriculture, topography, continuity and change among the gentry and aristocracy, genealogy, women's history, legal history, diplomatic and sigillography.

Several collections have wider politico-geographical significance, as sources for military, colonial and diplomatic history. The Spring Rice Collection, for example, contains valuable comments on the political and economic situation in Britain, on the administration of the Foreign Office, and on the troubles in Ireland in the 1840s.

The muniment and charter collections are complemented by the Library's excellent collection of 18th- and 19th-century published County Histories (p. 112).

Select alphabetical list of resources:

Arderne Deeds

Date range: 17th–19th centuries.

Muniments relating to the Arderne family of Alvanley, Cheshire, and the related Done family of Utkinton, Cheshire, and their estates. The documents relate chiefly to Alvanley, Utkinton, Tarporley, Rushton, Eaton, Oulton, Clotton, Kingsley, Norley, Duddon and Stockport. They include title deeds, rentals, maps, enclosure awards, and 17th- and 18th-century deeds concerning apprentices' charities. There are numerous marriage settlements and wills from the 17th and 18th centuries. A number of items also relate to the Crewe family of Crewe, Cheshire.

Finding aids: unpublished handlist.

Astle Deeds

Date range: 17th–19th centuries.

Muniments of the Astle estate near Chelford, Cheshire. They comprise deeds of conveyance, assignments, surrenders, mortgages, marriage settlements, wills and probate records, certificates of baptism, marriage and burial, and abstracts of title relating to the Astle, Dixon and Parker families. Properties lie in Astle, Snelson, Chelford and Nether Alderley.

Finding aids: unpublished handlist.

Bagshawe Muniments

Date range: 1423–1866.

Archives of the Bagshawes of Ford Hall and the Oaks, Derbyshire, one of the oldest families in the county. Members of the family included the Rev. William Bagshawe (1628–1702), the 'Apostle of the Peak', and Colonel Samuel Bagshawe (1713–62), who had a distinguished military career in Gibraltar, Ireland and India. The Bagshawes were related by marriage to two other families: the Caldwells of Castle Caldwell co. Fermanagh, Ireland, and the Murray family. Sir James Caldwell, 4th Baronet (c.1722–84), involved himself in the political, social and economic affairs of Britain and Ireland and came into contact with many of the leading literary and social figures of the late 18th century. Lord John Murray and Lieutenant General William Murray, formerly Foxlowe (d. 1818), were both distinguished soldiers.

The Bagshawes played a prominent part in local and county affairs within Derbyshire and Yorkshire, and historians of those areas, as well as economic and social historians, will find much of value among the numerous household, business and estate records. There are large numbers of deeds and estate papers for properties in Derbyshire, particularly in Castleton, Chapel-en-le-Frith, Ford, Hope, Norton and Wormhill; and in Ecclesall Bierlow, Fulwood and Sheffield in Yorkshire. The collection also contains important material on military history, particularly on military service in Ireland and India in the mid-18th century and the American War of Independence, and on economic history (e.g. lead mining in Derbyshire during the 18th century). There are several volumes of sermons, treatises and journals of the 'Apostle of the Peak' and other early Nonconformist ministers. Caldwell family papers include correspondence of Sir James Caldwell with many leading figures of his day, including George Townshend, Lady Mary Wortley Montagu, Dr Samuel Johnson, Dr John Hawkesworth, David Garrick and Arthur Young.

Finding aids: published handlist, F. Taylor, *Hand-List of the Bagshawe Muniments Deposited in the John Rylands Library* (Manchester, 1955).

Muniment & Charter Collections

Beaumont Charters

Date range: 12th–17th centuries.

Collection of over one hundred charters relating to abbeys in Normandy, part of a collection assembled by the Abbé de la Rue (1751–1835), the noted Norman scholar. The documents comprise deeds, licences, grants and legal agreements concerning lands belonging to the Abbeys of Notre Dame at Ardenne and Barbery, and to abbeys at Caen, Fécamp, Fontenay-le-Tesson, Gouffern, Troarn and Vignats. Much of the material dates from the 12th and 13th centuries, constituting a significant source for studies of land-holding and the organization of religious houses in medieval France.

Finding aids: published handlist, Robert Fawtier, *Handlist of Charters, Deeds, and Similar Documents in the Possession of the John Rylands Library*, vol. 1 (Manchester, 1925).

Bellot Papers

Date range: 18th–19th centuries.

Collection of correspondence, personal papers and legal records relating to the Bellot, Hale, Killer and Thyer families, donated in 1969 by Hugh Hale Bellot, Professor of American History at London University. Among the papers are some 60 items relating to Robert Thyer (1709–81), Librarian of Chetham's Hospital from 1732 to 1763 and editor of *The Genuine Remains in Verse and Prose of Samuel Butler, with Notes* (1759). He was the stepfather of Elizabeth Killer, whose grand-daughter Frances married William Henry Bellot in 1847. The Bellot family included several surgeons, practising especially in Stockport. Among Thyer's papers are a protection from arrest which Richard Vaughan, 2nd Earl of Carbery, issued to Samuel Butler in 1667, a transcript of some of the verse remains of Butler, 28 letters from Robert Thyer, a collection of his essays and verses, and papers relating to his wife Silence.

Finding aids: unlisted; Robert Thyer's letters and speeches are discussed and extracts therefrom printed in Edmund Ogden, 'Robert Thyer. Family Letters and some Speeches

See also the Bellot Printed Collection (p. 146).

written for Public Recitation', *Transactions of the Lancashire and Cheshire Antiquarian Society*, vol. 47 (1930–31), pp. 58–83. See also Edmund Ogden, 'Robert Thyer, Chetham's Librarian, 1732–1763', *TLCAS*, vol. 41 (1924), pp. 90–136; note in *Bulletin of the John Rylands Library*, vol. 52 (1969–70), pp. 237–8; *Notes and Queries* (September 1993), pp. 324–5.

Bromley Davenport Muniments

Date range: 12th–20th centuries.

Important family papers of the Bromley Davenport family of Capesthorne near Macclesfield, Cheshire. The collection contains correspondence, family papers, muniments of title (including large numbers of medieval deeds and charters), estate accounts, rentals, surveys and associated documents. As well as the Davenports of Capesthorne, two other branches of the family in Cheshire are also represented, the Davenports of Calveley and the Davenports of Woodford, together with two Warwickshire families, the Bromleys of Baginton and the Throckmortons of Haseley.

The properties represented lie in many counties but primarily in Cheshire (especially in Nether Alderley, Calveley, Capesthorne, Davenport, Gawsworth, Henbury, Heswall, Macclesfield, Marton, Siddington, Somerford, Swettenham, Upton and Woodford), Staffordshire (especially Ellastone and Wootton), Warwickshire (Baginton, Churchover, Finham, Haseley, Hatton, Oxhill, Shrewley and Southam) and Buckinghamshire (Great Marlow). The extensive papers of Edward Davies Davenport (1778–1847) include political and personal correspondence with Thomas Attwood, Richard Cobden, Richard Grosvenor, 2nd Marquis of Westminster, Reginald Heber, Bishop of Calcutta, Harriet Martineau, Sir Charles Napier, Lord John Russell and Sydney Smith. Other material includes the Crimean War diary of William Davenport Bromley, who was attached to British forces as a freelance observer/soldier, and papers relating to Sir William Bromley Davenport's service in the South African War (Boer War), 1899–1902.

Access: post-1918 material may be consulted only with the permission of the depositor. Finding aids: outline list. See also Evelyn Lord, 'In Love and War: Episodes in the Life of a Country Gentleman' [re Crimean War diary], *Archives*, vol. 20, no. 89 (1993), pp. 42–7.

Brooke of Mere Muniments

Date range: 13th–20th centuries.

Family papers of the Brooke family of Mere Old Hall, near Knutsford, Cheshire. Mere was held by the Mere family until 1652 when the estate was sold to Peter Brooke, younger son of Sir Richard Brooke of Norton. During the 18th century the Brookes expanded their estates by purchasing the Frodsham estate at Elton, the Marton estate at Holford, and other properties in Lostock Gralam, Mottram St Andrew and Plumley. In the late 18th century Peter Brooke married Maria Langford and thereby inherited plantations on the island of Antigua in the West Indies.

The collection consists of medieval deeds, muniments of title, marriage and family settlements, mortgages, leases, wills, Chancery papers and other legal records, rentals, estate papers and correspondence, primarily concerning properties in Bollington, Dutton, Frodsham, Holford, Lostock Gralam, Mere, Mottram St Andrew, Plumley, Stretton, Thelwall and Walton Superior in Cheshire. There are also papers relating to the sale of estates in Ireland in the 1750s, and records such as accounts, inventories and correspondence concerning the plantations in Antigua in the early 19th century.

Finding aids: outline list.

Clowes Deeds

Date range: 13th–19th centuries.

Correspondence, papers and deeds relating to the Clowes and Chetham families, and to the Clowes estates, mainly in south-east Lancashire and particularly Manchester. The collection includes several fine medieval documents relating to the manors of Butterworth and Crompton, east of Rochdale, and Moston and Nuthurst, north-east of Manchester; arbitration awards; marriage settlements; and many letters and papers of the Chetham family.

Finding aids: unpublished handlist.

Cornwall-Legh Muniments

Date range: 13th–19th centuries.

Muniments of the Cornwall-Legh family of High Legh near Knutsford, Cheshire. The collection comprises medieval charters, later deeds and papers relating to the Cornwall-Leghs, the Leghs of East Legh, Cheshire (13th–19th centuries), the Leghs of Swineyard (or Swinehead) in High Legh, Cheshire (17th–18th centuries), the Cornwalls of Shropshire (15th–18th centuries), and the Chambres of Plas Chambres, Denbighshire (18th century). Material includes deeds, business and estate correspondence, papers and plans for High Legh, Knutsford, Lymm and Manley in Cheshire, Barton upon Irwell and Openshaw in Lancashire, and Birstall in Yorkshire; and records relating to the manors of Sale (14th–18th centuries) and Thornton-le-Moors (13th–18th centuries) in Cheshire. There are also correspondence and papers relating to the Cheshire militia and magistracy and to Bucklow Hundred in the early 19th century.

Finding aids: unpublished handlist; manuscript calendar of deeds by J.P. Earwaker (1892–93). See also Evelyn Lord, 'The Cornwall-Leghs of High Legh: Approaches to the Inheritance Patterns of North-West England', *Bulletin of the John Rylands University Library of Manchester*, vol. 73, no. 2 (1991), pp. 21–36.

Crutchley Muniments

Date range: 12th–19th centuries.

Muniments of the Coke family of Longford, Derbyshire, and Holkham, Norfolk. The family's estates lay principally in Derbyshire, Lancashire and Suffolk, and the majority of documents relate to these counties. More than half concern Derbyshire and principally Longford. Other documents relate to the manors of Wherstead, Bourn Hall and Pannington Hall in Suffolk, and estates in south-east Lancashire, notably Reddish, Great and Little Heaton and Crumpsall. There are also documents concerning the former owners of these properties, the families of Longford of Longford, Reddish of Reddish, Hulton, Langley, Prestwich, Browne, Radcliffe and Hall. The collection is particularly rich in manorial records from Longford, Over Haddon, Newton Solney and Hathersage in Derbyshire, Wherstead and Goddelsford (i.e. Gusford Hall) in Suffolk, and Prestwich and Reddish in Lancashire. There are also many fine seals.

Finding aids: published handlist, F. Taylor, *Hand-List of the Crutchley Manuscripts in the John Rylands Library* (Manchester, 1951).

Ducie Muniments

Date range: 13th–19th centuries.

The Manchester (Strangeways) portion of the muniments of the Earl of Ducie of Tortworth, Gloucestershire was transferred to the John Rylands Library in 1954. The collection contains muniments of title, rentals, plans, legal records, agents' accounts and correspondence, and allied estate documents concerning the Reynolds, Hartley and Strangeways families of Strangeways near Manchester. Included are 14th-century charters, which enable the early street patterns of Manchester to be reconstructed, and records such as Parliamentary Bills and Acts concerning roads, bridges and railways in the area. The documents relate to properties in Manchester (particularly the Millgate, Market Street and Deansgate areas), the neighbouring townships of Cheetham, Gorton and Levenshulme, and the township of Castleton near Rochdale.

Finding aids: unpublished handlist.

Egerton of Tatton Papers

Date range: 14th–19th centuries.

Collection of letters, papers and allied documents belonging to the Egerton family of Tatton, Cheshire. These chiefly relate to Samuel Egerton (1711–80) and his uncle Samuel Hill (1691–1758) of Shenstone Park, Staffordshire. They include Egerton family accounts and receipts, 17th–18th centuries; Pickering of Thelwall family correspondence and papers, 17th–18th centuries; miscellaneous accounts and receipts, 18th century; records of the court leet and view of frankpledge for the manors of Knutsford and Tatton, c.1700–58; and over 100 constables' presentments for various townships in Bucklow Hundred, early 18th century.

Finding aids: unpublished detailed catalogue.

Finney of Fulshaw Muniments

Date range: 15th–20th centuries.

Small collection of deeds and documents relating to the Finney family of Fulshaw Hall near Wilmslow, Cheshire. They concern property in Fulshaw, Styal and Wilmslow and the families of Finney, Davenport, Newton, Wilbraham and Worthington. They include deeds of conveyance, mortgages, assignments, leases, settlements, bonds, agreements, wills, and certificates of baptism, marriage and burial.

Finding aids: unpublished handlist.

Grey (Stamford) of Dunham Massey Papers

Date range: 13th–20th centuries.

A very large collection of papers of the Grey family, Earls of Stamford, and their predecessors from Dunham Massey Hall near Altrincham, Cheshire. The Grey family inherited

Dunham Massey in the mid-18th century from the Booths, Earls of Warrington, who are also represented. The collection contains the personal papers of the Booth and Grey families; title deeds and settlements; important manorial records from the courts leet of the barony of Dunham Massey and the borough of Altrincham, the court leet with court baron for the manor of Bollin cum Norcliffe (Wilmslow), courts baron for the manors of Dunham Massey, Carrington and Ashton upon Mersey, and Altrincham fair court; household records including 18th- and 19th-century accounts and inventories, and correspondence relating to the restoration of Dunham Massey Hall; papers relating to local schools and charities; and large quantities of estate papers, principally from the 19th and 20th centuries, including deeds, leases, rentals, valuation books, rent ledgers, cash books, income and expenditure accounts, invoices and vouchers, plans and correspondence files. The deeds and other papers relate to properties in Altrincham, Ashley, Ashton upon Mersey, Bollin Fee (Wilmslow), Bollington, Bowdon, Carrington, Dunham Massey, Hale, Hattersley, Matley, Millington, Partington, Pownall Fee (Wilmslow), Sale, Stayley, Thornton-le-Moors and Timperley in Cheshire, and Ashton-under-Lyne and Warrington in Lancashire.

Muniment &
Charter Collections

See also Rylands
Charters 3850–4317
(leases for lives in
Wilmslow parish,
presented to the Library
by the 10th Earl of
Stamford).

Among the personal papers of the Booth family are an account roll of Sir Robert Booth as sheriff of Cheshire, c.1445–50; a detailed compendium of family and estate accounts of Sir George Booth, 1648–51/2; personal correspondence and accounts of George Booth, 2nd Earl of Warrington, 1693/4–1758; and papers of his daughter Mary, Countess of Stamford, relating to the construction of the Bridgewater Canal, 1758–67. The personal papers of the 5th and 6th Earls of Stamford contain material relating to the lord lieutenancy of Cheshire, the magistracy and local militia, the defence of the county against possible French invasion and internal security measures in the late 18th and early 19th centuries, including printed matter relating to the Peterloo Massacre of 1819. Among the papers of the 6th Earl of Stamford are colourful letters written by his son while on the Grand Tour in the 1820s. There are also manuscripts of, and papers pertaining to, the naturalist Gilbert White of Selborne (1720–93) and other members of the White family; papers of the Lumsden family concerning service in the East India Company (*q.v.*) and colonial life and administration before and during the Indian Mutiny; and papers of the Rev. William Grey, a missionary in Newfoundland, Canada, 1849–53.

Access: papers of members of the family alive during the 20th century may be consulted only with the written permission of the National Trust. Finding aids: unpublished detailed catalogue with index (17 vols).

Jodrell Muniments

Date range: 13th–18th centuries.

Muniments of the Jodrell family of Yeardsley cum Whaley, Cheshire. The collection primarily comprises deeds and allied documents such as grants, final concords, releases, leases, surrenders, wills, marriage agreements, inventories, receipts, bonds, extracts of court rolls and letters of attorney. These relate to properties in Cheshire (particularly Disley Stanley, Kettleshulme, Macclesfield Forest, Taxal and Yeardsley cum Whaley), Derbyshire (Hartington, Hayfield and Makeney), Lancashire (Chatburn), Staffordshire (Marchington, Tunstall and Waterfall), and Yorkshire (Waddington). There are also papers relating to Edmund Jodrell's two terms as sheriff of Cheshire , 1650–51 and 1670–71.

Finding aids: published handlist, Robert Fawtier, *Hand-List of the Mainwaring and Jodrell Manuscripts at present in the custody of the John Rylands Library* (Manchester, 1923); unpublished outline list of additional material.

Muniment & Charter Collections

Legh of Lyme Muniments

Date range: 12th–19th centuries.

Extensive family papers of the Leghs of Lyme Park, Cheshire. These comprise muniments of title, including large numbers of medieval deeds and charters, 17th- and 18th-century manorial court records, original architect's plans of Lyme Hall, surveys, wills, abstracts of title, estate correspondence, accounts and other papers. The muniments relate to the Lancashire estates (the manors of Newton and Golborne, and property in Newton-le-Willows, Golborne, Lowton, Haydock, Ashton-in-Makerfield, Ince-in-Makerfield, Warrington, Burtonwood, Poulton and Fearnhead, Bold, Pemberton and Dalton), and the Cheshire estates (with property in Lyme Handley, Disley, Pott Shrigley, Macclesfield, Grappenhall, Norbury, Marple, and Broomedge and Heatley in Lymm).

There is an extensive and important selection of personal correspondence, dating from the 16th century onwards, including correspondence with members of the Gerard, Egerton and Chicheley families, with much material on 18th-century Northern politics.

Finding aids: partially listed: calendar of deeds and typescript list of correspondence.

Leycester of Toft Muniments

Date range: 13th–19th centuries.

Muniments of the Leycester family of Toft near Knutsford, Cheshire, and the related Gerard family of Crewood in Kingsley, Cheshire. The muniments of title relate chiefly to estates in Cheshire (especially Acton, Chester, Chorley, Cotton Abbotts, Crowton, Kingsley, Knutsford, Mobberley, Northwich, Over Peover, Plumley, Toft and Woodford), with smaller numbers relating to properties in Berkshire (Cookham), Lancashire (Manchester, Speke and Whittle-le-Woods), Lincolnshire (Sotby and Bleasby), Staffordshire (Colwich and Leek) and Flintshire (Hawarden). They include 900 medieval charters, 17th- and 18th-century manorial court records, estate correspondence and papers. There is extensive family correspondence ranging from the late 16th century to the 20th, roughly half being 17th-century.

Finding aids: unpublished lists of correspondence and muniments.

Mainwaring Manuscripts

Date range: 12th–19th centuries.

Manuscripts of the Mainwaring family of Peover Hall, Cheshire. The collection contains state papers, diaries, manorial records, rentals, pedigree rolls and household records, as well as a large number of deeds and charters relating to estates in Cheshire and other counties. Some 400 charters predate the reign of Henry VIII, the earliest consisting of charters granted by the Earls of Chester in the 12th century. Deeds relate to numerous Cheshire townships, but particularly to Allostock, Astle, Baddiley, Goostrey cum Barnshaw, Chelford, Knutsford, Nantwich, Over Peover, Great Warford, Little Warford, Waverton, Wharton, Withington and Worleston.

Finding aids: published handlist, Robert Fawtier, *Hand-List of the Mainwaring and Jodrell Manuscripts at Present in the Custody of the John Rylands Library* (Manchester, 1923); unpublished outline list of additional material. Note that numerous items recorded by Fawtier were removed by the depositor in 1972 and sold at Sotheby's.

Medici Records

Date range: 11th–18th centuries.

Documents from the archives of the younger branch of the Florentine family of Medici, formerly in the possession of the Marquis Cosimo and the Marquis Averardo de' Medici. They include a grant from Pietro di Pietro Petroni to the church and monastery of St Barnabas of Gamungno, Faenza, in 1085; a papal bull of Pope Pius II to the Archdeacon of Florence concerning the foundation of a canonry in the church of San Lorenzo, 1462; a letter from Pope Leo X to Zanobi de' Medici, 1521; credentials of Francesco de' Medici as envoy of Pope Clement VII to Charles de Bourbon, Count of Saint Pol, 1529; letters from Francesco I, Grand Duke of Tuscany, to Raffaello de' Medici, 1575–77; letters from Ferdinando I, Duke of Florence, to the Marquis Biagio Capizucchi in Avignon and others, 1589–1608; and numerous medieval and post-medieval grants, letters patent, court orders, records of judgements, agreements, correspondence and accounts.

Finding aids: published handlist, Robert Fawtier, *Handlist of Charters, Deeds, and Similar Documents in the Possession of the John Rylands Library*, vol. 1 (Manchester, 1925).

Nicholas Papers

Date range: 14th–18th centuries.

Records forming part of the archives of the Nicholas family of West Horsley, Surrey. They relate chiefly to Sir Edward Nicholas (1593–1669), Secretary of State to Charles I and Charles II, to his sons John and Edward, and to the Nicholas estates in West Horsley, Surrey, and Gillingham, Dorset. There are letters to Sir Edward Nicholas as Secretary of State, 1643–44; account books of Edward Nicholas esq. as Treasurer and General Receiver, 1694–1715; important manorial court rolls for West Horsley, 1385–1709; manorial court records for Gillingham, including a court book, survey, rental, perambulation and accounts, 1469–1725; and other documents relating to property in West Horsley and Gillingham, including deeds of conveyance, mortgages, leases and accounts.

Finding aids: published handlist, Robert Fawtier, *Handlist of Charters, Deeds, and Similar Documents in the Possession of the John Rylands Library*, vol. 1 (Manchester, 1925).

Orford Papers

Date range: 17th–19th centuries.

Collection donated by Mr Lewis H. Orford, a Manchester solicitor and trustee of the John Rylands Library. The collection contains deeds and personal papers formerly belonging to several families: the Brewis family of Manchester and Buckinghamshire; the Scholes family of Manchester; the Oldham family of Stockport; the Taylor and Town families of Shropshire; branches of the White family in London and Manchester; and the Lees family of Hollingworth, Cheshire. Most of the deeds and other papers relate to properties in Manchester and its environs: Blackley, Cheetham, Broughton, Stockport, Sale,

Cheetwood, Salford, Gorton, Levenshulme and Hollingworth. However, there is material for properties further afield: at Ibstone in Buckinghamshire and Oxfordshire, Richard's Castle and Brimfield in Herefordshire, Ludlow and Stanton Lacy in Shropshire, Audley in Staffordshire, and Bethnal Green in Middlesex.

Perhaps the most interesting aspect of the collection, however, is that it contains the residuary papers of Mrs Enriqueta Augustina Rylands, founder of the John Rylands Library. These include the accounts of her executors, papers relating to the memorial monument for the Rylands family, photographs, plans and documents concerning the building of the Library, and deeds and papers relating to properties owned by Mrs Rylands and sold after her death.

Finding aids: unpublished detailed catalogue.

Phillipps Charters

Date range: 12th–17th centuries.

Assortment of over five hundred charters and other records which once formed part of the collection of Sir Thomas Phillipps (1792–1872), antiquary and bibliophile, at Middle Hill, Broadway in Worcestershire. They were acquired by the Library either directly at the Phillipps sales or through various booksellers. There are numerous medieval charters and other records relating to religious houses and bishoprics throughout France and Belgium, and deeds relating to secular estates, particularly in Tournai. The former include papal bulls of Hadrian IV (1157), Clement III (1191), Gregory IX (1236), Alexander IV (1255), Nicholas V (1451), Paul IV (1556) and Gregory XIII (1572), and briefs of Popes Paul V (1616) and Innocent X (1650). Other notable medieval documents are: the settlement for the unrealized marriage of Isabella (1332–79), daughter of Edward III, and Louis, Count of Flanders (1347); compotus rolls from Norfolk (1277–1576); accounts of royal silver mines near Calstock, Cornwall (1317); and royal wardrobe accounts (1313–14).

In addition, the collection incorporates many medieval charters, such as grants, quitclaims, agreements, bonds and letters of attorney, for numerous English counties, particularly Derbyshire (especially Ashbourne, Castleton, Swadlincote and Taddington), Durham (Stainton), Huntingdonshire (Stilton), Kent (Charing and Willesborough), Staffordshire (Enville and Whittington), and Yorkshire (Beswick, Lockington and Middleton near Rothwell).

Finding aids: published handlist, Robert Fawtier, *Handlist of Charters, Deeds, and Similar Documents in the Possession of the John Rylands Library*, vol. 1 (Manchester, 1925).

Pluscarden Charters

Date range: 1233–1565.

Charters relating to Pluscarden Priory near Elgin, Morayshire. Pluscarden was founded in 1230 by Alexander II, King of Scots, for monks of the Valliscaulian Order, whose mother house at Val-des-Choux in Burgundy had been established for a mere thirty years when it sent its Rule into Scotland. The only other foundations of the Order outside France were at Beauly near Inverness and Ardchattan in Argyll. The collection comprises twelve of the earliest surviving charters of the house, including a confirmation by Andrew, Bishop of Moray, in 1233 of grants made by Alexander II, the King's second charter of 1236, and a transumpt which purports to summarize all charters granted during the first ten years of the monastery's existence, among them the lost foundation charter. There are also two precepts of the Abbot and Convent of Kinloss, 1559 and 1565.

Finding aids: unpublished handlist. See also note in *Bulletin of the John Rylands Library*, vol. 38 (1955–56), pp. 274–6.

Roundell Muniments

Date range: 13th–20th centuries, but mainly 18th and 19th.

Muniments relating to the families of Tomkinson, Tollemache and Roundell of Dorfold Hall near Nantwich, Cheshire, and to properties in nine English counties. The collection comprises title deeds, abstracts of deeds, rentals, surveys, valuation books, poll books, tithe books, estate and business correspondence and papers, such as minute books, memoranda books and letter books, and accounts (mainly 18th and 19th centuries).

The deeds and other documents relate chiefly to Cheshire, and in particular to the townships of Acton, Alpraham, Antrobus, Aston juxta Mondrum, Audlem, Broxton, Burland, Croxton, Davenham, Dodcott cum Wilkesley, Dorfold, Henhull, Hurleston, [Church] Lawton, Nantwich, Stanthorne, Tattenhall, Tiverton, Warmingham, Wettenhall and Wimboldsley. In addition there are small quantities of documents relating to Lancashire (particularly Westhoughton), Staffordshire (Madeley), Warwickshire (Nuneaton) and other counties.

Finding aids: partial unpublished handlist.

Rylands Charters

Date range: 13th–19th centuries.

A miscellaneous sequence of several thousand deeds, charters and other documents acquired by gift or purchase from various sources. Most counties in England and Wales are represented, with particularly good coverage of Cheshire, Derbyshire, Lancashire and Lincolnshire. Items include charters, deeds of conveyance, settlements, mortgages, leases, wills, rentals, manorial records, accounts and miscellaneous papers. Although documents are numbered consecutively, the separate provenances of collections have been respected. Among the larger collections are:

a collection of deeds relating to Lancashire (Rylands Charters 285–700);

deeds relating to Cheshire presented by Lord Stanley of Alderley (Ryl. Ch. 776–913: see p. 85);

deeds mainly concerning the Salusbury family, acquired with the Thrale-Piozzi Manuscripts (p. 144) from Mrs R.V. Colman (Ryl. Ch. 914–1262);

deeds chiefly concerning properties in Cheshire, particularly townships on the Wirral such as Higher and Lower Bebington, Bromborough, Eastham, Hooton, Mollington, Storeton and Tranmere, and also properties in Flintshire and Denbighshire, purchased from the Rev. P.G. Langdon (Ryl. Ch. 1263–1942);

deeds and manorial records relating to the Aston family of Aston by Sutton in Cheshire, acquired from R.H. Linaker esq. (Ryl. Ch. 2012–2130);

deeds relating to the Hadfield family of Hadfield in Derbyshire (Ryl. Ch. 2245–2477);

deeds from the Clayton MSS relating to Lincolnshire (Ryl. Ch. 2478–2808);

deeds relating to the Rochdale and Rossendale areas of Lancashire, particularly Bacup, Brandwood, Haslingden, Newchurch in Rossendale, Rawtenstall, Todmorden and Whitworth, presented by G. Calvert esq. (Ryl. Ch. 2891–2976);

business and legal papers associated with Sir Robert Clayton (1629–1707), MP for the City of London, and his fellow apprentice and partner, Alderman John Morris (d. 1682) (Ryl. Ch. 3632–3849);

leases from Dean Row and Styal and manorial records relating to the manor of Bollin cum Norcliffe in Wilmslow, Cheshire, presented by the 10th Earl of Stamford (Ryl. Ch. 3850–4317);

records of the township of High Legh in Cheshire, including settlement and removal orders, apprenticeship indentures, constables' accounts, and records of the overseers of the poor and surveyors of highways (Ryl. Ch. 4318–4510).

Finding aids: published handlists, Moses Tyson and Frank Taylor, *Hand-List of Charters, Deeds and Similar Documents in the Possession of the John Rylands Library*, 3 vols (Manchester, 1935–75).

Spring Rice Collection

Date range: 19th century.

Over 500 letters and papers of the Spring Rice family were presented to the Library in 1957 by Mrs Charles Booth of Ulverscroft, Leicestershire. The bulk, some 300 items, comprises correspondence of Rt. Hon. Thomas Spring Rice (1790–1866), 1st Baron Monteagle of Brandon, and his two sons, Stephen (1814–65) and Charles (1819–70). Monteagle was Chancellor of the Exchequer from 1835 to 1839, and Comptroller General from 1839 to 1865. His sons served in the Board of Customs and the Foreign Office respectively. The letters are varied in content and, in addition to the information they contain about the family itself, provide many valuable comments on political and economic events at home and abroad, and on the troubles in Ireland in the 1840s. Among the letters is a lengthy epistle from Macaulay to Monteagle, written in August 1834 from India, dealing with party politics and parliamentary affairs.

A further 200 letters were exchanged between Monteagle's grandsons, Cecil and Stephen Spring Rice, and the latter's wife Julia, 1873–1902. Cecil Spring Rice (1859–1918) was a career diplomat who held posts in America, Japan, Berlin, Persia and Russia, before serving as Ambassador in Washington from 1913 to 1918.

The collection also contains over 400 letters, papers, newspaper cuttings and photographs relating to Julia's father, Sir Peter Fitzgerald (1808–80), 19th Knight of Kerry, and fifty letters of his son Sir Maurice (1844–1916), 20th Knight. The material dates mainly from the 1870s and '80s, when Sir Maurice was equerry to Prince Arthur, Duke of Connaught. Among the correspondents are Prince Arthur, Gladstone, Arthur Penrhyn Stanley, Dean of Westminster, and Lord Lansdowne. The papers provide useful insights into court and society life, and contemporary political events.

Finding aids: recorded in published handlist of English Manuscripts (English MSS 1187–1190).

Stanley of Alderley Deeds and Papers

Date range: 13th–19th centuries.

Almost 250 deeds relating to Cheshire were presented to the Library by Lord Stanley of Alderley in April 1927 (Rylands Charters 776–913). Among them are deeds of the Jodrell family and their estates in Yeardsley cum Whaley and Sutton (Ryl. Ch. 776–813), the Tatton of Wythenshawe family and their lands in Northenden (Ryl. Ch. 814–840), and the Winningtons and their property in Northwich and Winnington (Ryl. Ch. 841–913). The latter section includes deeds relating to salt-houses in Northwich in the 13th century. The deeds, which range in date from the 13th century to the 19th, comprise grants, quitclaims, leases, letters of attorney and bonds.

Among the English Manuscripts are boyhood letters and a diary of Arthur Penrhyn Stanley, later Dean of Westminster, 1824–28 (Eng MSS 1089–1090); family and miscellaneous letters addressed to Edward Lyulph Stanley (1839–1925), 4th Lord Stanley, between 1853 and 1874, including a three-page letter written at Balaclava by Augustus Lane Fox (later Pitt-Rivers) in which he describes the fighting in the Crimean War (Eng MSS 1092–1095); a Stanley family household account book, 1784–85 (Eng MS 1096); and a rental of Sir John Thomas Stanley, 1781–85 (Eng MS 1097).

Finding aids: recorded in published handlists of Rylands Charters (Ryl. Ch. 776–913) and English Manuscripts (English MSS 1089–1097). See also Nancy Mitford, *The Stanleys of Alderley: Their Letters Between the Years 1851–1865* (1939).

Stapleton Manuscripts

Date range: 15th–19th centuries, but mainly 17th and 18th.

Correspondence, papers and deeds of the Stapleton family. They relate in particular to Sir William Stapleton, 1st Baronet (d. 1686), Deputy Governor of Montserrat and Governor of the Leeward Islands, and Sir William Stapleton, 4th Baronet (1698–1740). There is important material relating to the West Indies in the 17th and early 18th centuries, including commissions and appointments to offices, public accounts, militia lists, correspondence, grants and leases of land, plantation accounts, plantation inventories, lists of slaves and sugar accounts. There are also Stapleton marriage settlements, title deeds relating to property in Kent and Berkshire (15th–19th centuries), rentals and terriers (16th–18th centuries), manorial court rolls for the manor of Tildens and Tubbins in Marden parish, Kent, and the manors of Shottesbrooke and Clewer in Berkshire (16th–18th centuries), accounts and household records.

Finding aids: unpublished handlist.

Tabley Muniments

Date range: 19th century.

The collection consists mainly of the personal papers of the poet John Byrne Leicester Warren (1835–95), 3rd Baron de Tabley, of Tabley near Knutsford, Cheshire. He published under the pseudonyms George F. Preston and William Lancaster and later under his own name. The papers reflect his interests in literature, politics, botany and numismatics and include correspondence with numerous prominent later Victorian figures. Attention

Muniment & Charter Collections

See also the Clinton Papers (p. 121) and the Spring Rice Collection (p. 84).

There is correspondence with the 3rd Baron de Tabley among the Edward Freeman Papers (p. 187). See also the Tabley Book Collection (p. 26).

should also be drawn to de Tabley's extensive and important collection of armorial book-plates.

Finding aids: preliminary survey list.

Muniment &
Charter Collections

Tatton of Wythenshawe Muniments

Date range: 13th–19th centuries.

Collection of medieval charters, deeds, estate papers and correspondence of the Tatton family of Wythenshawe, Cheshire. Documents relate chiefly to lands in Cheshire, particularly to Wythenshawe, Northenden, Northen Etchells, Stockport Etchells and Macclesfield, with smaller numbers concerning Aldford, Altrincham, Bowdon, Bredbury, Godley, Great Warford, Hale, Kenworthy, Knutsford, Pownall Fee, Romiley and Werneth, and a handful bearing on properties in Derbyshire, Flintshire, Lancashire and Nottinghamshire. In addition there are 17th-century letters and personal papers of the Tatton family, including material relating to the English Civil War.

Finding aids: unpublished handlist.

Thomson Byrom Collection

Date range: 17th–18th centuries.

Records of the Byrom family of Kersal and Manchester, whose best known member is John Byrom (1692–1763), author of *Christians Awake*. The collection comprises muniments of title relating to properties in Kersal and Salford and in the Market Place, Shambles and Deansgate areas of Manchester; several 17th- and early 18th-century wills; a marriage settlement of 1684; and pedigrees of the Byroms of Byrom, the Byroms of Salford and the Byroms of Manchester.

Finding aids: unlisted. See notes in *Bulletin of the John Rylands Library*, vol. 44 (1961–62), p. 272; vol. 46 (1963–64), pp. 2–3.

Warburton of Arley Muniments and Related Collections

Date range: 12th–19th centuries.

There are three components to the Warburton collections:

The Arley Charters (12th–17th centuries) constitute a muniment collection of national importance, noted for the large number of early charters, including charters of the constables of Chester and several monastic examples, and its fine seals. They mainly concern the Dutton and Warburton families and their Cheshire estates in Appleton, Aston by Budworth, Aston by Sutton, Chester, Dutton, Great Budworth, Lower Walton, Lymm, Newton by Chester, Northwich, Poulton, Pulford, Sutton, Thelwall, Warburton, Wincham and Winnington. In addition there are 13th- and 14th-century deeds relating to Beverley in Yorkshire.

The main, deposited, collection comprises the muniments of the Warburton family of Arley Hall, Cheshire (16th to 19th century). It consists of muniments of title, settlements, mortgages, leases, bonds, rentals, manorial records, Acts of Parliament, plans, estate correspondence, papers relating to enclosure, roads in Warburton, Great Budworth church and other churches and schools, Croxton family papers, and an extensive collection of 18th-century accounts for the house and estate at Arley and the family residence in London. The deeds and other papers relate to properties in Appleton, Aston by Budworth, Aston by Sutton, Comberbach, Crowley, Higher Whitley, Sutton and Warburton.

The third component consists of papers relating to the navigation of the River Weaver in Cheshire from the 1750s and 1760s, including correspondence of Sir Peter Warburton, accounts, and contemporary official documents.

Finding aids: published calendar of Arley Charters, W. Beamont, *A Calendar of Ancient Family Charters Preserved at Arley Hall, Cheshire* (London, 1866); unpublished manuscript handlist of main collection; River Weaver papers unlisted.

Wickstead Papers

Date range: 16th–19th centuries.

Papers of the Wickstead family of Nantwich, Cheshire, comprising over 150 documents relating to properties in the townships of Acton, Chorley, Coole Pilate, Dodcott cum Wilkesley, Haughton, Henhull, Nantwich, Wardle, Wigland, Wolstanwood and Wybunbury in Cheshire. Documents comprise deeds of conveyance, assignments, mortgages, leases, settlements, wills, accounts and correspondence.

Finding aids: unpublished handlist.

ECONOMIC & INDUSTRIAL HISTORY

Manuscript Resources

The Library has a wealth of primary sources for the study of Britain's economic and industrial history. Major sources for the textile industry are the archives of Samuel Oldknow, McConnel & Kennedy, Sun Mill, Rylands & Sons, W.M. Christy & Sons, and Fielden Brothers of Todmorden, and also the Greater Manchester Mill Survey Archive, which contains information on all textile mills still extant in the county during the 1980s. These are supplemented by a variety of smaller collections. There are significant holdings relating to coal and iron (Thomas Botfield & Co.), pharmaceuticals (James Woolley, Sons & Co. and Manchester Pharmaceutical Association), engineering (William Dale & Sons and the B.R. Faunthorpe collection re Joseph Whitworth), African railways and mining (Tanks Group), ceramics (Josiah Wedgwood), international trade (Heald Family Papers, Hodgson, Robinson & Co., John Micklethwaite, Owen Owens and Pietro Tealdi), and watermills and windmills (E. Mitford Abraham). The development of the computer industry, in which Manchester played a pioneering role, is comprehensively recorded in the National Archive for the History of Computing.

Trade union archives date from the earliest years of the mass organization of labour and cover textiles (the Bolton and District Operative Cotton Spinners' Provincial Association and the Amalgamated Association of Operative Cotton Spinners), engravers, and professional and clerical staff. Trade and employers' organizations include the Ashton Textile Employers' Association, the Oldham Textile Employers' Association and the Manchester Pharmaceutical Association. The Library also holds a collection of documents submitted to the public inquiry which considered the proposed second runway at Manchester Airport, and the archives of two committees charged with examining and improving accounting standards and auditing practices.

See also the papers of the scientists Sir William Boyd Dawkins (coal industry and water-supply industry in the 19th century), and R.S. Hutton (electro-chemistry and metallurgy in the first half of the 20th century).

Printed Resources

The Library holds numerous secondary sources which support its rich holdings of archive materials relating to the textile industry. There are also individual works on general economic and industrial history, and on specific industries such as engineering and chemical manufacture.

Special attention should, however, be drawn to the Kenneth Brown Railway Collection, and to several associated collections. These contain a wealth of information on all aspects of railway history and operations, and in particular on the early development of railways in Britain. They include monographs, periodicals, Parliamentary papers and plans, and much ephemera.

Select alphabetical list of resources: (MS: Manuscript/Archive; PR: Printed)

MANUSCRIPT RESOURCES

E. Mitford Abraham Windmills and Watermills Collection

Date range: c.1900–52.

Photographs of windmills and watermills collected by E. Mitford Abraham, a distinguished Quaker from Ulverston, Cumbria. 47 albums contain over 1,200 views of mills he visited during the first half of the 20th century, chiefly in Cambridgeshire, Cheshire, Cumberland, Lancashire, Lincolnshire, Norfolk, Suffolk, Westmorland and Yorkshire. There are also negatives, cuttings from newspapers and periodicals, and notes on the location, history, construction and condition of many mills.

Finding aids: unpublished handlist.

Accounting Standards Committee Archive

Economic &
Industrial History

See also the Auditing
Practices Committee
Archive (p. 91).

Date range: 1952–90.

Papers of the Accounting Standards Committee of the Consultative Committee of Accountancy Bodies (CCAB). The ASC was established in 1976 to develop a system of definitive standards for financial reporting and accounting, following the accounting scandals of the late 1960s and early 1970s.

Material includes agendas and agenda papers, minutes, correspondence, memoranda, press releases, press cuttings, government and other reports, draft and published copies of standards, offprints and copies of articles and extracts from books. The collection also contains the papers of the ASC's predecessor body, the Accounting Standards Steering Committee (ASSC).

Finding aids: catalogue available on disk from the Department of Accounting & Finance, University of Manchester.

Amalgamated Association of Operative Cotton Spinners of Lancashire and Cheshire Archive

Date range: c.1880–1976.

See also the archive of
the Bolton and District
Operative Cotton
Spinners' Provincial
Association (p. 91).

Textile industry trade union collection covering the Association's activities in Lancashire, Cheshire and parts of West Yorkshire. Records include: correspondence files; compensation claim books for personal injuries suffered by operatives; cash books and other financial records; correspondence files relating to pensions, negotiations with employers, the TUC, the Cotton Industry Act 1959, the Industrial Relations Bill 1971 and the Labour Party; printed reports of Council; and other printed literature relating to trade unionism, socialism and the cotton industry. The archive is an important source for the history of the trade union movement in Britain, and of the rise and fall of the cotton industry.

Finding aids: cataloguing in progress.

Ashton Textile Employers' Association Archive

Date range: 1891–1969.

Records of the Ashton Textile Employers' Association, formerly the Ashton and District Cotton Employers' Association which was formed in 1891 in the face of increasing trade union activity in the mills of Ashton-under-Lyne in south-east Lancashire. The Glossop, Hyde & District Cotton Employers' Association amalgamated with the Ashton Association in 1921.

See also the Oldham
Textile Employers'
Association Archive
(p. 95).

The archive comprises minute books of the Ashton and Glossop Associations, a volume concerning holiday entitlements at mills, papers relating to strikes and employment agreements, and published works on the cotton industry. There is also a small quantity of material relating to the Manchester and District, Stockport and District, and Wigan and District Cotton Employers' Associations.

Finding aids: unpublished catalogue.

Auditing Practices Committee Archive

Date range: 1971–91.

Papers of the Auditing Practices Committee of the Committee of Consultative Accountancy Bodies (CCAB). The APC was established in 1976 to produce professional standards and working guidelines for auditors and to facilitate debate in the field of auditing. It was born out of the business and financial crises of the late 1960s and early 1970s, which resulted in criticism of auditors.

Material includes agendas, minutes, correspondence, faxes, drafts of standards, guidelines and exposure drafts, reports, memoranda, press releases, press cuttings, government and other reports, published copies of APC documents, copies of articles, academic papers and extracts from books.

Finding aids: catalogue available on disk from the Department of Accounting & Finance, University of Manchester.

Economic & Industrial History

See also the Accounting Standards Committee Archive (p. 90).

Bolton and District Operative Cotton Spinners' Provincial Association Archive

Date range: 1857–1975.

The Bolton and District Operative Cotton Spinners' Provincial Association was formed in March 1880 by the amalgamation of two Bolton cotton-workers' organizations: the Hand-Mule Spinners' Association and the Self-Actor Minders' Association. The Association acted as a trade union, providing sickness benefit, unemployment benefit and strike-pay for its members, representing its members in wage negotiations and trade disputes, and participating in wider political activities.

The collection comprises minute books, account books, cash and contribution books, benefit books, accident registers and other records of the main Bolton branch and of branches in ten other Lancashire towns: Atherton, Chorley, Farnworth, Hindley, Leigh, Manchester, Pendlebury, Reddish, Tyldesley and Wigan. In some instances the records of the local branches incorporate those of earlier workers' associations which were absorbed or superseded by the Bolton Association. There are also annual reports, other printed material, and excellent correspondence files relating to the textile employers, who were organizing themselves into their own associations by the 1870s. The archive is an important source for the history of the trade union movement in Britain, and of the rise and fall of the Lancashire cotton industry.

Finding aids: large section provisionally listed; cataloguing in progress.

See also the archive of the Amalgamated Association of Operative Cotton Spinners (p. 90).

Botfield Papers

Date range: 1758–1873.

Records of the firm of Thomas Botfield & Co., charting the activities of a Shropshire coal and iron company through and beyond the Industrial Revolution. Thomas Botfield built furnaces at Old Park in 1790 and by 1815 Old Park was the largest ironworks in Shropshire, consisting of four blast furnaces, a forge and associated collieries. In 1830 a forge was built at Stirchley and in the next few years two blast furnaces were built at Dark Lane. The company also owned collieries at Clee Hill and Hinkshay in Shropshire, and at Mancott and Sandycroft in Flintshire.

Records comprise copy letter-books and large quantities of in-letters; ledgers, journals, cash books, wages account books and other financial records; sales, delivery and production records; property records such as inventories and valuations of works; and a few Botfield family records.

Finding aids: provisional outline list. See also Barry Trinder, *The Industrial Revolution in Shropshire* (Chichester, 1981).

W.M. Christy & Sons Ltd Archive

Date range: 1833–1966.

Records of W.M. Christy & Sons Ltd, the famous towel manufacturers from Droylsden, Manchester. The company, founded by William Miller Christy in the early 1830s, owed its success to the Royal Turkish Towel with its looped surface, exhibited at the Great Exhibition of 1851 and favoured by Queen Victoria. Christy continues to manufacture towels although since 1966 it has been part of the Courtaulds Group.

Records include stock books and financial, legal and statutory documents, as well as some correspondence and an interesting series of patents and samples of towel labels. The collection also contains histories of W.M. Christy & Sons and of the House of Christy in London.

Finding aids: unpublished detailed catalogue.

Dale Papers

Date range: 18th–20th centuries.

Papers of Messrs William Dale & Sons, a firm of agricultural engineers from Sandle Bridge near Alderley Edge, Cheshire. These consist of 34 ledgers relating to the firm (1794–1921). The collection also contains records of the Overseers of the Poor (18th–19th centuries) and Surveyors of the Highways (19th century) for the township of Marthall with Little Warford, Cheshire, and records of the Overseers of the Poor (19th century) and Parish Council (19th–20th centuries) of Great Warford.

Finding aids: unpublished handlist.

Engravers' Trade Unions Archive

Date range: c.1888–1973.

Records of the Amalgamated Union of Engravers to Calico Printers and Paper Stainers, and of the United Society of Engravers. Records comprise minute books; ledgers; contribution books; registers of members and apprentices; files relating to wallpaper and textile industry agreements; printed matter such as annual reports and rule books; photographs of machinery manufactured by Lockett Crossland Ltd; and annual reports of other organizations such as the Trades Union Congress, World Trades Union Congress, Women Workers' Annual Congress and Wall Paper Manufacturers Association.

Finding aids: unpublished outline list.

B.R. Faunthorpe Collection re Joseph Whitworth

Date range: 19th–20th centuries.

Papers collected by Commander Bertram R. Faunthorpe in connection with an intended biography of Sir Joseph Whitworth (1803–87). Whitworth's contributions in the fields of mechanical engineering and scientific measurement were manifold: he invented a method of manufacturing truly plane surfaces, conceived and developed a micrometer which was accurate to two-millionths of an inch and, perhaps most significantly, devised a uniform system of screw threads. At his extensive works in Openshaw, near Manchester, Whitworth also experimented to improve the design of rifles and artillery pieces. The business was converted into a limited liability company in 1874, and in 1897 it merged with Armstrong's of Elswick. After his death Whitworth's executors donated £118,000 to found the chair of engineering and establish laboratories at Owens College, Manchester.

Papers include material on Whitworth's work on firearms and screw threads, notes on the history of the engineering industry, copies of articles by or about Whitworth, photographs, and papers relating to Whitworth's estate at Stancliffe in Darley Dale, Derbyshire. Among the latter are a farm stock book, a quarry stock book and Joseph Dawson's letter-books.

Finding aids: unpublished outline list.

Greater Manchester Mill Survey Archive

Date range: 1985–91.

A survey to identify and record all surviving textile mills within Greater Manchester was undertaken by the Royal Commission on the Historical Monuments of England and the Greater Manchester Archaeological Unit in 1985–86. The results of the survey were published in 1992 (see below).

The archive contains the research materials compiled in the course of the project. These comprise correspondence concerning the establishment and funding of the project, the progress of the survey, and the final publication; general research materials such as notes and photocopies of articles and monographs on the history of the textile industry, cotton mills and industrial archaeology; photocopies of aerial photographs of mills; ground-level photographs (b/w prints) of mills; survey data sheets for individual sites; and files on particular mills.

Mills were divided into four categories. Category A sites were selected for detailed recording; files contain a full written report, a surveyed plan and elevation, historical and documentary information, photocopies of plans and documents, 35mm and large-format photographs and aerial photographs. Category B sites were selected for detailed recording but without a full written report; files contain historical and documentary information and various combinations of plans and photographs. Category C sites are recorded in the archive with site survey sheets, a printout of the county Sites and Monuments Record database entry, and ground and aerial photographs. Category D sites are no longer extant but are mentioned in the text of the publication.

Finding aids: unlisted. See Mike Williams and D.A. Farnie, *Cotton Mills in Greater Manchester* (Preston, 1992).

Hodgson, Robinson & Co. Archive

Hodgson, Robinson & Co. had links with two other firms represented at the Library: Owen Owens (p. 96) and the Fielden Brothers (p. 104).

Date range: 1811–86.

The archives of Hodgson, Robinson & Company (formerly Green & Hodgson) provide a valuable insight into the workings of a British import/export house working in South America during the 19th century. James Hodgson went into partnership with Joseph Green of Liverpool in 1818, trading between Britain and Argentina. The partnership was dissolved in 1829 and in the following year Hodgson joined John Robinson, his former accountant, in a partnership which lasted until 1844. Thereafter Hodgson continued to trade on his own account, and still owned a ranch in Argentina.

The archive comprises financial records such as invoice books, sales books, cash books and ranch accounts; letter-books; personal notebooks and diaries; and a large quantity of loose correspondence.

Finding aids: unpublished detailed catalogue.

McConnel & Kennedy Archive

Date range: 1795–1888.

Important textile archive of a Manchester cotton-spinning company at the height of the Industrial Revolution. The partnership of McConnel & Kennedy was founded in 1795 by two natives of Kirkcudbrightshire, James McConnel (1762–1831) and John Kennedy (1769–1855). The firm was originally involved in both machine making and cotton spinning, but by the close of the 18th century it was devoted exclusively to cotton spinning, becoming the largest such concern in Manchester in the 19th century.

The collection contains letter-books recording all the firm's correspondence until 1836 and a volume covering 1868–69. There is also a large quantity of letters and bills to the firm, 1795–1826, and financial records including day books, ledgers, sales journals etc.

Finding aids: unpublished detailed catalogue.

Manchester Airport Second Runway Inquiry Archive

Date range: 1994–97.

The collection comprises copies of documents submitted to a public inquiry held to consider the planning application for the construction of a second runway at Manchester Airport. Documents were presented by Manchester Airport plc and other interested parties, both for and against the runway, such as Manchester City Council, Cheshire County Council, the Department of Transport, Liverpool Airport, Manchester Airport Environment Network, the National Rivers Authority, the National Trust, and numerous individuals. Reports and studies contain detailed information on the regional transport infrastructure, actual and forecast traffic flows, pollution, tourism, industrial development and the environment. The collection also contains a copy of the Inspector's final report which summarizes the evidence.

Finding aids: unpublished handlist.

Manchester Pharmaceutical Association Archive

*Economic &
Industrial History*

Date range: 1828–1977.

The Manchester Pharmaceutical Association was founded in 1828 as the Apothecaries, Chemists and Druggists Society. By 1868 the title had been modified to the Manchester Chemists and Druggists Association, and the name was changed again in 1883 to the Manchester Pharmaceutical Association. In 1922 the Manchester, Salford and District Branch of the Pharmaceutical Society of Great Britain was established, and the Branch and Association have since worked in parallel.

The archive comprises minute books of the MPA and its predecessors, account books and other financial records, membership registers and lists, publications, general correspondence and correspondence relating to subscriptions, records relating to the MPA's educational and training activities, ephemera and miscellaneous papers.

Finding aids: unpublished handlist.

Micklethwaite Correspondence

Date range: 1786–1838.

Business and family correspondence of John Micklethwaite, merchant, of Leeds and Ardsley, West Yorkshire, mostly from correspondents in various Yorkshire towns (Leeds, Wakefield, Sheffield, Barnsley etc.) and in London, with some letters from abroad (Amsterdam, Baltimore, Philadelphia).

Finding aids: recorded in published handlist of English Manuscripts (English MS 1138).

Oldham Textile Employers' Association Archive

Date range: 1870–1960.

Records of the Oldham Textile Employers' Association, which supported the interests of the cotton industry in Oldham, arbitrated in disputes between firms, lobbied both local and national government on behalf of the industry, and in later years helped to co-ordinate industrial reorganization and redundancy schemes.

*See also the Ashton
Textile Employers'
Association Archive
(p. 90).*

Records include a complete run of letter-books, files relating to other organizations such as the British Cotton Growing Association, official government reports and a large amount of printed material concerning the cotton industry, including a set of the *Cotton Factory Times*, 1889–1937. There is a wealth of information on working conditions, relations between employers and employees, the state of both domestic and overseas trade, and the decline of the Lancashire cotton industry.

Finding aids: unpublished catalogue.

Oldknow Papers

Date range: 1782–1820.

Collection of papers relating to Samuel Oldknow's cotton-manufacturing firm based at Mellor near Stockport (until 1934 part of Derbyshire). Material includes accounts of creditors and employees, ledgers and account books for weavers, pickers, spinners and bleachers, wages books, pay tickets, warping books, costing books, output books, time books, stock books, inventories and information on female labour. A large notebook records mistakes made by women workers, with a conduct report. Records shed light on the common practice among early industrial concerns for employers to provide housing, food and drink for their workers and to deduct the cost from their wages (the truck system). The collection is an important source for studies of the early Industrial Revolution.

Finding aids: recorded in published handlist of English Manuscripts (English MSS 751–840); additional unlisted material. See also George Unwin, *Samuel Oldknow and the Arkwrights*, 2nd edition (Manchester, 1968).

Owen Owens & Sons Archive

Date range: 1813–57.

Records of the Manchester merchant trading company of Owen Owens & Sons. The company was founded by Owen Owens, a native of Holywell, Flintshire, who moved to Manchester in early adulthood. He was joined in partnership by his son, John Owens (1790–1846) in 1817, and thereafter the company expanded greatly. John Owens was considered to be one of the best buyers of cotton in the Manchester market. He purchased calicoes and coarse woollen cloths for export to China, India, the east coast of South America, and New York, importing hides, wheat, raw cotton and other goods in return.

See also the Hodgson,
Robinson & Co.
Archive (p. 94).

The archive includes correspondence, sales books, ledgers, cash books and other financial records. These contains details of the company's import and export trade and reveal the investments which the firm made, particularly in new railway companies.

Finding aids: outline list printed as Appendix 1 in B.W. Clapp, *John Owens, Manchester Merchant* (Manchester, 1965).

Rylands & Sons Archive

Date range: 1742–1969.

Records of Rylands & Sons Ltd, cotton manufacturers. The firm was founded in 1819 by Joseph Rylands of St Helens, Lancashire, and his three sons, Joseph, Richard and John. John Rylands assumed control of the company in the 1840s and developed it into one of the largest textile manufacturing and trading companies in Britain. The company continued to expand until the early 1920s when, in common with most of the Lancashire cotton industry, it began to decline and finally ceased trading in 1971.

The archive comprises directors' minute books, accounting records, sales records and catalogues, wages and employment records, and details of property owned by the firm. There are also papers relating to the Rylands family itself.

Finding aids: unpublished detailed catalogue.

Sun Mill Archive

Date range: 1860–1960.

Sun Mill, at Chadderton near Oldham, was built between 1860 and 1862 by a company which was founded in 1858 by members of the Oldham Industrial Co-operative Society. The Sun Mill Company was the first of the so-called 'Oldham Limiteds', the limited-liability companies which proliferated during the joint-stock boom of 1873–75. The mill was originally built to accommodate 60,000 spindles, three times the average number then found in local mills. It was enlarged in 1875 to house 142,000 spindles, becoming the largest mill in Oldham.

The records are incomplete, but include minute books for the board of directors, shareholders' ledgers and registers, annual reports and accounts, a visitors book and a volume of newspaper cuttings relating to the mill.

Finding aids: unpublished catalogue.

Tanks Group Archive

Date range: c.1900–50.

Archive of Tanks Group Services Ltd, a London-based holding company for several railway and mining concerns in Central and East Africa. Papers relate to the Benguela Railway, Geita Gold Mining Company Ltd, Rhodesia Katanga Company Ltd, Tanganyika Concessions Ltd, Tanganyika Concessions Union Minière, Zambesia Exploring Company Ltd and The Nile Congo Divide Syndicate Ltd. Papers include correspondence files, annual reports, minutes, accounts, contracts and legal documents. As well as being of interest to industrial historians, they are a valuable source for studies of colonialism and development in Africa.

Finding aids: partial unpublished handlist.

Tealdi Correspondence

Date range: 1836–38.

Miscellaneous business correspondence, mostly relating to the cloth trade, addressed to Pietro Ascagno Tealdi, merchant of Manchester. Almost all the letters are from Italy (mainly Ancona, Genoa, Leghorn and Turin) and are written in Italian, with a few from Amsterdam, Brussels and Paris.

Finding aids: recorded in published handlist of English Manuscripts (English MS 1130).

Wedgwood Correspondence

Date range: 1758–1804.

Ten volumes containing 19th-century copies of private and business correspondence of the Wedgwood family, notably the ceramic manufacturer Josiah Wedgwood senior (1730–95). Among the correspondents are Wedgwood's partner Thomas Bentley (1731–80), James Watt (1736–1819) and James Watt jun. (1769–1848), Erasmus Darwin (1731–1802), David Garrick (1717–79), Sir Joshua Reynolds (1723–92), Sir Richard Arkwright (1732–92), Benjamin Franklin (1706–90) and Anna Seward (1742–1809). The original letters are now dispersed and some are thought to be no longer in existence.

Finding aids: recorded in published handlist of English Manuscripts (English MSS 1101–1110).

James Woolley, Sons & Co. Ltd Archive

Date range: 1838–1967.

Records of the Manchester pharmaceutical firm of James Woolley, Sons & Co. Ltd, which manufactured and sold a wide range of products, including tablets, pills and capsules of all types, surgical equipment and trusses, talcum powder, health cordials and photographic equipment.

Records include legal documents, financial records such as ledgers, cash books and wages books, photographs of the company's premises and commercial vehicles, scrapbooks, printed histories of the company, and material relating to the pharmaceutical industry in general. There is also a small quantity of personal papers of the Woolley family.

Finding aids: provisional outline list.

PRINTED RESOURCES

Kenneth Brown Railway Collection

1,300 items.

The collection amassed by E. Kenneth Brown, a London solicitor and former President of the Railway Club, comprises over 1,300 volumes, including 220 bound maps, 280 volumes of periodicals, 225 pamphlets and 600 monographs. It contains material of interest to the social historian, the engineer, the cartographer and the student of publishing history. There are numerous 19th-century Parliamentary Acts and plans, and the collection is rich in the reports of civil engineers such as Robert Stephenson, Edward L. Stephens, Nicholas Wood, Sir John Hawkshaw and Isambard Kingdom Brunel. There is much pictorial material including John Cooke Bourne's *History of the Great Western Railway* (1846), Thomas Talbot Bury's *Views on the Liverpool and Manchester Railway* (1831), and Thomas Fairbairn's *Britannia and Conway Tubular Bridges* (1849). Periodicals include the *Railway Magazine* from 1837, the *Railway Record* from 1852 and the *Railway Times* from 1839. There are also issues of *Bradshaw's Railway Guides*.

The Library also holds a smaller railway collection, that of the late Graham Moss, comprising some 280 volumes; a collection of early Edmondson railway tickets, and ephemera relating to the tickets and machines patented by Thomas Edmondson (1792–1851); and the George Miller and Eric Dyckhoff collections which contain ephemera such as postcards, leaflets, timetables and magazines relating to railways and steamships.

Finding aids: Kenneth Brown collection recorded in general printed-book catalogue; see also note in *Bulletin of the John Rylands Library*, vol. 41 (1958–59), pp. 277–9; Graham Moss collection recorded in general printed-book catalogue; handlist of George Miller collection. See also John P. Tuck, 'Some Sources for the History of Popular Culture in the John Rylands University Library of Manchester', *Bulletin of the John Rylands University Library of Manchester*, vol. 71, no. 2 (1989), pp. 168–71.

SOCIAL & POLITICAL HISTORY

Manuscript Resources

The *Manchester Guardian* Archive is a major source for studies of the political, military, economic, social and technological developments of the 20th century. It contains correspondence with a large number of politicians and statesmen, and almost every major political event and social trend is documented in the correspondence and despatches. The papers of W.P. Crozier, former editor of the *Manchester Guardian*, contain interviews with leading politicians and statesmen, while the manuscript collection of A.P. Wadsworth, another former editor, is important for the social and economic history of Lancashire, and includes material relating to the Peterloo Massacre.

The great social campaigns of the 19th and early 20th centuries, such as the abolition of slavery, factory reform and the emancipation of women, are documented in the Raymond English Anti-Slavery Collection, the Papers of the Fielden Brothers (including material on John Fielden and William Cobbett), and the Women's Suffrage Movement Archives. The history of slavery in the West Indies is illuminated in the Stapleton Manuscripts and the Brooke of Mere Muniments, while Manchester's social history is reflected in the archives of Agecroft Rowing Club, Manchester Reform Club, and the charities Henshaw's Society for the Blind and Wood Street Mission.

The Library holds papers of several national and local politicians, including Prime Minister James Ramsay MacDonald; Thomas Spring Rice (1790–1866), 1st Baron Monteagle of Brandon, Chancellor of the Exchequer; Sir John Bowring (1792–1872), MP for Bolton and Anti-Corn Law League campaigner; J.W.T. Newbold, Britain's first Communist MP; and the Manchester councillor Dame Mabel Tylecote. The Pink Papers contain copious biographical information on Members of Parliament. Political parties are represented by the Accrington Conservative Club Archive.

Other collections include the Aladin Papers (mainly pre-Revolution Russia); the Axon Papers (Manchester local history, journalism, social reform); the Leonard Behrens Papers (United Nations, Liberal Party, social and cultural life of Manchester); the Dale Papers (Cheshire poor law and parish records); the Heald Family Papers (trade, military and physical medicine); the Hibbert-Ware Papers (local history, military history and antiquarian); the Kay-Shuttleworth Papers (education, poor relief and social reform); the Simon Papers (the Frankfurt Parliament and Revolution of 1848); and the D.A. Wilson Papers (socialism and trade unionism). The papers of Dorothy Richardson comprise detailed accounts of travel in England during the late 18th century, illustrated with drawings, and offer extensive scope for cultural, social, gender and art historical studies.

The Library also holds papers of two historians of government and politics: Samuel Finer, Professor of Government at Manchester University and later Gladstone Professor of Government and Public Administration at Oxford; and Sir Lewis Namier, Professor of History at Manchester University, 1931–53, and author of *The Structure of Politics at the Accession of George III* (1929).

See also the sections on Economic and Industrial History (p. 88) and Muniment and Charter Collections (p. 73).

The Library has attempted to acquire all the major printed sources for the social and political history of Britain. The coverage is wide-ranging, from Tudor texts to the literature of 20th-century social and political movements such as socialism and the campaign for family planning.

It is estimated that the Library has some 8,000 pre-Civil War English publications, of which about half are theological and the rest are almost equally divided between historical and literary works. Of later publications, many are extra-illustrated copies; for example, the 1807 edition of Clarendon's *History of the Rebellion* which was increased from three volumes to 21 volumes by Lord Spencer's grangerization.

The Sir John Neale Collection includes works covering almost every aspect of the reign of Elizabeth I. The English Tract Collection comprises over 15,000 items relating to political, social and theological subjects; many date from the Civil War period. Further tracts of the late 17th and early 18th centuries are to be found within the Sutherland Collection. The Ferguson Collection is particularly valuable for the study of Scottish history and literature in the 16th and 17th centuries. The Poll Book Collection comprises some 1,000 poll books, broadsides, posters and leaflets relating to English parliamentary elections in the 18th and 19th centuries.

The history of English socialism and radicalism is comprehensively documented. The Benson Collection comprises early socialist periodicals such as *Hog's Wash* and monographs by Robert Owen, Jacob Holyoake and other radicals. It also includes all the major publications of the Independent Labour Party. The massive collections of pamphlets, reports and newspaper cuttings from the Labour Party Library document the history of British and international socialism in unparalleled detail, and are key sources for studies of the major events and trends of the 20th century. The Dame Mabel Tylecote Printed Collection holds material relating to the Fabian Society and the fledgling Labour Party. Publications of all the major political parties are represented in the 20th-century Election Literature Collection. The campaign for the abolition of slavery is recorded in the H.J. Wilson Anti-Slavery Collection. The history of education for the deaf is the subject of the Deaf Education Collection, while the Marie Stopes and Birth Control Collection is concerned with the family-planning movement of the 20th century. On a lighter note, sport, and cricket in particular, is documented in the Brockbank Cricket Collection.

The Library's excellent collection of 18th- and 19th-century County Histories reveals the warp and weft of English social life at the local level, although the authors were primarily concerned with the gentry and landed classes. These volumes are an invaluable accompaniment to the Muniment and Charter Collections (p. 73). Other general historical collections include the Ashburne Hall Collection, which holds many 17th- and early 18th-century items, and the Edward Freeman Printed Collection.

French history is also well represented. The period of the Fronde, 1648–53, is documented in the Mazarinades Collection, while the Preston Pearce Collection contains documents from the century before the French Revolution, constituting a fascinating resource for the social and political history of the country in the 17th and 18th centuries. The French Revolution Collection is acknowledged to be one of the finest in Britain, if not the world, comprising some 40,000 monographs, periodicals, newspapers, proclamations and broadsides, from the time of the Revolution up to the restoration of the Bourbons.

In addition to primary source materials, the Special Collections Division holds a full range of secondary literature, including key historical monographs, periodicals, numerous series of record society publications, and a complete set of the Calendars of Rolls, State Papers and other public records published by the Public Record Office.

Bibliography

Dorothy Clayton, *British History: a Guide to Research Resources in the John Rylands University Library of Manchester* (Manchester, 1993).

David W. Riley, 'English Books of the Seventeenth to Nineteenth Centuries in the John Rylands University Library of Manchester, with Particular Reference to History and Literature', *Bulletin of the John Rylands University Library of Manchester*, vol. 71, no. 2 (1989), pp. 87–102.

John P. Tuck, 'French Studies: a Guide to Research Resources in the John Rylands University Library of Manchester', *Bulletin of the John Rylands University Library of Manchester*, vol. 72, no. 2 (1990), pp. 3–25.

Select alphabetical list of resources: (MS: Manuscript/Archive; PR: Printed)

MANUSCRIPT RESOURCES

Accrington Conservative Club Archive

Date range: 1880–1966.

Records of the Accrington Conservative Club, Lancashire. These include general and executive committee minute books; minute books of specific committees such as the municipal, political, entertainment and financial committees; subscription and visitors books; newspaper cuttings books; and miscellaneous papers such as brochures, programmes, photographs and documents relating to General Elections.

Finding aids: unpublished handlist.

Papers of the Agecroft Rowing Club

Date range: 1864–1980.

Agecroft Rowing Club was founded in 1861 to encourage the sport of rowing on the River Irwell near Manchester. The Club held regattas and participated in events organized by other clubs, but it was primarily a social club for rowing enthusiasts. Records include minute books, correspondence files, log books and regatta notes. The collection is rich in photographs, not just of Club members and of rowing activities on the Irwell, but also of the social aspects of the Club. A series of journals records one member's travels in Europe between 1900 and 1938, profusely illustrated with photographs.

Finding aids: unpublished catalogue.

Aladin Papers

Date range: c.1905–27.
Papers, in Russian and English, of Alexis Aladin (d. 1927), member of the first Russian Duma (pre-Revolutionary assembly), leader of the Trudoviks, and subsequently an emigré in England. The collection includes extensive correspondence with (Sir) David Russell and Miss E. Constance Nightingale concerning the Russian Revolution and subsequent Civil War, with photographs, articles and newspaper cuttings.
Finding aids: unpublished handlist of English-language correspondence.

Axon Papers

Date range: 1864–1947.
Papers of Dr William Edward Armytage Axon (1846–1913) and his son Ernest A. Axon (1868–1947). Dr Axon was a librarian (1861–74), a journalist with the *Manchester Guardian* (1874–1905), bibliographer, local historian, folklorist and social reformer. He was also a Unitarian of very liberal tendencies. The archive contains some 6,600 letters to him arising from these various interests. There is also a collection of some 600 autographs of famous contemporaries sent to or collected by him.
Ernest Axon was a librarian for over 50 years, a historian of Manchester and the North-West, and the author of several Unitarian local histories. His papers consist of almost 1,500 in- and out-letters, 1897–1947.
Finding aid: card index of correspondence.

Leonard Behrens Papers

Date range: 1916–76.
Papers of Sir Leonard Frederick Behrens (1890–1978), Manchester businessman. The collection contains diaries; personal correspondence; files relating to the United Nations (1946–75), the Liberal Party (1949–74), the BBC (1944–58), the Serbian Relief Fund (1916–19), and the Hallé Orchestra (1952–72); and volumes of newspaper cuttings and photographs on the Irish rebellion, the United Nations, the Liberal Party, the Hallé, and the German Democratic Republic.
Finding aids: outline list.

W.P. Crozier Papers

Date range: 1931–44.
Accounts, both typescript and holograph, of interviews conducted by William Percival Crozier (1879–1944), editor of the *Manchester Guardian*, 1932–44, with statesmen and politicians. The interviews are concerned with European politics and the Nazi threat, the Jewish National Home and the Far East (India and China). There are 175 major interviews with 23 leading politicians, including Stanley Baldwin, Neville Chamberlain, Winston Churchill, Anthony Eden, David Lloyd George, Jan Masaryk and Herbert Morrison. There are also 57 other interviews with other notable figures such as Leo Amery, Lord Halifax, Neville Laski, Jawaharlal Nehru, Eleanor Roosevelt and Chaim Weizmann.
Finding aids: outline list.

Raymond English Anti-Slavery Collection

Date range: 1824–86.

Important source for the history of the abolition of slavery. The archive contains letters, letter-books, diaries, lectures and printed works of and concerning the anti-slavery campaigners George Thompson (1804–78), his daughter Amelia Chesson, and son-in-law Frederick Chesson. Much of the correspondence relates to Thompson's work in India, Ceylon (Sri Lanka) and America. There are diaries of George Thompson, Frederick Chesson and Amelia Chesson. The latter recorded her father's anti-slavery activities in notebooks. In addition, there are original minutes of the London Emancipation Committee and a letter-book of the Aborigines Protection Society.

Finding aids: unpublished detailed catalogue.

Papers of the Fielden Brothers

Date range: 1811–1906.

Collection of papers concerning the cotton-spinning firm of Fielden Brothers and the career of John Fielden MP (1784–1849), important for the social, political and economic history of the 19th century. The partnership of Fielden Brothers was formed in 1816, based at Waterside Mill in Todmorden, West Yorkshire, and it became one of the most important and profitable textile firms in the country. John Fielden, a practising Unitarian, was elected MP for Oldham in 1832 with William Cobbett. He was known for his radical politics, taking an active part in the movement to limit the hours of factory labour and attempting to get a minimum wage agreement for handloom weavers.

Company records include accounts and correspondence concerning the running of the mills and trading activities at home and overseas. There are also papers concerning John Fielden's political activities, especially factory reform and the Ten Hour Bill, including correspondence with John, James and Richard Cobbett.

Finding aids: unpublished detailed catalogue. See also Brian R. Law, *The Fieldens of Todmorden: a Nineteenth Century Business Dynasty* (Littleborough, 1995).

Guardian *(formerly* Manchester Guardian*) Archive*

Date range: 1821–1970s.

The *Manchester Guardian* was founded by John Edward Taylor (1791–1844) in 1821, two years after the Peterloo Massacre. In the 1880s and '90s, under the editorship of the legendary Charles Prestwich Scott (1846–1932), it was transformed from an essentially provincial journal into a newspaper of national and international standing. Scott pursued a consistently radical, liberal editorial stance during his fifty-seven years in the post, even in the face of public hostility. He championed Irish Home Rule, condemned the excesses of imperialism, and criticized British policy in South Africa immediately before and during the Boer War. The *Manchester Guardian*'s radicalism continued under successive editors. In 1959 the title of the newspaper changed to the *Guardian*, to reflect its national distribution and news coverage, and in 1970 the main editorial offices and production facilities moved to London. The newspaper and its archive are a major source for studies of the political, military, economic, social and technological developments of the 20th century.

The archive consists of three elements: printed copies of newspapers and related publications; the records of the newspaper as a business; and editorial correspondence and despatches from reporters.

The archive contains a complete hard-copy set of the *Guardian* newspaper from 1821 onwards, with a subject card-index from 1929 to 1985; copies of regional issues and other *Guardian* publications such as the *Guardian Weekly*; and a large collection of cuttings from the *Guardian* and other newspapers, originally intended as research material for the paper's journalists (subsequently returned to the newspaper).

Social & Political History

Business records include partnership contracts and legal documents relating to the foundation and subsequent ownership of the paper, leases of properties, and libel actions; financial records such as ledgers, cash books, balance sheets and financial correspondence; circulation and distribution records, including detailed sets of statistics; and employment records and records relating to the production of the newspaper, containing information on developments in printing technology, changes of premises, working conditions, wage rates and trade union employment agreements.

The correspondence and despatches are a source of immense importance for studies of almost every aspect of the late 19th and 20th centuries. The period of Scott's editorship (1872–1929) is represented by two classes of correspondence. There are nearly 4,400 personal letters to and from Scott, exchanged with some 1,100 individuals. The second class comprises editorial correspondence, numbering 13,000 items from over 1,300 persons. Scott's correspondence reveals his close personal and political contacts with many of the leading statesmen and politicians of his time, such as Herbert Asquith, David Lloyd George, Winston Churchill, Lord Haldane, Lord Grey of Fallodon, Ramsay MacDonald (*q.v.*), Lord Beaverbrook, Lord Beveridge, Sir Samuel Hoare and Leslie Hore-Belisha. His interest in causes such as women's suffrage, Irish nationalism and the establishment of a Jewish homeland is illuminated in correspondence with the suffragette Emmeline Pankhurst, the subsequent Irish rebel Sir Roger Casement, and the Zionists Chaim Weizmann and Sir Lewis Namier (*q.v.*). Leading literary figures also feature in the correspondence, such as George Bernard Shaw, William Butler Yeats, John Masefield and Arthur Ransome.

See also the papers of: W.E.A. Axon, journalist (p. 103); W.P. Crozier, editor, 1932–44 (p. 103); A.N. Monkhouse, critic (p. 140); C.E. Montague, journalist (p. 140); Howard Spring, journalist (p. 143); and A.P. Wadsworth, editor, 1944–56 (p. 109).

In the post-war period, under the editorships of Alfred Powell Wadsworth (1944–56) and Alastair Hetherington (1956–75), Labour politicians figure prominently, such as George Brown, James Callaghan, Richard Crossman, Hugh Gaitskell, Roy Jenkins and Harold Wilson, while Jo Grimond represents the Liberals. Among the prominent *Guardian* staff members who feature in the correspondence are Neville Cardus, Alistair Cooke, Bernard Levin, Malcolm Muggeridge, Peter Preston, Terence Prittie, Arthur Ransome and Brian Redhead.

The large collection of despatches submitted by the *Guardian*'s foreign and war correspondents is perhaps the richest source for the historian. Almost every major event and crisis of the 20th century is represented in the archive: the First World War, the Russian Revolution, the Abdication Crisis of 1936, the rise of Fascism and the Second World War, the founding of Israel and the later Middle East conflicts, the Suez Crisis, the Korean and Vietnam Wars, the Cold War, the development of the European Economic Community and so forth. There are also files on industry, technology, transport, the churches, the police, and social issues such as housing, employment and poverty.

Finding aids: various unpublished handlists. See also Peter McNiven, 'The Guardian Archives in the John Rylands University Library of Manchester', *Bulletin of the John Rylands*

University Library of Manchester, vol. 74 (1992), pp. 65–84. Alternative form: published microfilm of C.P. Scott papers: *The Papers of C.P. Scott, 1846–1932, from the John Rylands University Library of Manchester* (Marlborough: Adam Matthew Publications, 1992).

Location: JRULM (Main Library).

Heald Family Papers

Date range: 1866–1987.

The original donation of Heald family papers, made in 1958, consists of 400 letters, five letter-books and six volumes of diaries. The bulk relates to Walter Heald (1841–1925), a merchant who went to South America in 1866, to his wife Emily Isabel, née Krabbé (1852–1926), whom he met there, and to the firm of Krabbé, Higgins & Co. of Buenos Aires, general merchants. Most of the correspondence consists of business letters from this country and from South America written and received by Walter Heald, who seems to have acted as a representative for the company. There are also four diaries written by Heald during his voyage to and residence in Buenos Aires, 1866–70, and a two-volume diary kept by his future wife in Quinta, 1869–71.

Additional material acquired in 1996 and 1997 chiefly comprises the papers of Charles Brehmer Heald (1882–1974), formerly consultant physician in physical medicine at the Royal Free Hospital. C.B. Heald had the distinction of serving as a medical officer in all three branches of the armed forces during the First World War. After the war he took a keen interest in electrotherapeutics and played a leading role in the development of physical medicine. His papers include a typescript copy of his unpublished autobiography relating his colourful wartime experiences, scrapbooks, printed matter, correspondence and personal papers. These will be of interest to students of the history of medicine and particularly of the military medical services. There are also further family papers relating to the Heald, Hall and Krabbé families.

Finding aids: earlier material recorded in published handlist of English Manuscripts (English MSS 1217–1223); unpublished accession list of later material.

Records of Henshaw's Society for the Blind

Date range: 1833–1982.

Records of Henshaw's Society for the Blind, formerly known as Henshaw's Blind Asylum which was opened in Old Trafford, Manchester, in 1837 to provide education, employment and welfare for the blind. Henshaw's has gradually broadened the scope of its activities in relation to blindness, and since 1971 it has provided a service for the visually impaired as well as the blind. The Asylum was re-named Henshaw's Institution for the Blind in the 1920s and assumed its present name in 1971. Today the Society provides a wide range of services for the blind and visually impaired.

Records consist of the minutes and financial accounts of Henshaw's Society for the Blind and its precursors, including a wide variety of committees, departments and meetings. Many of the minutes of individual committees include reports from other committees, relevant correspondence, and reports of joint meetings between committees, and many of the volumes are indexed.

Finding aids: unpublished catalogue.

Hibbert-Ware Papers

Date range: 1770–c.1880.

Papers of the Hibbert-Ware family. The collection includes notes and papers of Dr William Hibbert, surgeon in the Second Queen's Royals, relating to his service in India, 1836–38; papers of Lieut. Col. George Hibbert (1790–1847), commander of the 40th Regiment, 1838–48; letters from Captain G.H. Hibbert-Ware during the Crimean War, 1854–56; a household account book of Thomas Hibbert, merchant of Manchester, 1770–95; over 2,000 family letters and papers, the majority relating to Dr Samuel Hibbert-Ware (1782–1848), geologist and antiquary, 1797–1849; a commonplace book of Samuel Hibbert jun., 1799–1815; Lancashire tradesmen's bills, 1802–15; documents concerning the history of Ireland and the Jacobite Rebellion of 1715, and other historical and topographical notes.

Social & Political History

Finding aids: recorded in published handlist of English Manuscripts (English MSS 989–1038).

Kay-Shuttleworth Papers

Date range: c.1820–77.

Papers mainly relating to Sir James Phillips Kay-Shuttleworth (1804–77), public-health reformer and founder of the English system of public education. The collection chiefly comprises letter to James Kay-Shuttleworth from his family, friends, colleagues and associates, including Lord John Russell, 1st Earl Russell, and Sir William Cavendish, 7th Duke of Devonshire. There are also letters to Sir James's son, Ughtred James Kay-Shuttleworth, 1st Baron Shuttleworth (1844–1939), and printed materials relating to poverty and its relief, education and social reform.

Finding aids: handlist by B.C. Bloomfield (College of S. Mark & S. John Occasional Papers No. 2). See also Frank Smith, *The Life and Work of Sir James Kay-Shuttleworth* (London, 1923); R.J.W. Selleck, *James Kay-Shuttleworth: Journey of an Outsider* (Ilford, 1994); *On the Punishment of Pauper Children in Workhouses by James Phillips Kay (later Sir J.P. Kay-Shuttleworth, Bart.)* (College of S. Mark & S. John Occasional Papers No. 1).

Ramsay MacDonald Papers

Date range: 1893–1937.

Correspondence and papers of the Labour and National Government Prime Minister James Ramsay MacDonald (1866–1937). The correspondence relates to a wide range of subjects, political and personal. There are discussions upon political questions with colleagues, instructions on government policy during his premiership, affectionate notes to family and friends and day-to-day working correspondence. There are files relating to the Independent Labour Party, the Union of Democratic Control, the Coal Dispute and General Strike of 1926, the Zinoviev Letter, Communism, Palestine, China, India and Egypt. There are also appointment diaries, notebooks and Cabinet papers from 1934–37.

Finding aids: unpublished detailed catalogue. See also D. Howell, 'The Ramsay MacDonald Papers in the John Rylands University Library of Manchester: an Initial Discussion', *Bulletin of the John Rylands University Library of Manchester*, vol. 72, no. 2 (1990), pp. 101–20.

Date range: 1886–1988.

Manchester Reform Club was established in 1867 as a gentlemen's club for Liberal politicians and supporters in the Manchester area. The Club's fortunes paralleled those of the Liberal Party. Faced with declining membership in the 20th century, it merged with the Engineers' Club in 1967 to form the Manchester Club, which was eventually wound up in 1988.

Records include minute books of the Club's many committees, financial papers, membership records, records relating to the building, cuttings books and a photograph album. As well as illuminating the history of the Club, the collection has wide significance for studies of 19th-century radicalism and the history of the Liberal movement in Manchester.

Finding aids: unpublished catalogue.

Newbold Papers

Date range: c.1913–43.

Papers of John Walton Turner Newbold (1888–1943), socialist and historian. Newbold was briefly Britain's first Communist MP (representing Motherwell, 1922–23), but resigned from the Party in 1924, and gradually drifted to the right of politics.

Papers comprise notes on historical, political and economic subjects, including the history of capitalism, international finance, banking and trade, the electricity and chemical industries, armaments and the two World Wars. There are also autobiographical materials relating to Newbold's political life, the Labour Party, the Communist Party and Russia, and copies of articles written by him.

Finding aids: provisional outline list. See also Robert Duncan, 'The Papers of John Walton Turner Newbold, 1888–1943: an introductory guide', *Bulletin of the John Rylands University Library of Manchester*, vol. 76, no. 2 (1994), pp. 195–203.

Pink Papers

Date range: late 19th and early 20th centuries.

Papers collected by Mr W. Duncombe Pink of Leigh, Lancashire, mainly in connection with an unpublished biographical dictionary of Members of Parliament. Papers include indexes of and biographical notes on MPs in the Tudor and Stewart periods, notes on London MPs from the 13th to the 19th century, notes on the Long Parliament and Pride's Purge, transcripts of poll books, and miscellaneous notes and papers.

Finding aids: recorded in published handlist of English Manuscripts (English MSS 296–333).

Simon Papers

Date range: 1816–40.

Eight volumes of papers of August Heinrich Simon (1805–60). Born in the Prussian town of Breslau (now Wrocław, Poland), Simon trained for the legal profession and was a prominent advocate of constitutional and educational reform. He was a leading member of the revolutionary Frankfurt Parliament of 1848–49. Arraigned for high treason, Simon fled to Switzerland in 1849, taking with him the Parliament's seal. The volumes contain letters, diaries and documents relating to Simon's life in Breslau, and in particular to his training and early career as a lawyer. They provide interesting background information for the study of August's nephew, Henry Simon (1835–99), who came to Manchester from Germany in 1860 and founded the engineering companies Henry Simon Ltd and Simon-Carves Ltd, still in existence as the Simon Engineering Group.

Social & Political History

Finding aids: unpublished detailed catalogue. See also Brian Simon, *In Search of a Grandfather: Henry Simon of Manchester, 1835–1899* (Leicester, 1997).

Dame Mabel Tylecote Papers

Date range: 1914–79.

Personal papers of Dame Mabel Tylecote née Phythian (1896–1987), mainly concerning her career in the Labour Party, Manchester local politics, and adult education. The collection comprises: general correspondence, both personal and official; letters of congratulation and condolence; files relating to particular topics such as adult education, by-elections and general elections, her career in Manchester politics and Mechanics' Institutes; Phythian family correspondence; letters to Lucile Keck of Chicago, Illinois, from Tylecote and others; Sidebottom family correspondence, including earlier letters from A.J. Balfour (1888, 1893), John Bright (1848, 1864) and Richard Cobden (1864); personal diaries; and photograph albums. There is also a collection of 67 watercolours and drawings of scenes from the First World War by her brother Wilfrid Phythian.

See also the Dame Mabel Tylecote Printed Collection (p. 117).

Finding aids: incomplete provisional handlist.

Wadsworth Manuscripts

Date range: 18th–20th centuries.

The historical collections of Dr Alfred Powell Wadsworth, former editor of the *Manchester Guardian* and a governor of the John Rylands Library, were presented by his daughter, Miss Janet Wadsworth. In addition to Wadsworth's own notebooks and papers concerning his researches into the textile industry, Manchester Sunday schools and the history of Rochdale, there are significant original materials collected by him. These include letters from Mrs Linnaeus Banks, author of *The Manchester Man*, 1882–95; a collection of papers relating to the Peterloo Massacre of 1819, including original placards and notices; correspondence of Isaac Hawkins Browne the younger, 1788–1802; miscellaneous letters and papers of the Rev. William Robert Hay, vicar of Rochdale, 1781–c.1836; a 'minute book' of William Hough of Chorley, Lancashire, attorney, 1783–1836; ledgers, stock books and inventories of Lancashire cotton manufacturers, Messrs Cardwell, Birley & Hornby of Blackburn, 1768–1858, Nathaniel Dugdale & Bros of Padiham, 1807–51, and Ashworth Cotton Mills at Eagley near Bolton, 1831–79.

Finding aids: recorded in published handlist of English Manuscripts (English MSS 1195–1207).

D.A. Wilson Papers

Date range: 1926–37, 1968.

Papers of David Arnold Wilson (b. 1897), a Yorkshire railway clerk, trade unionist and socialist. His papers comprise diaries, correspondence, socialist and trade union pamphlets, circulars and reports, newscuttings, copies of articles, and printed books and journals. Subjects covered include the General Strike of 1926, the Minority Movement, municipal elections in Bradford, housing in Leeds, the organization and condition of the Communist Party, the Comintern, and the Labour Party and Independent Labour Party in Bradford. There is also a brief autobiography and personal reminiscence of the General Strike, compiled in 1968. The printed books concern socialism, the Labour Party, the Communist Party and the Soviet Union.

Finding aids: unpublished catalogue.

Women's Suffrage Movement Archives

Date range: 1892–1920.

The Library holds archives for: the Parliamentary Committee for Women's Suffrage (1892–1901); the Manchester Men's League for Women's Suffrage (1909–18); the National Union of Women's Suffrage Societies (1910–14); and the International Woman Suffrage Alliance (1913–20).

The Parliamentary Committee for Women's Suffrage was founded in 1894 and its members included 24 MPs. The object of the all-party Committee was to secure the Parliamentary franchise for women and they promoted the passage of all Bills and amendments which would further their cause. The archive consists of four minute books and a couple of annual reports for the period 1895–1901, and a few printed items relating to the women's suffrage movement, dated 1892.

The Manchester Men's League for Women's Suffrage was founded in 1908 and was active in propaganda activities until the outbreak of the First World War. Initially affiliated to the London Men's League for Women's Suffrage, it later became independent. It dissolved after the passing of the Representation of the People Act 1918. The archive consists of minute books, chronological correspondence files, League ephemera, ephemera collected by the League and news cuttings indexed by subject, covering the period 1909–18.

The National Union of Women's Suffrage Societies was founded in 1897 to provide an umbrella organization for the various regional societies devoted to the cause of women's suffrage. Its headquarters were in London and its President was Millicent Garrett Fawcett. Its methods were constitutional. The archive consists of 30 bound volumes of news cuttings, 1910–14, which offer a very full chronological record of the social and political position of women and of all aspects of the women's suffrage movement during this period.

The International Woman Suffrage Alliance was founded in 1902 at the initiative of Carrie Chapman Catt, President of the National American Woman Suffrage Association, and by the end of 1920 it had affiliated societies in 30 countries throughout the world, with its headquarters in London. The aim of the Alliance was to aid the enfranchisement of the women of all nations through the international co-operation of the national societies. The Alliance held biennial international Congresses, published a monthly journal, *Jus Suffragii*, and ran an international Information Bureau. The archive consists of almost 300 files from the period 1913–20: subject files relating to the work of the IWSA; alphabetical correspondence files; and files of news cuttings classified by subject.

All the collections are valuable for the study of the women's suffrage movement in Britain. The archives of the MMLWS, the NUWSS and the IWSA give valuable insights into the social and economic, as well as political, position of women in the early 20th century and also touch upon the concerns of other reform movements of the period: prostitution and the 'white slave trade'; divorce law; venereal disease; prisons; poor law; and others issues. The archive of the IWSA is also a source for the study of international conditions and attitudes during the First World War and its immediate aftermath.

See also the correspondence of C.P. Scott with Emmeline and Christabel Pankhurst within the Guardian Archive *(p. 104).*

Finding aids: unpublished handlist. Alternative form: published microfilm: *The Women's Suffrage Movement: Papers of the International Woman Suffrage Alliance, the National Union of Women's Suffrage Societies, the Parliamentary Committee for Women's Suffrage, and the Manchester Men's League for Women's Suffrage, from the John Rylands University Library, Manchester* (Woodbridge: Research Publications, 1990).

Wood Street Mission Archive

Date range: 1885–1995.

Wood Street Mission, known officially as the Manchester & Salford Street Children's Mission, was founded in 1869 by Alfred Alsop, to provide spiritual and practical support for poor children in the slum areas of central Manchester and Salford. In 1873 the Mission moved to its present premises on Wood Street (adjacent to the site where a few years later Mrs Rylands chose to build her Library). The practical necessities of life – food, clothing and shelter – were provided for hundreds of poor children and their families, while their spiritual and recreational needs were also attended to: church services and Sunday schools were held, and in 1897 a holiday camp was built at St Anne's on Sea near Blackpool. The Wood Street Mission is a registered charity which continues to provide services to the community, with particular emphasis on mitigating the effects of poverty and deprivation on children, young people and their families in the Manchester and Salford areas.

John Rylands was one of the founder trustees of the Mission, and Mrs Rylands made a generous bequest to the charity.

The archive comprises minute books, annual reports, cuttings books, account books, registers of donors and recipients of charity, wages books and other employment records, visitors books, diaries and photographs. The collection constitutes a vital record of the social history of Manchester and Salford, with particular emphasis on poverty and social deprivation, and on efforts to alleviate them.

Access: by written permission of the director of Wood Street Mission; confidential material is subject to a 75-year closure from the date of its creation. Finding aids: unpublished accession list.

PRINTED RESOURCES

Ashburne Hall Collection

3,000 items.

This includes three special groups of material, the Morley, Toller and Tootal Broadhurst collections. Many of the items date from the 17th and early 18th centuries, and there is a marked emphasis on the history of England, America and Europe, although the subject range of each collection is wide. The Morley Collection comprises works on philosophy, theology, political economy and political science, British, European (particularly French) and American history, and literature (Classical, English and European). The Toller Collection includes historical texts, foreign-language dictionaries and works on literature and theology, while the Tootal Broadhurst Collection contains works of general history, literature and illustrated books.

Finding aids: Morley Collection catalogued on cards in the Main Library card catalogue; Toller and Tootal Broadhurst collections recorded in separate card catalogue at Deansgate.

Location: JRULM (Deansgate); some items remain at Ashburne Hall.

Benson Collection

500 items (dispersed).

This collection, devoted to the history of English socialism, was formed by Sir George Benson (1889–1973), former Labour Member of Parliament for Chesterfield, and was donated between 1947 and 1952. The material ranges from the works of Robert Owen, Bronterre O'Brien, Jacob Holyoake, and William Thompson to the early socialist periodicals of the late 18th and early 19th centuries, *Hog's Wash*, *The Black Dwarf* and *The Crisis*. Also included are all the major publications of the Independent Labour Party.

Finding aids: recorded in general printed-book catalogue. See also notes in *Bulletin of the John Rylands Library*, vol. 32 (1949–50), p. 143; vol. 35 (1952–53), p. 288.

Brockbank Cricket Collection

1,200 items.

This important collection of cricket books was bequeathed to the Library by Dr William Brockbank (1900–84), a Manchester physician. Representative rather than comprehensive in nature, it nevertheless includes many rare individual items as well as runs of early statistical works, e.g. a virtually complete set of *Wisden*, including some facsimile editions and a fine series of 'Britchers', or rather Samuel Britcher's *A Complete List of All the Grand Matches*, 1793–1804/5. Also held are early classics of the game in many editions, e.g. Nyren's *The Young Cricketer's Tutor*, and early tour books such as Lillywhite's *The English Cricketers' Trip to Canada and the United States*, 1860.

Finding aids: recorded in general printed-book catalogue and separate card catalogue. See also John P. Tuck, 'Some Sources for the History of Popular Culture in the John Rylands University Library of Manchester', *Bulletin of the John Rylands University Library of Manchester*, vol. 71, no. 2 (1989), pp. 164–7; John P. Tuck, *The Game of Cricket: an Exhibition of Books Based on the Brockbank Cricket Collection* (Manchester, 1986).

County Histories Collection

500 items (dispersed).

The Library holds a fine collection of 18th- and 19th-century county histories, which are an important source for studies of local history and topography, antiquities, agriculture and commerce, the aristocracy and gentry, ecclesiastical history, and genealogy. They include Owen Manning and William Bray's *History and Antiquities of the County of Surrey* (1804–14); Sir Richard Colt Hoare's *Ancient History of South and North Wiltshire* (1812–19) and *History of Modern Wiltshire* (1822–44); three editions of John Hutchins's *History and*

Antiquities of the County of Dorset (1774, 1796–1815 and 1861–70); John Cussans's *History of Hertfordshire* (1870–81); George Baker's *History and Antiquities of the County of Northampton* (1822–41); John Nichols's *History and Antiquities of the County of Leicester* (1795–1811); the Rev. Stebbing Shaw's *History and Antiquities of Staffordshire* (1798 & 1801); the original 1819 edition of George Ormerod's *History of the County Palatine and City of Chester*, and the 1882 edition revised by Thomas Helsby; Edward Baines's *History of Lancashire* (first edition, 1836, second edition edited by John Harland, 1868–70); and Robert Surtees's *History and Antiquities of the County Palatine of Durham* (1816–40). The Library also boasts all the editions of John Stow's *A Survey of London*, from 1598 to 1633, and a grangerized copy of Thomas Pennant's *Some Account of London* (1805). Many of the volumes are extra-illustrated with the coats of arms hand-painted.

Social & Political History

Finding aids: recorded in general printed-book catalogue.

Election Literature Collection

380 items.

A small collection of election literature relating to British general elections, by-elections, and municipal elections between 1931 and 1966. There are 131 items produced by the Conservative Party, 87 by the Liberal Party, 97 by the Labour Party, and 66 by minor parties and independent candidates. In addition there are a dozen newspaper supplements for general elections, and miscellaneous leaflets and pamphlets.

See also the Poll Book Collection (p. 116).

Finding aids: unpublished handlist.

English Tract Collection

15,000 items.

The Library holds very extensive collections of tracts on political, economic, social and theological subjects. Many of these date from the Civil War period, with over 745 items associated with parliamentary matters, 55 relating to Oliver Cromwell and 351 specifically concerned with Charles I. This last figure includes eighteen editions of *Eikon Basilike* from the first edition of 1648 onwards.

Finding aids: recorded in general printed-book catalogue; a partial chronological index is available.

Ferguson Collection

363 items.

Frederick Sutherland Ferguson (1878–1967), managing director of Quaritch's from 1928 to 1943, made an outstanding contribution to the first edition of STC. This portion of his personal library, purchased in 1966, contains a large number of 16th- and 17th-century items relating to Scottish history and literature. The collection contains four works by the historian George Buchanan, including the first editions of his *De Iure Regni* (1579) and his *Rerum Scoticarum Historia* (1582). There are four editions of the Scottish royal book of King James, *Basilikon Doron*, and some 25 items relating to Scottish parliamentary administration. The Library also has a copy of Ferguson's own extensively annotated version of the first edition of STC.

STC: *A.W. Pollard & G.R. Redgrave, A Short-Title Catalogue of books printed in England, Scotland and Ireland and of English books printed abroad, 1475–1640, 1st edition (London, 1926).*

Finding aids: recorded in general printed-book catalogue. See also David W. Riley, 'English Books of the Seventeenth to Nineteenth Centuries in the John Rylands University Library of Manchester, with Particular Reference to History and Literature', *Bulletin of the John Rylands University Library of Manchester*, vol. 71, no. 2 (1989), pp. 88–9.

Edward Freeman Printed Collection

See also the Edward Freeman Papers (p. 187).

6,500 items (dispersed).

The library of Edward Augustus Freeman (1823–92), the 19th-century historian and commentator on a vast range of political and social issues, constituted the foundation of Owens College Library's history holdings when it was acquired by the Whitworth Legatees in 1892. The collection is especially rich in medieval history, and played a significant role in the development of the 'Manchester History School'.

Finding aids: recorded in general printed-book catalogues. See also James Tait, *Catalogue of the Freeman Library presented to the Owens College by the legatees of the late Sir Joseph Whitworth, Bart* (Manchester, 1894).

Location: JRULM (Main Library, and a small amount at Deansgate).

French Revolution Collection

40,000 items.

Acknowledged to be one of the finest collections of newspapers, periodicals and books published at the time of the French Revolution and up to the restoration of the Bourbons, it includes 15,000 proclamations, broadsides and bulletins as well as contemporary periodicals and newspapers (over 1,000 titles). The original folio edition of *Moniteur* (1789–1815) is present, together with an almost complete set of the *Bulletin de la Convention Nationale* (1792–95), more complete, in fact, than the set available at the Bibliothèque Nationale. The broadsides and proclamations are for the most part mounted in over 100 folio binders, and range in date from 1789 to 1871. There are substantial runs of laws and decrees, with much critical and biographical material.

Finding aids: books, periodicals and newspapers are recorded in the general printed-book catalogue. See also the following published guides: Albert Goodwin, 'The French Revolutionary Collection in the John Rylands Library: a Brief Survey', *Bulletin of the John Rylands Library*, vol. 42 (1959–60), pp. 8–14 (a few of the collections described have been subsequently withdrawn, and therefore parts of Professor Goodwin's article should be treated with caution); Bibliotheca Lindesiana, *Journaux et Publications Périodiques de la Révolution Française, le Premier Empire et la Restauration* (Wigan, 1911); Bibliotheca Lindesiana, *Collations and Notes. Bulletin de l'Assemblée Nationale, 1792, Bulletin de la Convention Nationale, 1792–95* (Wigan, 1902). See also John P. Tuck, 'French Studies: a Guide to Research Resources in the John Rylands University Library of Manchester', *Bulletin of the John Rylands University Library of Manchester*, vol. 72, no. 2 (1990), pp. 10–12.

Labour Party Library Collections

50,000 items.

The JRULM holds two very substantial collections of material acquired from the library at the Labour Party headquarters in London. These collections are known as the Labour

Party Pamphlets and Reports Collection (LPPRC) and the Labour Party Newspaper Cuttings Collection (LPNCC).

The Pamphlets and Reports Collection comprises some 10,000 pamphlets, reports and material published predominantly between 1900 and 1970. It may conveniently be divided into four sections. There is an incomplete collection of pamphlets, leaflets and conference reports published by the Labour Party itself between 1906 and 1968, which includes a number of publications issued jointly by the Labour Party and other bodies such as the TUC. Secondly, there are several thousand pamphlets on 20th-century events and conditions in countries throughout the world. The third section comprises over 100 pamphlets issued between 1887 and 1954 by such organizations as the Fabian Society, Independent Labour Party, Socialist League, Clarion Press and the Glasgow Reformers' Bookstall. The final and largest section contains reports of Royal Commissions, Select Committees of the House of Commons, and departments of the British Government; annual reports of private companies, nationalized industries and 'quangos'; publications of the Conservative Party; periodicals; newspapers; publications of international organizations such as the European Union, International Labour Organization and United Nations; publications of charities and societies; and local government publications.

The Labour Party Newspaper Cuttings Collection comprises approximately 40,000 envelopes containing some one million cuttings from British and foreign newspapers between 1909 and 1983. Most of the cuttings derive from British national daily and Sunday papers, such as the *Daily Telegraph, Daily Mail, Daily Herald, Daily Mirror, Daily Sketch, News Chronicle, The Sunday Times, The Times* and the (*Manchester*) *Guardian*. The collection covers all areas of 20th-century history and events, with the ironic exception of cuttings relating directly to the Labour Party itself, which have been retained by the Party. Events in all countries of the world from Abu Dhabi to Zimbabwe are documented.

Finding aids: unpublished handlist of the Cuttings Collection; see also *Reader Guide GS 1: Labour Party Library Collections* (John Rylands University Library of Manchester, 1996).

Location: JRULM (Main Library).

Mazarinades Collection

1,800 items.

The collection comprises more than 1,800 pamphlets, printed mainly between 1649 and 1652. These tracts, often scurrilous and mainly anonymous, were written in protest at, or sometimes in defence of, Cardinal Jules Mazarin (1602–61) and his policies at the time of the Fronde, the series of civil wars which afflicted France during the minority of Louis XIV. They provide a fascinating insight into the political and social turmoil in France at the time. More than one third of the items listed in the standard bibliographies of Moreau and of Lindsay and Neu are available. The collection is enhanced with engraved portraits of the political figures of the period.

Finding aids: annotated copy of Moreau bibliography. See also notes in *Bulletin of the John Rylands Library*, vol. 37 (1954–55), pp. 8–9; vol. 38 (1955–56), pp. 5–6; vol. 44 (1961–62), pp. 280–1; John P. Tuck, 'French Studies: a Guide to Research Resources in the John Rylands University Library of Manchester', *Bulletin of the John Rylands University Library of Manchester*, vol. 72, no. 2 (1990), pp. 9–10.

Sir John Neale Collection

Social & Political History

170 items.

The library of the Elizabethan historian Sir John Neale (1890–1975) was purchased from his widow and daughter on very favourable terms in 1979–80. Sir John had held the chair of modern history at Manchester from 1925 until 1927, but most of his academic career was spent as Astor Professor of English History at University College, London (1927–56). His abiding interest in Elizabeth I is reflected in the collection, which contains works covering almost every aspect of her reign. The 170 items of antiquarian interest held at Deansgate date mainly from the 17th and 18th centuries. They include William Camden's *Rerum Anglicarum et Hibernicarum Annales Regnante Elisabetha* (London, 1635), Sir Edward Coke's *The Second Part of the Institutes of the Laws of England* (London, 1642), and Jakob Spiegel's *Lexicon Iuris Civilis* (Basel, 1569): an edition not recorded in Adams. The Library also holds ten boxes of Neale's lecture notes.

Finding aids: antiquarian items recorded in general printed-book catalogue.

Location: JRULM (Deansgate); non-antiquarian material at Main Library.

Poll Book Collection

See also the Election Literature Collection (p. 113).

1,000 items (dispersed).

A collection of poll books dating from 1734 to 1868, with a large group from East Anglia. Some 300 broadsides, posters and leaflets relate to elections in Shrewsbury, 1790–1841, and in Cumberland, Westmorland and Northumberland, 1826–74.

Finding aids: recorded in general printed-book catalogue; unpublished handlist of former University Special Collections items.

Preston Pearce Collection

800 items (dispersed).

A collection of printed almanacs and 'companions' dating from 1681 to 1866 (including ten from 1684), donated by A. Preston Pearce between 1952 and 1954. The collection also contains miscellaneous French documents dating from the century before the French Revolution, formed to illustrate the history of revenue stamps. It includes records of all types relating to Paris and the regions of France, as far apart as Savoy, Brittany, Lorraine and Corsica, with wills and marriage settlements being particularly well represented. The collection provides a fascinating research resource for students of French social and economic life in the 17th, 18th and 19th centuries.

Finding aids: recorded in general printed-book catalogue. See also note in *Bulletin of the John Rylands Library*, vol. 35 (1952–53), pp. 287–8.

Sutherland Collection

600 items (dispersed).

John Gordon (1661–1733), 16th Earl of Sutherland, brought together this collection of late 17th- and early 18th-century tracts. Approximately one third consists of polemical works on the religious issues of the day, including many tracts by well-known divines such as Thomas Case, Rector of Stockport, Edward Stephens and Daniel Featley. The major portion reflects the Earl's interest in the affairs of his time, and in particular in the Union of Scotland with England, of which he was an active supporter.

Finding aids: recorded in general printed-book catalogue. See also note in *Bulletin of the John Rylands Library*, vol. 42 (1959–60), pp. 267–8.

Social & Political History

Dame Mabel Tylecote Printed Collection

400 items.

The collection contains material relating to the birth of the Fabian Society, the nascent Labour Party and British socialism generally. There are numerous Fabian Society tracts, research publications and Young Fabian pamphlets. In addition there are pamphlets published by the Anglo-Israel Association and publications relating to the foundation of Israel, the Middle East conflict, and many aspects of life in Israel.

See also the Dame Mabel Tylecote Papers (p. 109).

Finding aids: uncatalogued; recorded in accession register.

Location: JRULM (Main Library).

H.J. Wilson Anti-Slavery Collection

800 items.

A collection of 19th-century anti-slavery pamphlets received in 1923 from the executors of Henry Joseph Wilson (1833–1914), the distinguished Liberal Member of Parliament for Sheffield. The collection is of particular importance for the study of the activities of the provincial philanthropic societies, such as the Birmingham and Midland Freedmen's Aid Association, the Birmingham and West Bromwich Ladies' Negro's Friend Society, the Glasgow Emancipation Society, the Manchester Union and Emancipation Society, and the Sheffield Ladies Female Anti Slavery Society.

Finding aids: recorded in general printed-book catalogue.

Alternative form: published microfilm: *Anti-Slavery Materials: Regional Records and Other Pamphlets, 18th–19th Centuries – The Collection of the John Rylands University Library, Manchester* (London: World Microfilms, 1989).

(See pages 121–2)

'State of the Forces under the Command of Lieut General Sir John Moore K.B., Corunna, 14th Jany 1809', from a Weekly States Book. Clinton Papers.

State of the Forces under the Command of Lieut General Sir John Moore, K.B.
Corunna 14th Jany 1809

Regts	Colonels	L. Colonels	Majors	Captains	Subalterns	Staff	Paymrs of Cavalry	Sergeants	Trumpeters or Drummers	Present fit for duty	Sick	Command	Total	Wanting to complete effective strength	Horses	Batt. Mules	Arrived	Dead	Discharged	Deserted	Strayed	Remain	Bout	Dead
7 Light Dns	..	2	2	9	14	5	3	36	8	568	57	..	625	43	304	4	..	..	..	..	..	..	..	280
10 do	..	2	2	7	9	5	8	35	9	600	50	..	650	..	414	..	..	..	..	..	..	..	..	59
15 do	..	1	2	8	10	5	7	36	8	608	48	..	656	14	263	..	..	2	..	..	..	..	..	120
18 do	..	1	2	8	13	4	8	35	8	526	20	77	623	41	239	3	..	1	..	..	..	..	..	229
3 do KGL	..	..	2	5	13	3	8	34	8	328	41	171	540	14	299	..	..	1	..	2	..	..	..	179
Total	..	6	10	37	59	22	36	176	41	2630	216	248	3094	112	1519	9	1	3	..	2	..	..	..	867
Artillery	1	3	2	21	20	17	..	37	20	1268	65	..	1333	..	..	..	1	..						
Drivers	..	..	..	2	12	2	..	30	10	931	60	..	991	..	491	..								
Waggon Train	..	1	1	6	8	3	5	19	6	308	45	..	353	19	47	..								
Engineers	..	..	1	5	12	..	..	1	..	36	3	1	39	3	..	..	1							
Total	1	4	4	34	52	22	5	87	36	2542	173	1	2716	22	538	..	..	2						
Guards 1 Batt	..	..	..	7	32	5	..	78	23	1133	140	..	1273	74	..	..	..	10						
Guards 3 do	..	..	..	8	26	5	..	62	19	805	244	..	1049	64	..	..	..	1						
1 Foot 3	..	1	2	8	21	6	..	39	20	372	155	..	527	180	..	..	4	9						
2 .. 1	..	1	2	6	11	4	..	38	20	505	..	152	657	97										
5 Detachmt 1	..	..	..	1	3	..	..	4	1	62	6	..	68											
4 1	..	1	2	9	24	4	..	50	20	607	209	19	835	122	..	1	..	1						
5th 1	..	1	1	9	24	6	..	41	17	594	215	..	809	146	..								
6th 1	..	..	1	8	22	5	..	48	20	389	152	17	558	374	..	7	..	3						
9th 1	..	1	2	7	14	1	..	54	20	461	337	13	811	146	..	17	2							
14th 2	..	..	1	8	19	6	..	40	19	381	82	3	466	147	..	1	14							
20th 1	..	..	2	1	8	24	5	..	42	17	415	30	81	526	52	..	3	..	2					
23 2	..	1	2	9	17	6	..	37	16	349	76	..	425	149	..	..	8							
26 1	..	1	2	7	28	6	..	50	19	571	183	..	754	116	..	2	..							
28th 1	..	1	2	9	17	5	..	50	20	581	200	23	804	220	..	1	..	3						
32 1	..	1	2	5	24	4	..	50	22	633	161	..	794	60	..	..	1	6						
36 1	..	1	1	7	17	3	..	50	22	517	142	33	692	154	..	6	..	6						
38th 1	..	1	2	6	24	5	..	54	20	625	219	6	850	101	..	13	..	3						
42 1	..	2	2	7	23	5	..	52	21	706	123	6	835	91	..	13	..	3						
43 {1/2}	..	1	2	6	12	6	..	39	19	243	324	6	573	121	..	..	1							
50th 1	..	..	2	5	26	5	..	49	19	552	200	10	762	156	..	7	2							
51 1	..	1	2	6	14	6	..	35	17	311	236	..	547	66	..	..								
52 {1/2}	..	1	2	9	24	5	..	53	18	637	125	12	774	93	..	4	3	..						
59th 9..	..	1	..	4	21	5	..	28	17	446	61	..	507	127	..	..	5							
60th 2	..	1	..	4	8	4	..	31	22	224	18	..	242	15	..	..	1	..	7					
71st 1	..	1	1	6	18	4	..	53	21	573	214	10	797	92	..	..	..	3						
76th 1	..	1	2	9	16	6	..	44	16	456	150	86	692	86	..	2	..	3						
79th 1	..	1	1	9	22	4	..	51	21	703	168	14	885	100	..	..	3							
81 2	..	..	3	5	22	5	..	35	17	388	182	..	570	147	..								
82 1	..	..	1	5	17	4	..	46	15	518	89	6	613	244	..	..							
91 1	..	..	2	7	25	6	..	50	16	424	232	21	677	216	..	3								
92 1	..	1	2	8	27	6	..	51	21	704	114	28	876	91	..	3								
1	..	1	2	8	25	6	..	45	13	566	171	10	747	85	..	30								
95th {1/2}																								
Light Bns {1/2}																								
KGL {1/2}	..	1	..	1	3	..	..	5	3	91	8	1	100	10	..	..								
Staff Corps																								
Total	..	27	47	221	650	153	..	1454	591	16572	4946	557	22095	3942	..	47	28	113	..	13				

Note} No State received from the Regiments left Blank

MILITARY, COLONIAL & DIPLOMATIC HISTORY & TRAVEL

Manuscript Resources

Resources for military, colonial and diplomatic history range from substantial blocks of material in several muniment collections, such as the Bagshawe Muniments (Ireland and India) and the Grey (Stamford) of Dunham Massey Papers (India and Canada), to holdings relating to the British in India (e.g. the East India Company Papers, the Jackson Family Papers, the Melville Papers and the Thomas Munro Papers); the Napoleonic Wars (the Clinton Papers); the Crimean and Boer Wars (the Hibbert-Ware Papers and the Bromley Davenport Muniments); the First World War (W.M. Wills's Home Front Diaries, the T.F. Tout Papers, and the Tylecote Papers); and the Second World War.

Material relating to the Second World War includes the Auchinleck and Dorman O'Gowan collections, several holdings relating to Orde Wingate and the Chindits, papers of the military historian Roger Parkinson, and confidential dispatches to the *Manchester Guardian*. The *Guardian* archive itself is a massive resource for the events of the 19th and 20th centuries, and includes a wide range of correspondence covering many subject areas.

Diplomatic and colonial history is documented in the Bowring Papers (relating to Hong Kong and China); the Carrington Papers (Ceylon/Sri Lanka); the 18th-century consular correspondence of Viscount Mount-Stewart (France, Spain and Italy); the Spring Rice Collection (Irish affairs in the 1840s, Foreign Office administration, and diplomatic service in several countries); the Stapleton Manuscripts (colonial administration and slave plantations in Montserrat and the Leeward Islands, West Indies); the Brooke of Mere Muniments (slave plantations in Antigua, West Indies); and the Tanks Group Archive (mining and railways in Central and East Africa).

Printed Resources

Early printed texts relating to the art of war are to be found within the Bullock Collection and the Niccolò Machiavelli Collection, while the English Tract Collection embraces contemporary accounts of the English Civil Wars. The Library also holds numerous printed secondary sources relating to warfare throughout the ages.

The Library's outstanding manuscript holdings relating to India are complemented by the Indian Empire Collection of printed materials, including rare state papers, government reports and publications. The collection is especially valuable for the history of the East India Company and the Warren Hastings affair.

The collection of some 15,000 pamphlets from the Foreign and Commonwealth Office includes rare and valuable material on South America, Australia, the Near East and European politics in the period 1815 to 1919. The Voyages and Travels Collection features important atlases and first editions of the published accounts of travellers and explorers such as Hakluyt, De Bry and Cook. There are also many finely illustrated works. The Manchester Geographical Society Collection of atlases and books written by or for travellers and traders documents the 'opening up' of Africa and other areas as part of the Victorian imperialist enterprise, while the Booker and Mills Map Collection contains fine examples of English county maps and French and Dutch maps of Asia and the Far East.

Military, Colonial & Diplomatic History & Travel

MANUSCRIPT RESOURCES

Auchinleck Papers

Date range: 1919–62 (bulk 1940–48).

Papers of Field-Marshal Sir Claude Auchinleck (1884–1981), who commanded Allied campaigns in Norway and North Africa during the Second World War. Auchinleck assumed command of Allied operations in northern Norway in May 1940. After the evacuation from Dunkirk and the fall of Norway, in July 1940 he became General Officer Commanding-in-Chief, Southern Command, responsible for planning the defence of the south coast of England against the expected German invasion. After a brief period as Commander-in-Chief of the Indian Army in 1941 he was appointed Commander-in-Chief, Middle East. Auchinleck suffered a series of ignominious defeats in North Africa at the hands of Rommel, culminating in the fall of Tobruk, before the defensive line was stabilized at the First Battle of El Alamein. He was summarily dismissed by Churchill in July

1942. He returned to India and spent several years preparing the country's armed forces for independence.

Auchinleck's papers include typescript and autograph letters, cipher messages, telegrams, despatches, reports, military orders, memoranda, and the texts of speeches by Auchinleck. Correspondents include Field-Marshal Sir Alan Brooke (Viscount Alanbrooke), Sir Winston Churchill and Admiral of the Fleet Lord Mountbatten. The collection is of central importance for students of military history, particularly the Desert Campaign, and for research into the final years of British rule in India, the rise of the nationalist independence movement, the transfer of power from Britain to India, and the formation of Pakistan.

See also the papers of Major-General Eric Edward Dorman O'Gowan, Auchinleck's second in command during the Desert Campaign (p. 124).

Finding aids: published catalogue, M.M. Wright, 'The Military Papers, 1940–48, of Field-Marshal Sir Claude Auchinleck: a Calendar and Index', *Bulletin of the John Rylands University Library of Manchester*, vol. 70, no. 2 (1988), pp. 143–393; unpublished handlist of additional (post-World War II) material.

Bowring Papers

Date range: 1822–1905.

Personal and political correspondence of Sir John Bowring (1792–1872) and his family. There are letters from Sir John Bowring to his son Edgar Alfred Bowring at the Board of Trade, mainly concerning political and commercial affairs in the Far East at the time when Sir John was Consul at Canton, Plenipotentiary to China and, from 1854, Governor of Hong Kong and Chief Superintendent of Trade. These are an important source for studies of Anglo-Chinese relations and the opening of Japan. Earlier letters and papers date from Sir John's term as MP for Bolton and his activities in the Anti-Corn Law League. There also papers and diaries of Sir John's son Frederick Hermann Bowring, Fellow of Trinity College Cambridge.

Finding aids: recorded in published handlist of English Manuscripts (English MSS 1228–1234). See also note in *Bulletin of the John Rylands Library*, vol. 41 (1958–59), pp. 269–71.

Carrington Papers

Date range: 1798–1844.

Small collection of letters and papers of Sir Codrington Edmund Carrington (1769–1849), Chief Justice of Ceylon (Sri Lanka). After acting as a junior counsel for the East India Company in Calcutta in the 1790s, he served as Chief Justice from 1800 to 1806 when ill-health forced him to resign his position and return to England. He purchased an estate in Buckinghamshire and became a magistrate and deputy lieutenant of the county.

The collection comprises correspondence and papers relating to his service as Chief Justice, containing much information on the legal system and affairs generally in Ceylon, and later correspondence concerning his offices and private affairs.

Finding aids: unpublished handlist.

Clinton Papers

Date range: c.1760–1845.

The papers of General Sir Henry Clinton (1771–1829) and his brother General Sir William Henry Clinton (1769–1846) constitute an important source for the military and political history of the late 18th and early 19th centuries. They relate to the wars against France, in particular the Peninsular War (1808–13), but also campaigns in the Low Countries (1790s–1815), India (1803–04), Sicily (1806–08), and Portugal (1808–09 and 1826–28).

Documents include original letters, letter-books, diaries, order books, ordnance and other returns, reports on the progress of the campaign, returns of killed, wounded and missing, intelligence reports, maps and plans, regimental accounts and bundles of proclamations. The collection also includes personal and political correspondence of the Clinton, Stanley of Alderley (*q.v.*), Holroyd (Earls of Sheffield), Chester of Bush Hall, Hertfordshire, and Dawkins families, and papers of Henry Pelham Clinton (1785–1851), 4th Duke of Newcastle.

The entirely separate Kennedy Papers also concern the campaigns in the Peninsula and the south of France. Sir Robert Hugh Kennedy (1772–1840) was Assistant Commissary-General of HM Forces on the Continent, Deputy Commissary-General, and, from June 1810, Commissary-General during the Peninsular War. The Commissariat letters, papers and accounts relate most fully to the years 1810 and 1811.

Finding aids: Clinton Papers unlisted. Initial survey in *Bulletin of the John Rylands Library*, vol. 41 (1958–59), pp. 3–9, 273. Kennedy Papers recorded in published handlist of English Manuscripts (English MSS 1308–1309).

East India Company Papers

Date range: 18th–19th centuries.

See also the Indian Empire Printed Collection (p. 126), the Grey (Stamford) Papers (p. 78), the Jackson Family Papers (below), the Melville Papers (p. 123) and the Thomas Munro Papers (p. 123).

Collections of documents relating to the East India Company. Many originally belonged to Richard Johnson who for a time was assistant to Nathaniel Middleton in Lucknow and in 1784 was appointed Resident at Hyderabad. His papers include correspondence with Lord Cornwallis, Warren Hastings and others, reports, statements, legal papers and notes (Eng MSS 173–197). These are useful for anyone interested in Warren Hastings and in Indian affairs in the second half of the 18th century.

Another collection belonged to John Charles Mason (1798–1881), who in 1837 was appointed secretary of the newly-formed Marine branch, and in 1859 became secretary of the Marine and Transport Department (Eng MSS 141–169). Many of his papers are concerned with the Bombay Marine and the Indian Navy, and with arrangements for the transport of troops during the Indian Mutiny.

There is also a small collection of 18th-century manuscript maps formerly belonging to Warren Hastings (Eng MS 469), and a collection of papers on the tea trade, 1784–1828 (Eng MS 523).

Finding aids: recorded in published handlist of English Manuscripts.

Jackson Family Papers

Date range: 1763–1942.

Collection of personal and official papers of Lieutenant Colonel Robert Jackson, his son Major-General Alexander Cosby Jackson, their wives and several of their descendants. In the 18th and 19th centuries many members of the family were employed by the British East India Company and the British Army in India, and much of the collection reflects their military and legal interests in the subcontinent and elsewhere. The most prominent members of the family were Robert Jackson (1738–86), who fought at Plassey in 1757 and subsequently held several prestigious posts as an infantry officer in the East India Company, Alexander Cosby Jackson (1773–1827), who served in the Netherlands, Ireland, Egypt and India, and his son Charles Robert Mitchell Jackson (1813–74), who became a member of the Legislative Council of India in 1859.

Finding aids: unpublished catalogue.

Melville Papers

Date range: 1786–1847.

Correspondence and papers of Henry Dundas (1742–1811), 1st Viscount Melville, Home Secretary, 1791–94, and Secretary of War, 1794–1801, and his son Robert Saunders Dundas (1771–1851), 2nd Viscount Melville, First Lord of the Admiralty, 1812–27. They mainly concern India and the East India Company, Indian administration, finance, commerce and army matters, lists of applications and appointments, and papers concerning the mutiny of officers in the Madras army in 1809.

Finding aids: recorded in published handlist of English Manuscripts (English MSS 670–699, 926–927).

Mount-Stewart Collection

Date range: 1776–83.

Four volumes of consular correspondence and papers of John Stuart (1744–1814), Viscount Mount-Stewart, later 1st Marquis of Bute. The first three volumes contain some 660 letters from consuls, vice-consuls and agents at Nice, Leghorn, Genoa and elsewhere in Southern Europe, addressed to Mount-Stewart as Envoy Extraordinary and Minister Plenipotentiary at the Court of Turin, 1779–83, and to the *chargés d'affaires* there. Enclosures include intelligence reports from ports in France and Spain. The fourth volume contains official copies of memorials, correspondence and reports forwarded with his despatches, together with treaties and political documents. Among them are letters and papers relating to the capture of Fort St Philip, Minorca, 1781–82.

Finding aids: recorded in published handlist of English Manuscripts (English MSS 1145–1148).

Thomas Munro Papers

Date range: 1765–1883.

Papers of Sir Thomas Munro (1761–1827), who held various posts in the colonial administration of India, served as brigadier-general during the third Maratha War (1817–18) and was appointed Governor of Madras in 1819. The collection includes 19 autograph letters by Munro, for the most part to John Sullivan of the India Board in London. It also incorporates printed documents related to Indian affairs of the time, several memoranda, copy letters and extracts, and an autograph note by Lord Roberts concerning Sullivan's son. Munro's letters give detailed accounts of the problems of administration and revenue collection in India and display an intimate knowledge of the country, but they also include detailed descriptions of Munro's military activities in the third Maratha War. The majority of items are dated between 1814 and 1826.

Finding aids: unpublished handlist.

Military Papers of Major-General Eric Edward Dorman O'Gowan

Military, Colonial & Diplomatic History & Travel

See also the papers of Field-Marshal Sir Claude Auchinleck (p. 120).

Date range: 1926–69.

Papers of Major-General Eric Edward Dorman O'Gowan, formerly Dorman-Smith (1895–1969). He served as second in command to Field-Marshal Sir Claude Auchinleck in North Africa until his removal in 1942. He fell out with the military establishment, became disillusioned with Britain and in 1949 adopted the Irish name O'Gowan, later becoming an IRA sympathizer.

The archive contains correspondence relating to the war in the Western Desert, 1940–42, and to various works published after the war concerning the Desert Campaigns and other aspects of the Second World War; personal memoirs; and correspondence relating to general military thinking, notably on the Arab-Israeli conflict. Many of the documents deal with recurring themes, notably the reputations of Auchinleck, Winston Churchill, Field-Marshal Montgomery and others.

Finding aids: unpublished detailed catalogue.

Roger Parkinson Papers

Date range: 1960s–70s.

Papers of Roger Parkinson (b. 1939), military historian. Parkinson has written several books on the Second World War, and in particular on Dunkirk, the Desert Campaign and Pearl Harbour, and has published biographies of famous commanders such as Blucher, Clausewitz, Kutuzov, Ludendorff and Zapata. His papers include typescripts and drafts of books and articles, some of which were published under the pseudonym of Matthew Holden; notes and files on military history, including the Vietnam War, NATO and Malaya; notes and files on the War Cabinet papers; photographs; and reel-to-reel audio tape recordings.

Finding aids: provisional outline list.

W.M. Wills's Home Front Diaries

Date range: 1903–19.

15 volumes of manuscript diaries of Winifred Myers Wills, a member of the wealthy tobacco family. The pre-war diaries detail the routine of a well-off family in England and the United States, with comments on events in the wider world, such as the San Francisco earthquake and the sinking of the Titanic. During the First World War the volumes document the participation of members of the family in the conflict, and they constitute a rare record of home life during the war. The diaries are interspersed with photographs, newspaper cuttings, letters and postcards.

Finding aids: auctioneer's catalogue description.

Orde Wingate (Burma Campaign) Collections

Date range: 1942–84.

Three collections relating to Major-General Orde Wingate (1903–44), the Chindits and the Burma Campaign of the Second World War. In 1943 Wingate formed and trained a 'long-range penetration force' to operate behind Japanese lines after the Allied retreat from

Burma. Known as the Chindits, they were supplied by air and fought for some six weeks before withdrawing. Wingate trained and commanded a second, larger force which was landed by air in early 1944.

The collections were amassed by Derek Tulloch, Peter Mead and Dennis Hawley. The largest collection is that of Tulloch, whose papers relate mainly to his book *Wingate in War and Peace* (London, 1972), and include notes, drafts, correspondence, typescript accounts by ex-servicemen of their experiences with the Chindits, printed works on the Burma Campaign in English and Japanese, and contemporary Chindit papers. The latter comprise signals, despatches and reports by Wingate and other officers on operations, special force diaries of events, and correspondence.

Mead's papers were compiled in connection with his book *Orde Wingate and the Historians* (Braunton, 1987), but there are also unpublished writings, and papers on research into the medical aspects of the Chindit campaign. The small Hawley collection includes material relating to *The Death of Wingate and Subsequent Events* (Braunton, 1994), unpublished writings and maps.

Finding aids: unpublished outline lists.

PRINTED RESOURCES

Booker and Mills Map Collection

900 items.

The Booker and Mills Map Collection comprises British and foreign maps, the main strengths being English county maps and ornamental examples of the French and Dutch mapping of Asia. Virtually every county in England is represented, with works by Saxton, Norden, Speed, Blaeu, Bowen and other eminent cartographers. The Asian maps depict the Middle East, Siberia, India, Sri Lanka, Burma, Indo-China, the Malay Archipelago, Japan, Korea and China.

The maps originally formed the nucleus of a loan exhibition organized by William H. Barker in the Whitworth Hall in 1923 to stimulate interest in the study of geography, at a time when the University of Manchester was considering the introduction of a Department of Geography. They comprised the collections of Colonel Dudley Mills and Mr R.P.L. Booker, whose maps were loaned by his widow. After the successful exhibition had resulted in the establishment of a Department of Geography, with Mr Barker as its head, Mrs Booker gave permission for her husband's maps, while still on loan, to be made available for the use of students. Subsequently Colonel Mills gave his collection to the University and combined the two collections in one catalogue.

Finding aids: published catalogue, *University of Manchester, Catalogue of Historical Maps, arranged by Colonel Dudley Mills* (Manchester, 1937).

Location: JRULM (Main Library).

Foreign and Commonwealth Office Pamphlet Collection

15,000 items.

The Foreign and Commonwealth Office Library was established in 1968 from the libraries founded at the Foreign Office in 1801, at the Colonial Office a few years later, at the Dominions Office in 1925, and at the Ministry of Overseas Development in 1964. The pamphlet collection from the FCO Library was placed on permanent deposit in the John Rylands University Library of Manchester in 1993. It consists of 301 volumes of pamphlets collected by the Foreign Office and 359 volumes from the Colonial Office, comprising some 15,000 individual items in total. The great bulk of the Foreign Office material dates from 1815 to 1919. It consists largely of pamphlets acquired by ambassadors overseas and sent back to London as being of value for the formulation of policy. The following fields are particularly well represented in the collection: South America, where the British Government was the formal arbitrator in boundary disputes; the Near East, where the last century of the Ottoman Empire and the growth of Zionism are documented; and the various great European 'Questions', from the Congress of Vienna through to German material published during the First World War and smuggled out through Switzerland. The Colonial Office pamphlets are chiefly of local imprints, including unique early Australiana.

The value of the collection for political and diplomatic history is obvious, yet economic and social subjects are also well documented. A substantial portion of the pamphlets, particularly those of the Foreign Office, are likely to be otherwise unrepresented in British libraries, and much of the Latin American material may well be unique.

Finding aids: partially catalogued in the *Catalogue of Printed Books in the Library of the Foreign Office* (1926) and the *Catalogue of the Colonial Office Library* (1964).

Location: JRULM (Main Library).

Indian Empire Collection

For the East India Company see also the Grey (Stamford) Papers (p. 78), the East India Company Papers (p. 122), the Jackson Family Papers (p. 122), the Melville Papers (p. 123) and the Thomas Munro Papers (p. 123).

6,000 items.

In the 1920s, the John Rylands Library acquired an extensive collection of printed research material for the history of India in the 18th and 19th centuries, including state papers, government reports and publications, many of which, printed in remote parts of India, would have been unprocurable without the generous assistance of successive holders of the office of Secretary of State for India. For the history of the East India Company and Warren Hastings the material is especially rich, about 1,000 items in all.

Finding aids: recorded in general printed-book catalogue.

Manchester Geographical Society Collection

4,500 items.

The Manchester Geographical Society was one of the most important provincial geographical societies in Britain, in its heyday rivalling even the Royal Geographical Society of London. The Society was founded in 1884, stimulated by the commercial opportunities being created by the 'opening up' of Africa. For it was recognized that full exploitation of the new markets by British industry and commerce depended upon the dissemination of geographical knowledge. The Society grew rapidly, and likewise its library, which was eventually transferred to the University of Manchester Library on permanent loan in 1970.

The collection comprises 200 atlases, 4,000 printed books, of which some 250 pre-date 1850, and 300 periodical titles. Many of the books and journals date from the late 19th century and illustrate both the spirit of the late Victorian imperialist enterprise, and its geographical interests. The atlases range from the mid-18th century to the mid-20th, and include fine examples of 18th-century French cartography by Jean Baptiste Bourguignon d'Anville and Guillaume Delisle, 19th-century English atlases published by firms such as

A.K. Johnston, George Philip & Son and John Bartholomew & Sons, and more recent specialist atlases. Many of the earlier atlases are richly decorated and hand-coloured. Britain's dominance of the seas is reflected in the high number of maritime charts.

The book section includes a number of 17th-century items which contain significant mapping, such as Richard Blome's *A Geographical Description of the Four Parts of the World* (1670) and William Camden's *Britannia* (1610). A high proportion of the more modern books relate to Africa and Asia, many containing descriptions of original exploration. A large number of works also describe Polar exploration, reflecting the period of the Society's expansion. There are in addition some 300 periodical titles, many published by geographical societies in France and Germany.

Finding aids: published catalogues, Andrew Lloyd, 'Early Atlases and Printed Books from the Manchester Geographical Society Collection: A Catalogue', *Bulletin of the John Rylands University Library of Manchester*, vol. 73, no. 2 (1991), pp. 37–157; Andrew Lloyd, *Manchester Geographical Society Library Catalogue* (Manchester, 1992).

Location: JRULM (Main Library).

Voyages and Travels Collection

10,000 items (dispersed).

A very extensive series of accounts of early voyages and travels is available including first editions of such famous published collections as those of Sir Francis Drake, Sir Walter Ralegh, Richard Hakluyt, Samuel Purchas, the De Bry family, Louis Antoine de Bougainville, Edward Daniel Clarke, Alexander von Humboldt and Peter Simon Pallas. The collection has particularly significant holdings of the works of James Cook, and another circumnavigator well represented is Hon. Commodore John Byron. Other authors in the collection include Sir Henry Blount, Lady Isabel Burton, John Cabot, John Hunter and Robert Lyall.

Some examples of illustrated works are Bernard von Breydenbach's *Pilgrimage to the Holy Land* (Mainz, 1486), available in both German and Latin editions and in a French paraphrase; William Hodges' *Travels in India* (1793); Edward Dodwell's *Views in Greece* (1821); David Roberts's *Egypt and Nubia* (1846–49) and *The Holy Land* (1855); and Francis Frith's *Egypt and Palestine* (1858–63), one of the first books to be illustrated with pasted-in photographs. There are a number of early maps and atlases, among them Christopher Saxton's *Atlas of England and Wales* (1579) and Jan Blaeu's *Atlas Major* (1662) in eleven volumes.

Finding aids: recorded in general printed-book catalogue.

LITERATURE, DRAMA & MUSIC

Manuscript Resources

Collections of English literary papers date especially from the 18th century to the present, and overlap with material relating to the world of art and to other aspects of culture and society, particularly in the Victorian era. The Bellot Papers contain a small quantity of material relating to Samuel Butler. The Thrale-Piozzi Manuscripts, covering the literary circle of Mrs Thrale and Dr Samuel Johnson, and the Bagshawe Muniments, containing correspondence between Sir James Caldwell and many leading figures of his day, including Lady Mary Wortley Montagu and Samuel Johnson, are succeeded chronologically by 19th-century correspondence and papers featuring Walter Savage Landor, Charlotte Brontë, Elizabeth Gaskell, Charles Dickens, John Ruskin and the Pre-Raphaelites. The Tabley Muniments contain papers of the poet John Byrne Leicester Warren (1835–95), 3rd Baron de Tabley.

In the 20th century the novelists L.P. Hartley and Howard Spring and the children's writers Alison Uttley and Elfrida Vipont figure prominently among literary holdings which contain an increasing emphasis on modern drama. The Library houses the papers of several playwrights, theatrical directors and designers, impresarios and critics such as Basil Dean, Annie Horniman, Hugh Hunt, Stephen Joseph, A.N. Monkhouse, C.E. Montague, and Peter Slade. The Pit Prop Theatre Company archive illustrates the work of a radical, regional theatre which addressed social concerns such as unemployment, poverty and racism.

Two collections are particularly relevant to film and media studies. The Basil Dean Archive contains material relating to Dean's directorship of Associated Talking Pictures (which later became the Ealing Studios) during the 1930s, while the recently-acquired archive of the stage and screen actor Robert Donat (1905–58), best known for his leading roles in *Goodbye, Mr Chips* and *The 39 Steps*, is of major importance for the history of film and cinema.

A significant development of recent years has been the acquisition of contemporary literary material, most notably the growing Carcanet Press Archive (in which scores of prominent poets and authors feature), and the records of Norman Nicholson, Adam Johnson, Michael Schmidt, C.B. Cox and the *Critical Quarterly*, and the concrete poet dom silvester houédard. Although British literature predominates, France (Victor Hugo and Amable Tastu), Germany (Peter Huchel), Ireland (Katharine Tynan) and the USA (Walt Whitman and Wallace Stevens) are also represented.

Printed Resources

The Library's printed sources for students of literature are outstanding, while drama and music are also well served. The acquisition of the Spencer Collection by Mrs Rylands in 1892 ensured that her library would hold an incomparable collection of Classical Literature, including the first printed editions of some 50 Greek and Latin authors, and of the masterpieces of medieval and Renaissance Italian literature. There are substantial holdings of the most important editions of Dante Alighieri, Boccaccio, Petrarch, Machiavelli, Ariosto, Torquato Tasso and Guarini, and of Minor Sixteenth-Century Italian Writers. The Christie and Bullock collections are also rich in Italian literature.

There are important collections of works by, and relating to, all major English authors, from the introduction of printing to England by Caxton through to contemporary literature, with rare first editions and important ancillary material. The Edmund Spenser Collection contains a first edition of the *Faerie Queene*, and first or early editions of numerous other poetical works. The Shakespeare Collection embraces all four Folios, the first (1609) edition of the Sonnets, and a full range of later editions. The John Milton Collection includes no less than six variant issues of the first edition of *Paradise Lost*, while the John Bunyan Collection contains the rare first issue of the first edition of part one of *Pilgrim's Progress*. Many other landmarks of 17th-century literature are to be found in the Seventeenth-Century Literary Publications Collection.

The Eighteenth-Century Literary Publications Collection contains over 25,000 titles in 60,000 volumes, including many of the polemical writings of Swift and Defoe. Outstanding is the Samuel Johnson Collection, which features a copy of the fourth edition of his *Dictionary*, which was at one time owned by Sir Joshua Reynolds and contains over 250 corrections in Johnson's own hand.

All major 19th-century authors are represented, together with most of the minor and more obscure figures. However, particularly significant collections exist for certain literary figures, and special emphasis can be placed on the poets William Blake, Lord Byron, William Wordsworth, Samuel Taylor Coleridge, Percy Bysshe Shelley, Edward Fitzgerald, Arthur Hugh Clough, Alfred Lord Tennyson and Francis Thompson; the essayists Charles Lamb, William Hazlitt, Thomas Carlyle, James Henry Leigh Hunt and Matthew Arnold; and the novelists Sir Walter Scott, Charlotte Brontë, Charles Dickens, William Makepeace Thackeray and George Eliot. Three 19th-century writers with Manchester connections who are well represented in the Library are Elizabeth Gaskell, George Gissing and Mrs Linnaeus Banks (the E.L. Burney Collection).

The Nineteenth-Century Fiction Collection contains copies of Dickens's serialized novels in their original part wrappers, as well as numerous three-decker editions in attractive publishers' bindings. The Library also has its share of the bibliographical curiosities produced by the forger Thomas J. Wise. One author who came in for the Wise treatment was John Ruskin, of whom the Library has some 340 19th-century editions, the large majority of which happily are genuine.

Popular, working-class literature is represented by the Sharpe Collection of early 19th-century Chapbooks printed in Scotland and Newcastle. The E.L. Burney Collection, already referred to, embraces items of general and popular fiction and juvenilia. The Children's Literature Collections contain some 1,500 items from the late 19th and early 20th centuries, many illustrated of course. Children's literature of this period is also covered by the Bellot Printed Collection and the Satterthwaite Collection, the former emphasizing boys' adventure stories, while the latter is biased towards girls' literature. The Jack Cox Collection contains a virtually complete run of the *Boy's Own Paper*.

British literature of the 20th century is well represented in all its genres: the L.P. Hartley Book Collection of novels and short stories; the Harold Blundell (George Bellairs) Collection of popular detective stories; the Norman Nicholson Book Collection, in which almost all 20th-century poetry of note is represented, as well as the Cumbrian poet's own writings; the book collection amassed by the Benedictine monk and concrete poet, dom silvester houédard; and the ever-growing collection of poetry, prose and critical studies published by the Manchester-based Carcanet Press.

The Allardyce Nicoll and G.L. Brook Drama Collections each contain over 1,000 19th-century play texts and related works by major authors and minor farceurs, many of which are scarce. The latter collection also contains material from the 20th century. It should also be noted that the Deansgate building holds an invaluable printed book collection of Restoration plays, many of which are in early 18th-century illustrated editions. Authors such as William Congreve, George Farquhar, Sir George Etherege and William Wycherley figure prominently.

American literature is represented by the Walt Whitman Book Collection, and the Upton Sinclair Collection amassed by Edward Allatt. French writers include the novelist and dramatist Alexandre Dumas père (1802–70) (the Douglas Munro Dumas Collection); Victor Hugo; Joséphin Aimé Péladan (the K.G. Millward Collection); and Marcel Proust (the Marie Riefstahl Nordlinger Collection). The Library also holds the book collection of Eugène Vinaver, Professor of French Language and Literature at Manchester University. German literature is represented by the book collection of the 20th-century poet Peter Huchel.

In recent years the Library has considerably enhanced its Music Collections. In addition to medieval musical manuscripts there are several scores of 18th- and 19th-century British music; papers within the Methodist Archives of three musicians in the Wesley family; within the Arthur D. Walker Music Collection, rare scores and collected editions of the works of Handel and Bach, and research notes on Handel and Mahler; and among the papers of Michael Kennedy important material relating to Ralph Vaughan Williams, including correspondence with his widow, Ursula.

Bibliography

Barry Cooper, 'Catalogue of Pre-1900 Music Manuscripts in the John Rylands University Library of Manchester', *Bulletin of the John Rylands University Library of Manchester*, vol. 79, no. 2 (1997), pp. 27–101.

Stella K. Halkyard and C.B. McCully, '"Thoughts of Inventive Brains and the Rich Effusions of Deep Hearts": Some of the Twentieth-Century Literary Archives of the John Rylands University Library of Manchester', *Bulletin of the John Rylands University Library of Manchester*, vol. 77, no. 2 (1995), pp. 105–21.

Diana Howard, *Directory of Theatre Resources: a Guide to Research Collections and Information Services* (London, 1986).

John Laidlar, *Hispanic Studies: a Guide to Research Resources in the John Rylands University Library of Manchester* (Manchester, 1991).

Peter Nockles, *English Studies: a Guide to Research Resources in the John Rylands University Library of Manchester* (Manchester, 1989).

David W. Riley, 'English Books of the Seventeenth to Nineteenth Centuries in the John Rylands University Library of Manchester, with Particular Reference to History and Literature', *Bulletin of the John Rylands University Library of Manchester*, vol. 71, no. 2 (1989), pp. 87–102.

Brenda J. Scragg, *Children's Books of Yesterday: a Survey of 200 Years of Children's Reading* (Manchester, 1985).

John P. Tuck, 'French Studies: a Guide to Research Resources in the John Rylands University Library of Manchester', *Bulletin of the John Rylands University Library of Manchester*, vol. 72, no. 2 (1990), pp. 3–25.

John P. Tuck, *German Studies: a Guide to Research Resources in the John Rylands University Library of Manchester* (Manchester, 1987).

Select alphabetical list of resources: (MS: Manuscript/Archive; PR: Printed)

MANUSCRIPT RESOURCES

Carcanet Press Archive

Date range: 1969 to present.

The Carcanet Press was founded in 1969 by Michael Schmidt (*q.v.*) and Peter Jones with the aim of publishing and promoting new poetry. The Press moved with Schmidt from Oxford to Manchester in 1972 and its home was the Corn Exchange from 1975 until June

1996 when the building was severely damaged by a terrorist bomb. The Press continues to promote new poetry, but it has expanded and diversified over the years. In 1974 the Fyfield series was launched to provide editions of previously undervalued poets of the past. Other series include fiction, lives and letters, aspects of Portugal and film books.

The materials within the archive, which continues to expand, fall into two categories. First, there are papers relating to the Press as a business, such as accounts, publicity material, and letters from suppliers, printers, designers, binders and accountants. Secondly there is literary material, comprising typescripts and proofs of works, letters from poets, agents, editors and translators, as well as typescripts, proofs and letters relating to *PN Review*. The range of poets and authors represented is vast, and includes John Ashbery, W.H. Auden, Robert Bly, Eavan Boland, Tony Harrison, Robert Hass, Seamus Heaney, Ted Hughes, Philip Larkin, Edwin Morgan, Les Murray, Sylvia Plath, Vikram Seth, Anne Sexton, Robert B. Shaw, C.H. Sisson, R.S. Thomas and Jeffrey Wainwright. Art historians will find material relating to contemporary artists such as Adrian Stokes, Charles Tomlinson, Ian Hamilton Finlay and Stephen Raw.

Finding aids: unpublished accession lists. Listing in progress. See also Stella K. Halkyard and C.B. McCully, '"Thoughts of Inventive Brains and the Rich Effusions of Deep Hearts": Some of the Twentieth-Century Literary Archives of the John Rylands University Library of Manchester', *Bulletin of the John Rylands University Library of Manchester*, vol. 77, no. 2 (1995), pp. 105–21.

Literature, Drama & Music

See also the Carcanet Press Book Collection (p. 149) and Stephen Raw Papers (p. 167).

Richard Church Papers

Date range: 1920–72.

Papers of Richard Thomas Church (1893–1972), poet, novelist and literary critic, one-time President of the Royal Society of Literature. Church published numerous volumes of poetry from 1917 onwards, mainly of a Georgian flavour, as well as adult and children's fiction and three volumes of autobiography. The collection contains personal correspondence, correspondence with publishers, agents and other authors, business and financial papers, diaries, original manuscripts and typescripts of his major works, manuscript and typescript copies of essays and talks, typescripts and cuttings of reviews, and travel papers.

Finding aids: unpublished outline list.

C.B. Cox Archive

Date range: c.1970–93.

Personal archive of Professor C.B. Cox, former John Edward Taylor Professor of English at Manchester University. As well as being a poet in his own right, Cox has been deeply concerned with the teaching of English, serving as Chair and later President of the National Council of Educational Standards, and Chair of the National Curriculum English Working Group. But he is most famous as the originator of the Black Papers, first published in 1969, which initiated a major debate in education which still rages today. He was also the co-founder of the literary journal *Critical Quarterly* (*q.v.*).

The archive falls into two parts. The first and largest concerns education, including files relating to the Black Papers, the campaign for Freedom in the Academic Community, the National Council for Educational Standards and conferences for teachers of English. The second comprises material arising from Cox's literary activities, including letters relating to his poetry from Philip Larkin, Ted Hughes, Charles Tomlinson and Louis Simpson.

Finding aids: unpublished accession list. See also C.B. Cox, *The Great Betrayal: Memoirs of a Life in Education* (London, 1992); Stella K. Halkyard and C.B. McCully, '"Thoughts of Inventive Brains and the Rich Effusions of Deep Hearts": Some of the Twentieth-Century Literary Archives of the John Rylands University Library of Manchester', *Bulletin of the John Rylands University Library of Manchester*, vol. 77, no. 2 (1995), pp. 105–21.

Critical Quarterly *Archive*

Date range: 1958–89.

The influential literary journal *Critical Quarterly* was launched in 1958 by C.B. Cox (*q.v.*) and A.E. Dyson to promote contemporary poetry. Containing new poems, reviews and discussion articles, *Critical Quarterly* attracted new poets of the highest calibre and helped to establish poets such as Sylvia Plath, Philip Larkin, Ted Hughes and R.S. Thomas. It has also organized poetry conferences and competitions. The archive contains accounts and business papers; material relating to education, including the Black Papers; contributors' typescripts and proof copies; and letters files. There is also material on Iris Murdoch and A.S. Byatt.

Finding aids: unpublished handlist. See also Stella K. Halkyard and C.B. McCully, '"Thoughts of Inventive Brains and the Rich Effusions of Deep Hearts": Some of the Twentieth-Century Literary Archives of the John Rylands University Library of Manchester', *Bulletin of the John Rylands University Library of Manchester*, vol. 77, no. 2 (1995), pp. 105–21.

Basil Dean *Archive*

Date range: 1902–76.

Papers of Basil Dean (1888–1978), actor, dramatist and theatrical impresario. In 1907 Dean joined Annie Horniman's Gaiety Theatre in Manchester, leaving in 1911 to become the first Controller of the Liverpool Repertory Theatre, later to be called the Liverpool Playhouse. In 1919, with Alec Rea, he formed the ReandeaN company and this partnership made an outstanding contribution to the British theatre in the 1920s. Basil Dean was among the first to make British talking pictures, and in the 1930s his career combined both stage and films. In 1939 he created ENSA (the Entertainments National Service Association) and became its Director General.

The archive consists of some 16,000 items covering most aspects of Dean's career over 60 years. It is an indispensable source for students of the British theatre and cinema during the first half of the 20th century. It includes 11,000 items of correspondence with figures such as Richard Aldington, J.M. Barrie, H.E. Bates, Arnold Bennett, Lilian Braithwaite, James Bridie (Osborne Henry Mavor), Harold Brighouse, Benjamin Britten, Sir Alfred Butt, Agatha Christie, Sir Charles Cochran, Fay Compton, Gladys Cooper, Noël Coward, Clemence Dane (Winifred Ashton), Robert Donat (*q.v.*), Godfrey Elton, St John Ervine, Gracie Fields, John Galsworthy, Sir John Gielgud, Sir Eugene Goossens, Graham Greene, Annie Horniman, Sir Barry Jackson, Margaret Kennedy, Gertrude Lawrence, Sir Gerald du Maurier and his daughter Daphne, Walter MacQueen-Pope, Walter Monckton, Sir Laurence Olivier, Louis Parker, Sir Ralph Richardson, Flora Robson, George Bernard Shaw, Dodie Smith, Sir Godfrey Tearle, Sybil Thorndike, Robert Vansittart and Edward

Willis. There is material relating to Dean's directorship of Associated Talking Pictures Ltd (which later became the Ealing Studios) during the 1930s, and papers concerning two American film companies, Radio-Keith-Orpheum (R.K.O.) and Paramount Famous Lasky Corporation. In addition there are press cuttings of articles and reviews, scripts, prompt books, set and costume designs, programmes and photographs. There is a separate block of correspondence addressed to Arnold Bennett, comprising over 600 letters and replies relating to the theatre.

Literature, Drama & Music

Finding aids: published handlist, G.A. Matheson, 'The Basil Dean Archive in the John Rylands University Library', *Bulletin of the John Rylands University Library of Manchester*, vol. 79, no. 2 (1997), pp. 103–230. Alternative form: published microfiche: *Theatre History Series, No. 2: the Basil Dean Collection in the John Rylands University Library of Manchester* (Haslemere: Emmett Publishing Ltd, 1990).

Robert Donat Archive

Date range: c.1920–58.

Robert Donat (1905–58), actor and film star, was born at Withington, Manchester, on 18 March 1905. In 1924 he joined Sir Frank Benson's repertory company. His success in provincial theatre and later in the West End brought him important film work, especially with Sir Alexander Korda. His best known film role was as the eponymous schoolmaster in *Goodbye, Mr Chips*, for which he was awarded an Oscar. During the 1930s and '40s Donat continued to combine film and theatre work, but ill-health curtailed his career and brought his premature death on 9 June 1958.

The archive comprises: meticulously indexed correspondence, both personal and professional, including correspondence with Sir Bronson Albery, William Armstrong, Anthony Asquith, Enid Bagnold, Sir Michael Balcon, Sir Frank Benson, John Boulting, James Bridie (Osborne Henry Mavor), Noël Coward, Eleanor Farjeon, Walter Greenwood, Tyrone Guthrie, Alfred Hitchcock, Danny Kaye, Sir Alexander Korda, Vivien Leigh, Walter MacQueen-Pope, Sir Laurence Olivier, David Ormsby-Gore, Eden Phillpotts, J. Arthur Rank, Flora Robson, Margaret Rutherford, George Bernard Shaw, Peter Ustinov, Irene Vanbrugh, Rex Whistler and Harcourt Williams (some in photocopy form); personal diaries; boxes of press cuttings, scripts and theatre programmes; film and radio scripts, posters, and costume and set designs; photographs of Donat from childhood and throughout his career, both personal and professional, including press photographs, theatre stills and studio stills (some being copies); reel-to-reel tapes of radio performances, interviews and poetry readings; an 'emotion chart' on which Donat mapped character development in *The Citadel*; and commercial records and tapes. There is also a small amount of material relating to the executorship of Robert Donat's estate.

Finding aids: cataloguing in progress.

Elizabeth Gaskell Manuscript Collection

Date range: c.1840–67.

See also the Elizabeth Gaskell Printed Collection (p. 151).

Papers of Mrs Elizabeth Cleghorn Gaskell (1810–65), novelist, donated to the John Rylands Library by the executors of Miss M.E. Gaskell. They include letters from Charles Dickens to Elizabeth Gaskell; an autograph manuscript of Dickens's *A Child's Dream of a Star*; over 200 letters collected by Mrs Gaskell from contemporary writers, politicians and other notable persons; letters of William Makepeace Thackeray and Walter Savage Landor (*q.v.*); and original manuscripts of *The Grey Woman* and *Wives and Daughters* (both published in 1865). The Library also holds manuscripts of Gaskell's *Life of Charlotte Brontë* (1857) and *The Crooked Branch* (1859); autograph letters from Charlotte Brontë and Patrick Brontë to Mrs Gaskell, and other manuscripts relating to the Brontë family; a portrait miniature of Mrs Gaskell by W.T. Thomson; and Mrs Gaskell's ink-stand, paper-knife and other personal possessions.

Finding aids: most items recorded in published handlist of English Manuscripts (English MSS 726–734, 876–877); other material recorded in unpublished card catalogue of University MSS. Alternative form: published microfilm: *Elizabeth Gaskell and Nineteenth-Century Literature: Manuscripts from the John Rylands University Library, Manchester* (Woodbridge: Research Publications, 1989).

L.P. Hartley Papers

Date range: 1908–72.

Literary and personal papers of Leslie Poles Hartley (1895–1972), novelist, short-story writer and critic. His reputation as a writer was established with the publication of the trilogy of novels, *The Shrimp and the Anemone* (1944), *The Sixth Heaven* (1946), and *Eustace and Hilda* (1947). The *Go-Between* (1953) was later made into a highly successful film.

See also the L.P. Hartley Book Collection (p. 152).

The papers comprise general letters to Hartley, including letters from Lady Cynthia Asquith, Daphne du Maurier, Aldous Huxley, Lady Ottoline Morrell, Harold Pinter, Anthony Powell, J.B. Priestley, Siegfried Sassoon, Edith, Osbert and Sacheverell Sitwell, Stevie Smith and Sir Hugh Walpole; business letters; letters to Hartley concerning his CBE; letters from Hartley to his family and others; original manuscripts of 13 novels and 44 short stories; proofs and corrected proofs of novels and short stories; press cuttings; scripts of broadcasts, talks and reviews; scripts, screenplays and photographs of the film production of the *Go-Between*; and bound copies of the *Weekend Review*.

Additional material donated in 1998 by Hartley's long-time friend, Mrs Joan Hall of Bramhall, Cheshire, comprises several hundred letters sent by the novelist to Mrs Hall during the last decade of his life, annotated typescripts of *The Collections* (1972) and *The Will and the Way* (1973), and auction catalogues for the sale of his effects.

Finding aids: unpublished handlist. See also note in *Bulletin of the John Rylands University Library of Manchester*, vol. 64 (1981–82), pp. 1–2.

Annie Horniman Papers

Date range: 1890s–1980s.

Annie Elizabeth Fredericka Horniman (1860–1937) was a pioneer of the modern repertory theatre movement. Her involvement with the theatre began in 1894 when she financed a season of plays at the Avenue Theatre, London, which saw the first public production of plays by W.B. Yeats and George Bernard Shaw. As a result of her friendship with Yeats, in 1904 she agreed to fund the opening of the Abbey Theatre in Dublin as a home for the Irish National Theatre. The Abbey, with regular subsidies from Miss Horniman, quickly established a wide reputation for its performance of new Irish plays and for the high standard of its acting. Following disagreements with the Abbey, in 1907 Miss Horniman transferred her activities to Manchester. She established a theatre initially at the Midland Hotel, and in 1908 she took over the Gaiety Theatre and transformed it into what is generally regarded as the first full-scale modern repertory theatre. The Gaiety's stock of plays was enormously varied, from Euripides to Shaw, but the theatre was most closely associated with writers of the so-called 'Manchester School', such as Harold Brighouse, Stanley Houghton, Basil Dean and Allan Monkhouse. Unfortunately the enterprise collapsed after the First World War and in 1921 the Theatre was sold to a cinema company.

The Annie Horniman Papers comprise four separate accessions. Miss Horniman herself donated to the Library in 1918 ten scrapbooks containing press cuttings relating to the Abbey Theatre (1903–18), and in 1921 a further seventeen relating to the Gaiety Theatre and the repertory movement in England (1907–21). These chart the history of the theatres in the form of reviews, reports, features and articles from a broad range of local and national publications. The Library also holds a collection of almost one hundred programmes for productions at the Gaiety Theatre (1908–20), donated by Mr J. Peacock in 1934.

See also the Basil Dean Archive (p. 134) and the A.N. Monkhouse Papers (p. 140).

Finally, an important collection of letters, photographs and other papers, both personal and professional, relating to Miss Horniman (1904–79) and amassed by her cousin, Mrs Marjorie Garrod, was purchased by the Library from Mrs Garrod's daughter, Elizabeth Cade, in 1984. There is a substantial number of letters to Annie Horniman from authors, journalists, playwrights, critics, actors, managers and other well-known figures of the day. Correspondents include J.M. Barrie, Arnold Bennett, James Bridie, Harold Brighouse, Millicent Garrett Fawcett, John Galsworthy, St John Hankin, C.H. Herford, Emmeline Pankhurst, George Bernard Shaw, Marie Stopes, Sybil Thorndike, Sir Herbert Beerbohm Tree, W.B. Yeats and Israel Zangwill.

Finding aids: unpublished detailed catalogue. Alternative form: published microfiche: *Theatre History Series, No. 1: the Annie Horniman Collection in the John Rylands University Library of Manchester* (Haslemere: Emmett Publishing Ltd, 1990).

dom silvester houédard Papers

Date range: c.1920s–1992.

Important collection of papers of dom silvester houédard (1924–92), a Benedictine monk of Prinknash Abbey, Gloucestershire. dsh, as he is correctly known, made significant contributions in many fields. His contribution to theology was outstanding, particularly in the ecumenical movement (he was an expert on Christian-Buddhist relations) and Biblical editing (he played a leading role in the *Jerusalem Bible* translation of 1961). In the fields of literature and art he was a prime exponent of concrete poetry (visual poetry), his most celebrated poem being 'Frog-pond-plop'. dsh also corresponded widely with leading poets, artists, theologians and philosophers: his address book was said to have contained 3,000 names.

See also the dom silvester houédard Book Collection (p. 152).

Throughout his life dsh amassed a substantial archive which reflects his wide interests. There is a vast series of in-letters, as well as three address books which confirm his legendary status as a letter-writer. There is also a large collection of artworks, including three-dimensional poems, poster poems, artists' books and magazines by dsh and John Furnival of the Openings Press, as well as material by other artists in the forefront of the Concrete Poetry Movement, such as Mary Ellen Solt, Augusto de Campos, Eugen Gomringer and Ian Hamilton Finlay. The archive has wide significance for students of literature, particularly concrete poetry and the Private Presses, theology and biblical studies, philosophy, art history and cultural studies.

Literature, Drama & Music

Finding aids: unpublished accession lists. See also Stella K. Halkyard and C.B. McCully, '"Thoughts of Inventive Brains and the Rich Effusions of Deep Hearts": Some of the Twentieth-Century Literary Archives of the John Rylands University Library of Manchester', *Bulletin of the John Rylands University Library of Manchester*, vol. 77, no. 2 (1995), pp. 105–21.

Victor Hugo Papers

See also the Victor Hugo Book Collection (p. 153) and the Amable Tastu Papers (p. 144).

Date range: c.1827–88.

Collection of correspondence of the French novelist, dramatist and poet Victor Marie Hugo (1802–85), author of *Les Misérables* and *Notre-Dame de Paris*. There are approximately 800 letters to Hugo and 170 original letters written by him, the majority of which were collected by Professor Jean Gaudon between 1962 and 1966. They cover virtually the whole of Hugo's literary career. Correspondents include many prominent French writers of the period such as Théodore de Banville (1823–91), and Alfred de Vigny (1797–1863). Other letters, including five written to Hugo's mistress Juliette Drouet (1806–83) and six addressed to Madame Victor Hugo by Ulric Guttinguer (1785–1866), shed light on the author's personal life. Six letters exchanged with Louis Blanc (1811–82) relate to Hugo's involvement in the Shakespeare Tercentenary celebrations of 1864. Further letters reflect Hugo's political activities and focus on a visit made to Brussels during the Paris Commune of 1871 and the controversial offer of asylum to all *communards*.

Other manuscript items include four page-proofs of the first edition of *Châtiments*, with holograph corrections by Hugo, a manuscript of *La Voix de Guernesey*, dated 1867, and a famous watercolour drawing by Hugo, produced as a New Year card, dated January 1856.

Finding aids: catalogue in course of preparation.

Hugh Hunt Papers

Date range: 1924–80.

Papers of Professor Hugh S. Hunt (1911–93), Professor of Drama at Manchester University, 1961–73. There are files on plays produced at the Abbey Theatre, Dublin (including three plays jointly written by Hugh Hunt and Frank O'Connor), the Sydney Opera House and the Bristol and London Old Vic Companies; volumes of press cuttings concerning the Bristol and London Old Vics; programmes from the Abbey Theatre and English provincial theatres; correspondence relating to Hunt's appointments with the Bristol Old Vic, 1945–49, the London Old Vic, 1949–53, and the Australian Elizabethan Theatre, 1954–58; miscellaneous articles and newsletters; and a photograph album for the Oxford University Dramatic Society production of *King John* in 1933.

Finding aids: unpublished outline list. Alternative form: published microfiche: *Theatre History Series, No. 3: the Hugh Hunt Collection in the John Rylands University Library of Manchester* (Haslemere: Emmett Publishing Ltd, 1990).

Location: JRULM (Main Library).

Adam Johnson Papers

Date range: 1965–93.

Papers of the Stalybridge-born poet Adam Johnson (1965–93), who died in 1993 from an AIDS-related virus. This small but diverse archive includes personal documents (birth and death certificates, letters, diaries and family photographs) alongside literary material on computer disk and on paper (typewritten and holograph). It also contains artefacts previously owned by the poet such as his typewriter and baby shoes. It forms an invaluable source for literary critics and historians of 20th century literature, especially those concerned with the issue of sexuality and poetry.

Finding aids: unpublished handlist.

Stephen Joseph Papers

Date range: 1946–67.

Papers of Stephen Joseph (1921–67), theatre director, producer and designer. Joseph is best remembered as one of the champions of new theatre forms, especially theatre-in-the-round. In the early 1950s he founded the Studio Theatre Company, which was the first professional repertory group set up for the express purpose of performing plays in the round. In 1955 the company began to present summer seasons in Scarborough, and from 1956 it toured all over England. A permanent base was created in 1962 when Stephen Joseph founded the Victoria Theatre in Stoke-on-Trent. In the same year he was appointed the first fellow of the newly-established Department of Drama at Manchester University. Joseph was also closely involved in the setting up of the Association of British Theatre Technicians, and advised on the design of many new theatres. While some of his ideas were ahead of their time and failed to gain acceptance, he was responsible for introducing many innovations, such as theatre-in-the-round, which are now commonplace.

Material includes private correspondence with family and friends; professional correspondence relating to the theatres in Scarborough and Stoke, Manchester University Drama Department, the ABTT, visits to America, and Joseph's writings; many original manuscripts and typescripts of books, articles and plays; photographs; plans of the Octagon Theatre, Bolton, the Victoria Theatre, Stoke, the University of Lancaster Arts Centre, the Fish and Chip Theatre, and other theatres; and set designs in watercolour.

Finding aids: unpublished detailed catalogue.

Walter Savage Landor Papers

Date range: 1802–64.

Papers of Walter Savage Landor (1775–1864), the irascible poet and prose author. Although he wrote several volumes of lyric and epic poetry, today Landor is best remembered for his *Imaginary Conversations of Literary Men and Statesmen*, published in five volumes between 1824 and 1829, which took the form of imagined dialogues between historical figures. An ardent classicist, he returned to the same genre many years later with his *Imaginary Conversations of Greeks and Romans* (1853).

The collection contains forty-one letters written by Landor, mainly in Italy. These record in intimate detail his daily life, his appraisal of his own works, and his views on classical and contemporary writers. There is also a larger volume of correspondence concerning the

Literature, Drama & Music

Among the Elizabeth Gaskell Manuscripts (p. 135) are three letters from Landor, a manuscript poem 'To the author of Mary Barton', and corrected page-proofs of part of Giovanna of Naples.

publication of *Imaginary Conversations*. This principally comprises sixty letters written between March 1823 and November 1828 by Julius Charles Hare, who was acting as Landor's agent, to the publisher John Taylor of Taylor and Hessey; two letters to Taylor's partner, James Augustus Hessey; and a single letter to Robert Southey, who assisted the publication. There are also drafts of letters from Taylor to Hare, Southey, and Landor's cousin, Walter Landor. The correspondence reveals the freedom which Landor allowed Hare and Southey to emend his text.

Finding aids: recorded in published handlist of English Manuscripts (English MSS 1237–1238).

A.N. Monkhouse Papers

Date range: 1892–1949.

Papers of Allan Noble Monkhouse (1858–1936), playwright, novelist and newspaper critic. Monkhouse was a novelist and dramatist in his own right (several of his plays were produced at Annie Horniman's Gaiety Theatre), but he is best remembered today as the dramatic and literary critic of the *Manchester Guardian* from 1902 until his retirement in 1932. During this time he developed extensive contacts within the literary and theatrical worlds.

There are letters from Monkhouse among the papers of Samuel Alexander (p. 186).

The collection primarily consists of letters sent to Monkhouse by friends, authors, playwrights, actors, directors and publishers, relating to literature in general, their own work, Monkhouse's writings and his work as critic. Correspondents include such figures as H.E. Bates, Arnold Bennett, Joseph Conrad, John Galsworthy, Harley Granville-Barker, Annie Horniman (*q.v.*), Arthur Ransome, Sybil Thorndike and Virginia Woolf. In addition there are cuttings of reviews, along with a smaller number of theatre programmes and photographs.

Finding aids: unpublished detailed catalogue.

C.E. Montague Papers

Date range: 1874–[1979].

Papers of Charles Edward Montague (1867–1928), novelist, playwright and *Manchester Guardian* journalist. He was on the staff of the newspaper from 1890 until 1925, except for the years 1914–19 when he served in the First World War. His most prolific period as a writer was the 1920s with works such as *Disenchantment* (1922), *Fiery Particles* (1923), *The Right Place* (1924), *Rough Justice* (1926) and *Action* (1928).

There are letters from Montague among the papers of Samuel Alexander (p. 186).

The collection contains material reflecting the whole of C.E. Montague's career as a journalist and an author. Volumes of press cuttings include Montague's varied contributions to the *Manchester Guardian*, 1890–1928, as well as his writings for other journals and newspapers. There is also some correspondence relating to his journalistic career and his retirement from the paper. His literary career is represented by the numerous notes, drafts, manuscripts and typescripts of his books. There is also correspondence concerning his books with publishers, writers and artists.

Finding aids: unpublished detailed catalogue. See also Keith Grieves, 'C.E. Montague, Manchester and the Remembrance of War, 1918–25', *Bulletin of the John Rylands University Library of Manchester*, vol. 77, no. 2 (1995), pp. 85–104.

Norman Nicholson Archive

Date range: 1914–87.

Archive of the Cumbrian poet Norman Nicholson (1914–87). Nicholson was a writer in the widest sense: he wrote novels, plays, short stories, topographies, criticism, essays, reviews and biographies, but he was first and foremost a poet. A strong sense of place permeated his writing, which was largely inspired by the landscape and industry of his native Millom, a small mining town in south-west Cumbria. He spent the whole of his life, except for a period of two years in his adolescence when he was forcibly removed to a sanitorium in Hampshire to recover from tuberculosis, in his birthplace, 14 St George's Terrace, Millom. The archive consists of 27 boxes containing literary manuscripts, typescripts and publishing material, letters, photographs, news cuttings and private documents.

Finding aids: unpublished accession list. See also Stella K. Halkyard and C.B. McCully, '"Thoughts of Inventive Brains and the Rich Effusions of Deep Hearts": Some of the Twentieth-Century Literary Archives of the John Rylands University Library of Manchester', *Bulletin of the John Rylands University Library of Manchester*, vol. 77, no. 2 (1995), pp. 105–21.

Literature, Drama & Music

The Library also holds the Norman Nicholson Book Collection (p. 156).

Henry Pettitt Papers

Date range: 1870s–90s.

Papers of the Victorian dramatist Henry Pettitt (1848–93). Apart from the occasional comedy, Pettitt's work consisted mainly of melodramas. In the early years of his career his principal colloborator was the actor-manager George Conquest, but from 1880 onwards he worked in partnership with Paul Merritt, Augustus Harris and George Sims. Though the *DNB* described his characters as conventional and his style as being "without literary quality", Pettitt was a popular and prolific writer, and many of his plays were performed in the West End during the 1880s and '90s, most frequently at the Adelphi and Drury Lane theatres. His plays also enjoyed runs in America and Australia.

The collection comprises 51 volumes of playscripts, for the most part manuscript and annotated. Enclosed within them are theatre programmes, colourful fliers and posters redolent of the period, sketches and memorabilia. There is also a selection of Pettitt's personal letters and papers, his main correspondent being the novelist Charles Reade. The collection constitutes a useful source for studies of art history, popular culture and drama.

Finding aids: unpublished catalogue.

Pit Prop Theatre Company Archive

Date range: 1979–94.

The Pit Prop Theatre Company was founded in 1979, and throughout its 15-year life was based in Leigh near Wigan, Lancashire. It was a radical company which set out to challenge many of the assumptions and attitudes prevalent in society. For example, productions were inspired by the miners' strike of 1984–85, the anti-apartheid movement and racial prejudice. Almost all productions were commissioned by the Company. It was particularly active in the theatre-in-education movement pioneered by Peter Slade (*q.v.*), touring schools and community theatres. The Company was forced to close in 1994 as a result of funding cuts.

The archive contains papers relating to productions, including scripts, research notes, programmes, publicity materials and photographs. There is also correspondence relating to funding, administration and the closure of the Company. The collection will be of particular interest to drama students and theatre historians, but it also has wider significance for the history of popular culture, social studies and research into arts funding in the 1980s and early 1990s.

Finding aids: unlisted.

John Ruskin Papers

Date range: 1813–1919.

Manuscript collection comprising over 2,000 items relating to John Ruskin (1819–1900), his work and his contemporaries, complementing the printed Ruskin Collection. The collection sheds light on Ruskin himself and his works, his personal affairs and his domestic and financial problems. There is also a section comprising some 500 items relating to Ruskin's cousin and heir, Joan Severn (née Askew), and her husband Arthur, which include detailed accounts of Ruskin's illnesses and death, with correspondence between the Severns and the eminent pathologist, (Sir) John Simon.

See also the Fairfax Murray Papers (p. 166), the Holman Hunt Papers (p. 165), the Spielmann Collection (p. 168) and the John Ruskin Book Collection (p. 158).

Ruskin's own letters fall into three categories: those written to friends and relations, those dealing primarily with the Guild of St George, and those concerned with the arts and with Ruskin's books. Major correspondents include William Henry Harrison (his first editor), Henry Jowett (printer and manager of Hazell, Watson & Viney of Aylesbury), Peter Bayne (author and editor of the Edinburgh *Witness* and the *Weekly Review*), the booksellers F.S. Ellis and David White, Ralph Nicholson Wornum (Keeper of the National Gallery), his cousin George Richardson, Mrs Fanny Talbot (Ruskin's close friend and patron of the Guild), his god-daughter (Emma) Constance Oldham, and Miss Blanche Atkinson of Liverpool. In addition to letters there are manuscript fragments, photographs, business papers, and papers of Ruskin relating to Sir Walter Scott (1771–1832).

Finding aids: recorded in published handlist of English Manuscripts (English MSS 1161–1166, 1193, 1245–1267, 1304). Alternative form: published microfilm: *John Ruskin, the Pre-Raphaelite Brotherhood, and Arts and Crafts Movement: the Ruskin, Holman Hunt, Fairfax Murray, Spielmann and Related Collections from the John Rylands University Library, Manchester* (Woodbridge: Research Publications, 1990).

Michael Schmidt Archive

Date range: 1948–92.

Papers of Michael Schmidt (b. 1947), poet, novelist and publisher. Schmidt founded the literary publishing house, Carcanet Press (*q.v.*), in 1969. He continues to manage the Press while editing the magazine *PN Review* (formerly *Poetry Nation*), which he also founded, lecturing and publishing his own poetry and novels.

The archive contains: personal papers; notebooks with particular emphasis on recent and contemporary writing (Octavio Paz, W.S. Graham, Donald Davie, Jeffrey Wainwright, Elaine Feinstein, Daniel Weissbort, Dawson Jackson etc.); appointment diaries throughout Carcanet's existence; and literary papers such as annotated typescripts of some of his works.

Finding aids: unpublished handlist. See also Stella K. Halkyard and C.B. McCully, '"Thoughts of Inventive Brains and the Rich Effusions of Deep Hearts": Some of the Twentieth-Century Literary Archives of the John Rylands University Library of Manchester', *Bulletin of the John Rylands University Library of Manchester*, vol. 77, no. 2 (1995), pp. 105–21.

Peter Slade Collection

Date range: 1936–89.

Peter Slade has waged a life-long struggle to prove the importance of drama as a means of personal expression and self-development. For over 60 years he has campaigned on behalf of educational drama, dramatherapy (as a means of combatting delinquency, disability and personal inadequacies) and children's theatre. He served as Drama Adviser to the City of Birmingham Education Committee, and in 1948 he was elected Director of the recently-formed Educational Drama Association.

The archive contains a wide range of material in a variety of media illustrating the work of Peter Slade and the Educational Drama Association, including correspondence, manuscripts of Slade's writings, scrapbooks, photographs of creative drama performances with children and adults, and audio-visual material.

Finding aids: unpublished detailed catalogue.

The Library also holds the archive of the Pit Prop Theatre Company which was active in the drama-in-education movement (p. 141).

Howard Spring Manuscripts

Date range: 1934–64.

Manuscripts of (Robert) Howard Spring (1889–1965), the Cardiff-born novelist and journalist on the *Manchester Guardian*. There are manuscripts of 20 works, chiefly novels such as *Shabby Tiger* (1934), *My Son, My Son!* (1938) and *Fame Is The Spur* (1940), but also including the three volumes of autobiography, and annotated typescripts of three published works by his wife Marion Howard Spring.

Finding aids: unlisted. See note in *Bulletin of the John Rylands University Library of Manchester*, vol. 59 (1976–77), pp. 5–6.

Wallace Stevens Collection

Date range: 1941–51.

Collection relating to the American poet Wallace Stevens (1879–1955). There are 106 letters, the majority typescript, from Stevens to the director or manager of the Cummington Press, Massachusetts, and copies of 85 letters to Stevens in reply, dealing chiefly with the publication of *Notes Toward a Supreme Fiction, Esthétique du Mal* and *Three Academic Pieces*, and a private work concerning the Stevens family portraits. The collection also contains a typescript of *Notes Toward a Supreme Fiction*, a proof copy of sections of *Three Academic Pieces*, two newspaper cuttings relating to Stevens, and a printed list of family portraits.

Finding aids: recorded in unpublished card catalogue of University MSS.

Amable Tastu Papers

Date range: 1827–65.

Papers of Amable Voïart Tastu (1798–1885), French poet, translator and writer of educational books and stories for children. These comprise some forty items, including versions of three poems and thirty-two letters. Seven of these are addressed to L.E. Audot, one to the actress and poet Marceline Desbordes-Valmore (1786–1859) and one to Victor Hugo. There is also a limited number of printed books.

Finding aids: recorded in unpublished card catalogue of University MSS.

Thrale-Piozzi Manuscripts

Date range: 18th–19th centuries.

Large collection of papers of Hester Lynch Thrale-Piozzi née Salusbury (1741–1821), friend and correspondent of Dr Samuel Johnson (*q.v.*) and the centre of a brilliant literary circle. Born Hester Lynch Salusbury, she married Henry Thrale in 1763 and, following his death in 1781, she married an Italian musician, Gabriel Piozzi, in 1784.

The collection contains over 150 letters from Hester to Samuel Johnson. Other notable correspondents include James Boswell, Dr Charles Burney, Fanny Burney, Lady Eleanor Butler and Miss Sarah Ponsonby (the ladies of Llangollen), John Delap, Robert Gray (later) Bishop of Bristol, Robert Merry, Elizabeth Montagu, Arthur Murphy, Samuel Lysons, Thomas Pennant, Anna Seward, Sarah Siddons and Helen Maria Williams. Further papers include family correspondence, accounts, business papers, sale catalogues, diaries, travel journals, literary manuscripts and memoranda.

Finding aids: recorded in published handlist of English Manuscripts (English MSS 530–660, 891–893). See also E.A. and L.D. Bloom and J.E. Klingel, 'Portrait of a Georgian Lady: the Letters of Hester Lynch (Thrale) Piozzi, 1784–1821', *Bulletin of the John Rylands University Library of Manchester*, vol. 60 (1977–78), pp. 303–38. Alternative form: published microfilm: *Hester Thrale-Piozzi, Samuel Johnson and Literary Society, 1755–1821: the Thrale-Piozzi and Related Manuscripts from the John Rylands University Library, Manchester* (Woodbridge: Research Publications, 1989).

Katharine Tynan Collection

Date range: 19th–20th centuries.

Collection of books and manuscripts relating primarily to the Irish poet and novelist Katharine Tynan (1859–1931), and to her husband Henry Hinkson (1865–1919) and daughter Pamela Hinkson, who also were novelists. Katharine Tynan published over 100 novels, collections of poems and five volumes of autobiography.

The collection contains the majority of published works by the three writers, as well as a body of correspondence. This emanates both from within the family and from their many friends in both British and Irish literary and political circles. Among these were the Yeats family, George William Russell ('A.E.'), Alice and Wilfrid Meynell, Lord and Lady Aberdeen, Louise Imogen Guiney and Jane Barlow. Included also are letters from such significant figures as George Bernard Shaw, Walter de la Mare and Eva Gore-Booth.

Finding aids: listing in progress.

Location: JRULM (Main Library).

Picture of St Luke, poised with pen and knife in hand, as he receives the Word of God, from the 12th-century Dinant Gospels.
Latin MS 11, fo. 88r.
(*see page 31*)

Volume containing labels for towels manufactured by W.M. Christy & Sons, 1910-20. Papers of W.M. Christy & Sons, wmc/4/4/16, pp. 46-7. (*see page 92*)

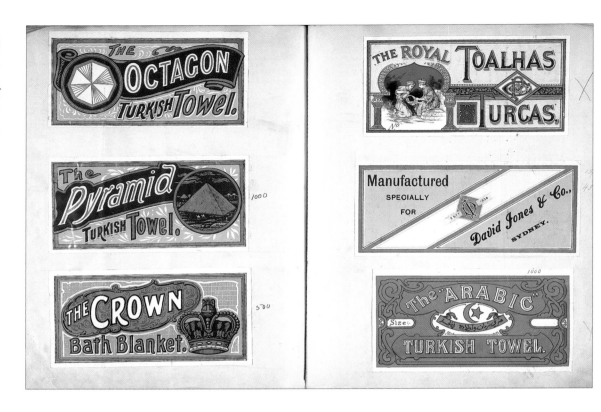

William Morris, *News from Nowhere: Or, An Epoch of Rest, Being Some Chapters from a Utopian Romance* (Hammersmith: Kelmscott Press, 1893). The house in the frontispiece, drawn by Charles M. Gere, is Morris's own Kelmscott Manor. (*see page 22*)

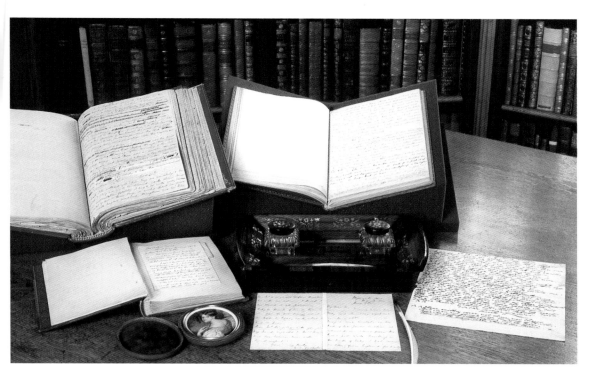

Gaskelliana. Clockwise, from top: manuscript of Elizabeth Gaskell's *The Crooked Branch*; letter from W.S. Landor to Mrs Gaskell (English MS 727); letter from Gaskell to Charles Kingsley, 6 June 1857; portrait miniature of Mrs Gaskell; letters from Charles Dickens to Gaskell (English MS 729); manuscript of Gaskell's *Life of Charlotte Brontë*. Centre: Mrs Gaskell's ink-stand, paper-knife, scissors and pen. (*see page 135*)

ken cox memorial   dsh 1968

'Ken Cox Memorial Poem' by dom silvester houédard, from *dsh* (Woodchester: Openings Press, 1992). Reproduced by courtesy of the Community of Prinknash Abbey. (*see pages 137 and 152*)

und macht in kul·Do bett ananias got an und sprach·Herre got du pist gerecht wir habē gesunt vñ hast uns in der heidē heut gebē unser opfer werd heut gros vor dinem anplick das es dir wol geuall·Do halff got den kinde das in nye kein leit geschahe·vñ satzē in dem ofen als in dē paradis·Do lobtē sie got und sprachē·Herre wir sein diner gnadē vol du must in den himeln und erdē gelobt sein·diner gnadn ist nicht gleich und die heiligē loben dich ewiglich·und sprechen·Heilig heilig heilig pistu herre·Nach dem machtē sie dē benedicite und sprachē alle auß einē mūd und lobtē got und sprachē·Gesegēt sei got vñ under vater und alle werck gotes sey genetter lobt in und erhohet in vō ewen zu ewen·Alle engel des himels seit gesegent des herrē·Alle wasser gotes gesegent got und die auff dē himel sein·Alle tugent unde krafft gotes gesegent got suñ

Alison Uttley Papers

Date range: 1903–94.

Papers of Alison Uttley (1884–1976), the well-known children's writer. Born Alice Jane Taylor in Cromford, Derbyshire, she developed a love of science at school, and won a scholarship to read physics at Manchester University; in 1906 she became only the second woman honours graduate of the university. Her writing career was born of necessity: her husband, James Arthur Uttley, died in 1930, his health broken by service in the First World War. In order to support herself and her son she began to write a series of stories about animals such as Little Grey Rabbit, Little Red Fox, Tom Pig and Hare. Her writing career blossomed, and she continued to write stories for young children, while expanding her range by writing for older children and adults. Alison Uttley was the author of over one hundred books, and was awarded an honorary Litt.D. by Manchester University in 1970.

The collection includes a good deal of very important information, not least 40 unpublished personal diaries, 1932–71; numerous notebooks containing rough drafts of stories, jottings of dreams, memories, experiences and quotations; scrapbooks containing press cuttings and reviews of Uttley's works; numerous copies of her works, in manuscript, typescript and proof copy form; copies of illustrations by artists such as Charles Tunnicliffe and Margaret Tempest; correspondence with Walter de la Mare and others; cuttings, postcards and photographs. In addition to Tunnicliffe and Tempest, many other notable illustrators are represented in the collection, including Arthur Rackham, Edmund Dulac, Harry Neilson and Randolph Caldecott.

The Library also holds a collection of books from Alison Uttley's personal library.

Finding aids: unpublished detailed catalogue of papers; books recorded in general printed-book catalogue.

Elfrida Vipont Collection

Date range: c.1910–90.

Personal collection of Elfrida Vipont Foulds née Brown (1902–92), writer of Quaker and children's literature. Vipont was born in Manchester but on the outbreak of the Second World War she moved to the north Lancashire village of Yealand Conyers. Her most famous book for children was *The Elephant and the Bad Baby* (Hamish Hamilton, 1969).

The collection contains manuscript and typescript copies of published and unpublished works, correspondence and other papers concerning her writings, papers relating to her other interests in music and Quakerism, audio dictation tapes, copies of her published books, articles and ephemera.

Finding aids: uncatalogued. For further information see Brenda J. Scragg, 'Elfrida Vipont: Quaker Children's Writer', *Bulletin of the John Rylands University Library of Manchester*, vol. 76, no. 3 (1994), pp. 249–65.

Walt Whitman Manuscript Collections

Date range: 1880–1948.

The Library holds two collections of papers relating to Walt Whitman (1819–92), the American journalist, essayist and poet, whose *Leaves of Grass* made him a revolutionary figure in American literature. The Sixsmith Collection (English MSS 1170, 1172, 1330, 1331) comprises papers of Charles F. Sixsmith of Anderton, Lancashire, respecting his Whitman interest. It includes 39 letters to Whitman from various correspondents, and miscellaneous correspondence of Horace L. Traubel, the intimate friend of Whitman, mostly addressed to J.W. Wallace, Dr John Johnston and Sixsmith.

See also the Walt Whitman Printed Collection (p. 161).

Another collection (English MS 1186) relates to James William Wallace (1850–1926), the friend of Walt Whitman, and the Bolton Whitman Fellowship. It contains 53 drafts or copies of letters from Wallace to Whitman, 1887–91, copies of 8 letters from John Addington Symonds, 1890–93, and a typescript diary of Wallace's visits to Whitman in 1891.

Finding aids: recorded in published handlist of English Manuscripts (English MSS 1170, 1172, 1186); unpublished detailed catalogues.

PRINTED RESOURCES

Lodovico Ariosto Collection

1,200 items (dispersed).

The Library's collection of early editions of the works of Ariosto is the second most important in Britain, comprising 83 of the 280 16th-century editions recorded by Agnelli and Ravegnani. There are fine copies, bound by Mackinlay, of both the first edition, 1516, and the first complete edition, 1532, of *Orlando Furioso*. Other rare editions include those of 1524, 1527 and 1530. The 16th-century editions of all the other works by Ariosto are available save for the prose version of *La Cassaria* and *Erbolato*. Dialect versions include the very rare 1558 edition, French translations date from 1720 and 1844, and of the twelve English translations published up to 1800, the Library has ten, including the first edition of Harington's translation, 1591, and a rare first issue of the first Croker edition of 1755.

Finding aids: recorded in general printed-book catalogue.

Bellot Printed Collection

5,000 items.

The working library of Hugh Hale Bellot, Professor of American History at London University, was bequeathed in 1969. The collection's strength is in 19th-century history, but it also includes quantities of 19th- and early 20th-century children's books and adventure stories. In particular there is a large number of novels by the well-known author of boys' stories, G.A. Henty. There are many examples of the firm of Ernest Nister of Nürnberg, including movable books. The series of *Dumpy Books for Children* contains scarce items. It should be noted that Professor Bellot donated numerous other books to the Library over many years; these have been incorporated into the general stock.

See also the Bellot Papers (p. 75).

Finding aids: children's books recorded in general printed-book catalogue; see also unpublished handlist.

Location: JRULM (Deansgate; children's books at Main Library).

Harold Blundell (George Bellairs) Collection

250 items.

Harold Blundell, a Manchester banker with close connections with the University of Manchester, was a Manx philanthropist who, in the mid-20th century, wrote over 40 detective stories under the pseudonym 'George Bellairs'. The Library has a complete collection of first editions, many of them autographed and annotated, translations of the novels into French, German and Spanish (146 volumes), manuscript drafts and final revisions of a number of the titles, and a substantial amount of correspondence with Blundell's literary agent, Christina Foyle.

Finding aids: uncatalogued. See John P. Tuck, 'Some Sources for the History of Popular Culture in the John Rylands University Library of Manchester', *Bulletin of the John Rylands University Library of Manchester*, vol. 71, no. 2 (1989), pp. 162–4.

Literature, Drama & Music

Giovanni Boccaccio Collection

6,000 items (dispersed).

Of the 192 15th- and 16th-century editions of Boccaccio recorded by Bacchi della Lega, the Library possesses 96 (compared with the British Library's 90). Pride of place must go to the only surviving complete copy of the Venetian 1471 edition of the *Decameron* printed by Christopher Valdarfer, which was sold by the Duke of Roxburghe in 1812 for the then record price of £2,200. However, the Library does also have what is thought to be the *editio princeps*: the Neapolitan Deo Gratias edition, previously dated 1472 but now dated 1470. Unfortunately the Manchester copy lacks the final two leaves. All but two of the incunable editions of the *Decameron* are available with a total of 47 editions present up to 1600. Noteworthy are the beautiful and rare Aldine edition of 1522, the famous Florentine edition of 1527 issued by Giunta, and the two notoriously emended texts of Ruscelli (1552) and Salviati (1587).

Of the seventeen early editions of *Ameto* the Library possesses twelve (1520–1723). Manchester also holds twelve of a possible twenty-three editions of *Il Filocolo* (1472–1724); eleven editions of *La Fiametta* (1480–1800); six editions of *Corbaccio* (1516–1723); two of *La Vita di Dante* (1576–1724); three of *La Teseida* (1475–1819); three of *Il Filostrato* (1480–1789); four of *Ninfale Fiesolano* (1480–1778); and three of the *Amorosa Visione* (1521–49). There are also several editions of Boccaccio's Latin works.

Finding aids: recorded in general printed-book catalogue.

G.L. Brook Drama Collection

3,000 items.

A collection of plays and books on theatrical history, amassed by George Leslie Brook (1910–87), the famous historian of English drama and Professor of English Language and Medieval English Literature at Manchester University, 1945–77. There are some texts printed before 1800 and approximately 1,000 19th-century works, the remainder being from the 20th century. They are predominantly in English, but most European languages are represented. Many of the items are scarce.

Finding aids: recorded in general printed-book catalogue.

Location: JRULM (Main Library).

See also the G.L. Brook Theology Collection (p. 66).

John Bunyan Collection

400 items (dispersed).

The collection includes the rare first issue of the first edition, without errata, of part one of *Pilgrim's Progress* (1678) and the first edition of another allegorical text, *The Holy War* (1682). The Library also holds the second edition of Bunyan's earliest printed work, the anti-Quaker *Some Gospel Truths Opened* (1656).

Finding aids: recorded in general printed-book catalogue.

E.L. Burney Collection

2,200 items.

The Wadsworth Manuscripts (p. 109) also contain letters from Mrs Linnaeus Banks, 1882–95.

The collection of Edward Lester Burney, donated in 1975, includes a large number of items associated with Mrs George Linnaeus Banks (1821–97), née Isabella Varley, the Manchester schoolmistress and authoress of *The Manchester Man* (1876). However, the subject coverage is wide, with items of local history, women's literature, general and popular fiction, book illustration and juvenilia. Women's literature is well represented, with works on the theme of etiquette and the role of women in Victorian society, such as *The House-maid: Her Duties, and How to Perform them* (c.1880) and Mrs Humphry's *Manners for Women* (1897). The whole collection resembles a private library put together in a piecemeal rather than systematic fashion, reflecting the tastes and preoccupations of a collector of diverse interests.

Finding aids: uncatalogued, but recorded in accession register. See also John P. Tuck, 'Some Sources for the History of Popular Culture in the John Rylands University Library of Manchester', *Bulletin of the John Rylands University Library of Manchester*, vol. 71, no. 2 (1989), pp. 176–7.

Byron Collection

400 items (dispersed).

Some two thirds of the published works of Lord Byron (George Gordon Noel Baron Byron) are available in first editions and most of the remainder, including the suppressed texts, in early editions. A substantial portion of the early Byron editions was received as part of the Lloyd Roberts bequest (p. 23). Copies of *English Bards and Scotch Reviewers* include the Lloyd Roberts copy of the fourth authorized edition (1810), the Spencer copy of the second authorized edition (1809), and a massively grangerized copy of the third authorized edition (1810), the work of Joseph Mayer, the 19th-century antiquary and book collector of Bebington, Merseyside. The grangerized copy, doubled in size, of Leigh Hunt's biography of Byron (1828) is also a source of much information.

Finding aids: recorded in general printed-book catalogue. See also David W. Riley, 'English Books of the Seventeenth to Nineteenth Centuries in the John Rylands University Library of Manchester, with Particular Reference to History and Literature', *Bulletin of the John Rylands University Library of Manchester*, vol. 71, no. 2 (1989), pp. 98–9.

Carcanet Press Book Collection

500 items.

The Library holds a collection of some 500 books printed by the Carcanet Press, the Manchester-based literary publishing house, which specializes in contemporary poetry and the revival of neglected writers. Especially rare are the first editions dating from 1969. Authors include John Ash, John Ashbery, Patricia Beer, Eavan Boland, Alison Brackenbury, Christine Brooke-Rose, Donald Davie, Michael Hamburger, John Heath-Stubbs, Elizabeth Jennings, P.J. Kavanagh, Grevel Lindop, Hugh MacDiarmid, Edwin Morgan, Andrew Motion, Les Murray, Octavio Paz, C.H. Sisson, Adrian Stokes, Michael Vince, Jeffrey Wainwright, Sylvia Townsend Warner, Andrew Waterman and William Carlos Williams. The collection complements the large and important Carcanet Press Archive (p. 132).

There are also twenty books by Ian Hamilton Finlay from the Wild Hawthorn Press.

Finding aids: recorded in general printed-book catalogue.

Literature, Drama & Music

Children's Literature Collections

1,500 items (dispersed).

The collection of late 19th-century and early 20th-century titles emphasizes the work of such artists as Randolph Caldecott, Walter Crane and Kate Greenaway. In addition to considerable manuscript holdings relating to Alison Uttley (p. 145), the Library has a collection of annotated first editions of her works, together with books finely illustrated by Arthur Rackham, Edmund Dulac and others. The collection of Elfrida Vipont (1902–92), author of *The Elephant and the Bad Baby* (p. 145), contains manuscript materials and copies of her published books and articles. The Bellot Printed Collection (p. 146) has a particular emphasis on boys' adventure stories, while the Satterthwaite Collection (p. 158) is biased towards girls' literature. The Jack Cox Collection (p. 150) comprises the working papers of the last editor of the *Boy's Own Paper*, together with a virtually complete run of *BOP*.

Finding aids: see under individual collection titles; Alison Uttley books and other works recorded in general printed-book catalogue.

Location: JRULM (Deansgate and Main Library).

Classical Literature Collection

5,000 items (dispersed).

Mrs Rylands's acquisition of the Bibliotheca Spenceriana in 1892 secured her one of the finest collections of Classical literature in the world. Few other libraries can boast that some 50 principal Greek and Latin authors are represented in their collections by the first edition. Cicero is represented by 75 editions before 1501, of which 64 are earlier than 1480. Particularly noteworthy is a vellum copy of *De officiis*, printed by Fust and Schöffer at Mainz in 1465, the first edition of any Classical author. The *editio princeps* of *De oratore*, printed by Sweynheym and Pannartz at Subiaco in 1465, is the first surviving work printed in Italy. There are no less than seventeen editions of Virgil printed before 1480, including the two 1469 editions of the complete works (Strasbourg, Mentelin; Rome, Sweynheym and Pannartz). There is also a vellum copy of the Aldine edition of 1501, the first book to be printed in italics. Of editions, translations and commentaries of Horace there are some 800 beginning with the Venetian edition of 1471. The Homeric epics are present in first edition,

See also the Spencer (p. 25), Christie (p. 19), Incunabula (p. 21), Aldine (p. 17), Baskerville (p. 18), Foulis Press (p. 21) and Sedbergh School (p. 24) collections.

and the many Greek writers represented by *editiones principes* include Hesiod, Aeschylus, Sophocles, Aristophanes, Herodotus, Thucydides, Plato, Aristotle, Apollonius Rhodius and Theocritus. Mention should also be made of the unique copy of the *Batracho-myomachia* probably printed by Thomas Ferrandus in Brescia in c.1474.

It should also be noted that the Library holds extensive collections of works published in the Loeb and Teubner series of Classical texts.

Finding aids: recorded in general printed-book catalogue. See also *The John Rylands Library: Catalogue of an Exhibition of the Earliest Printed Editions of the Principal Greek and Latin Classics and of a Few Manuscripts* (Manchester, 1926).

Jack Cox Collection

Jack Cox (1915–81) was the last editor of the *Boy's Own Paper*, familiarly known as *BOP*, which was published from 1879 to 1967. It was created by the Religious Tract Society, and was originally issued in weekly and monthly parts, but from 1913 it became monthly only. *BOP* also published an Annual for much of its life. The collection comprises all Cox's working papers as editor; a virtually complete run of *BOP* from volume 1; and books and papers relating to Scouting, camping and outdoor life written by Cox.

Finding aids: unlisted. See Jack Cox, *Take a Cold Tub, Sir!: the Story of the Boy's Own Paper* (Guildford, 1982).

Location: JRULM (Main Library).

Dante Alighieri Collection

6,500 items.

The Library's Dante Collection is justly famous. The nucleus of the collection came with the Spencer Collection (p. 25) in 1892, but there have been many significant additions since 1900. Few libraries can rival a collection which includes all but one of the fifteen incunable editions of the *Divina Commedia*, that of 1474 (but does offer all three 1472 editions). The 16th century is represented by 65 editions and variant copies. Only three editions of the *Divina Commedia* were published in the 17th century and the Library lacks only the 1613 edition (although this version of the text can be offered in a reprint of 1629). About 30 editions were published in the 18th century and of these the Library has 25. Attention can be drawn to the first Roman edition of 1791, printed on blue paper, with Lombardi's commentary, and the illustrated editions of Zatta published in Venice in 1757–58 and 1784. The bulk of the collection is, of course, formed by 19th-century texts and commentaries. The majority of the critical works were collected by Count Passerini.

Finding aids: recorded in general printed-book catalogue. See also Kathleen Speight, 'The John Rylands Library Dante Collection', *Bulletin of the John Rylands Library*, vol. 44 (1961–62), pp. 175–212.

Eighteenth-Century Literary Publications Collection

60,000 items (dispersed).

The collection contains nearly 25,500 separate titles, and all are recorded on the Eighteenth-Century Short Title Catalogue (ESTC) database. The major authors are represented by substantial collections of contemporary publications. Many of the polemical writings of both Jonathan Swift and Daniel Defoe are available. Particular emphasis can be placed on the tracts written at the time of the Union of Scotland with England, and the Library also has copies of both the first and second editions, the B issue, of *Gulliver's Travels* (1726–27). Among the works of other novelists, attention should be drawn to a first edition, presentation copy of Samuel Richardson's *Clarissa* (1751), and to a first-edition set of Laurence Sterne's *Life and Opinions of Tristram Shandy* (1760–67), with the author's signature present in two of the nine volumes.

Literature, Drama & Music

Eighteenth-century poetry is also well represented. Of the four parts of Thomson's masterpiece *The Seasons*, there are first editions of *Spring* (1728) and *Summer* (1727), while *Autumn* (1730) and *Winter* (1726) are present in second and third editions respectively. Pope's verse translations of the *Iliad* (1715–20) and *Odyssey* (1725–26) can be found in first edition, as can the first volume of his *Works* (1717), which includes the poem 'Eloisa to Abelard'.

Finding aids: recorded in general printed-book catalogue.

Elizabeth Gaskell Printed Collection

200 items (dispersed).

To complement the Library's important holdings of Elizabeth Gaskell Manuscripts (p. 135), there is available a significant collection of printed items which includes all of Sadleir's comparative scarcities, and all of the items for which he gives full bibliographical descriptions, save for the 1850 New York edition of *Lizzie Leigh* and the 1850 Manchester pamphlet *The Sexton's Hero*. Not recorded by Sadleir but available in Manchester are the 1840 *Clopton Hall*, the 1858 New York edition of *My Lady Ludlow* and the 1860 edition of *Right at Last*. Many of the volumes contain the author's own inscriptions and notes.

Finding aids: recorded in general printed-book catalogue.

George Gissing Collection

100 items.

The Library has a complete collection of first editions of the novels of George Robert Gissing (1857–1903), who was educated at a Quaker boarding school in Alderley Edge, Cheshire, and at Owens College, Manchester. Following his expulsion from Owens for theft and a month spent in prison, in 1876 he travelled to America, wandering for a year, before returning to London in 1877. The collection includes the Viscount Esher copy of *Workers in the Dawn* (1880), and the Hugh Walpole copy of *Born in Exile* (1892), together with the 1924 Chicago edition of *Sins of the Fathers*. Also available is the 1912 edition of *The Private Life of Henry Maitland* by Morley Roberts, extensively annotated by Edward Clodd and Clement Shorter. The only important items listed by Collie which are not available in the collection are Gissing's *Letters to Edward Clodd* (1914), and the undated *Letters to an Editor*.

Finding aids: recorded in general printed-book catalogue.

Giovanni Battista Guarini Collection

200 items (dispersed).

The Library has 36 editions of Guarini's pastoral tragicomedy *Il Pastor Fido* printed between 1590 and 1800. These include the first edition printed in Venice in 1590, together with another edition printed in the same year at Ferrara by Baldini in italic type; this is not available at the British Library. There are nine 18th-century editions here of *Il Pastor Fido*, including the Foulis Press edition of 1763 and the handsome large-paper copy of the Bodoni edition issued in Parma in 1793. Furthermore, there are six 17th-century English translations, including the earliest editions of Sir Richard Fanshawe's famous translation of *The Faithfull Shepheard*, dated 1647, 1648 and 1664. Attention can also be drawn to the 1694 altered version of Fanshawe's translation by Elkanah Settle.

Naturally, the Library has the first complete edition of the *Works* of Guarini, the Veronese text of 1737–38.

Finding aids: recorded in general printed-book catalogue.

L.P. Hartley Book Collection

The book collection complements an important collection of L.P. Hartley Papers (p. 136).

150 items.

A collection of printed first editions and critical studies of Leslie Poles Hartley (1895–1972), novelist, short-story writer and critic. Among the works represented in first edition are early writings, such as *Night Fears* (1924), *Simonetta Perkins* (1925) and *The Killing Bottle* (1932); the trilogy *The Shrimp and the Anemone* (1944), *The Sixth Heaven* (1944) and *Eustace and Hilda* (1947); *The Go-Between* (1953); and the later novels, *The Brickfield* (1964) and *The Betrayal* (1966). There are several advance copies, and not a few of the volumes carry inscriptions by the author.

Finding aids: recorded in general printed-book catalogue.

dom silvester houédard Book Collection

See also the dom silvester houédard Papers (p. 137).

2,000 items.

The book collection of dom silvester houédard (1924–92), the Benedictine monk of Prinknash Abbey, Gloucestershire, reflects his heterogeneous interests. There are theological and liturgical works; texts on eastern religion, philosophy and culture (in particular on Buddhism and Tibet); examples of concrete poetry, artists' books and the output of small presses in Europe and the United States; texts on literature in general, art and design; many rare 'fanzine'-style poetry magazines from the 1960s and '70s; and three-dimensional works of art such as an elephant maquette by the Scottish sculptor Eduardo Paolozzi.

Finding aids: uncatalogued.

Peter Huchel Collection of German Literature

350 items.

Part of the personal library of Peter Huchel (1903–81), the German poet and editor of the East German literary periodical *Sinn und Form*, this collection came to the Library from his daughter Susanne Huchel in 1989; related archival material followed in 1991. The significance of the collection lies in the fact that it contains texts with which the author can be seen to have worked; the main literary influences upon Huchel may be revealed through examination of the numerous annotations and marginalia. There are items of note from the late 19th century representing Private Presses such as Verlag der Bremer Presse and Blätter für die Kunst, as well as Kurt Wolff's Der jüngste Tag, and there are 35 texts from the famous Insel Bücherei series published by Insel Verlag. Stefan George, Hugo von Hofmannsthal, Rilke and Brecht are each well represented.

Finding aids: recorded in general printed-book catalogue. See also Stephen Parker, 'The Peter Huchel Collection of German Literature in the John Rylands University Library of Manchester', *Bulletin of the John Rylands University Library of Manchester*, vol. 72, no. 2 (1990), pp. 135–52; Stephen Parker, 'Recent Additions to the Peter Huchel Collection in the John Rylands University Library of Manchester', *Bulletin of the John Rylands University Library of Manchester*, vol. 74, no. 2 (1992), pp. 85–125; Stephen R. Parker, 'Dora Huchel's Account of her Life with Peter Huchel: an Edition and Commentary', *Bulletin of the John Rylands University Library of Manchester*, vol. 77, no. 2 (1995), pp. 59–84; Stephen Parker, *Peter Huchel: a Literary Life in 20th-Century Germany* (Berne, 1998).

Literature, Drama & Music

Victor Hugo Book Collection

1,100 items (dispersed).

The Library holds a collection of over 1,000 editions of works by or about Victor Hugo, including first editions of *Les Misérables* (1862) and *William Shakespeare* (1864), and a copy of *Hans of Iceland* (1825), an English translation of Hugo's first published novel, with illustrations by Cruikshank. These complement the valuable collection of Victor Hugo Papers (p. 138).

Finding aids: recorded in general printed-book catalogue.

Samuel Johnson Collection

600 items (dispersed).

To complement the Library's substantial manuscript collection of Johnsoniana, first editions and interesting association copies of most of the printed works of Johnson are available, including his very first published work, a Latin verse translation of Pope's *Messiah* which appeared in the 1731 edition of *A Miscellany of Poems by Several Hands* compiled by John Husbands. A Johnsonian Proposal for printing a translation of Sarpi's *History of the Council of Trent* in 1738 was discovered in an uncatalogued duplicate by a former Librarian: it is considered to be unique. There are many editions of the famous *Dictionary* available including the first issue of the first edition of the 1747 *Plan*, in which Johnson announced his intentions, and the first edition of the *Dictionary* (1755). Particular attention can be drawn to a copy of the fourth edition (1773), which was at one time owned by Sir Joshua Reynolds and contains over 250 corrections in Johnson's own hand: these were subsequently incorporated in the sixth and later editions. An equally strong collection of printed items relating to Boswell is available, including the first edition (1791) of his life of Johnson.

Finding aids: recorded in general printed-book catalogue. See also J.A.V. Chapple, 'Samuel Johnson's *Proposals for Printing the History of the Council of Trent*, [1738]', *Bulletin of the John Rylands Library*, vol. 45 (1962–63), pp. 340–69.

Correspondence with Samuel Johnson may be found within the Bagshawe Muniments (p. 74) and the Thrale-Piozzi Manuscripts (p. 144).

Niccolò Machiavelli Collection

1,000 items (dispersed).

Just over 200 different editions of the writings of Machiavelli were published in the 16th century, and of these 35 are available in the Library. Items of considerable rarity in Britain include the Venetian 1541 edition of *Libro dell'Arte della Guerra* (unique in Britain and one of only three copies recorded anywhere), and the Venetian 1543 edition of the *Discorsi*, also unique in this country although it can be found in six Continental libraries. The Aldine 1540 editions of *Il Principe*, the *Discorsi* and the *Historie* are all present.

Finding aids: recorded in general printed-book catalogue.

K.G. Millward Collection

100 items.

The collection, donated by K.G. Millward in 1971, includes some 60 volumes by and about Joséphin Aimé Péladan (1859–1918), the playwright and novelist, who in the late 1880s became associated with a revival of Rosicrucianism. Among these items are copies of Péladan's first novel, *Le Vice Suprême*, and fifteen volumes from the *La Décadence Latine* series. In addition there are 34 autograph letters, as yet uncatalogued, from Péladan to H. Bauquier, editor of *Le Petit Méridional*, dated 1903 to 1913. The correspondence concerns Bauquier's articles on Péladan and the staging at Nîmes in 1904 of Péladan's most successful play, *Sémiramis*.

Finding aids: recorded in general printed-book catalogue; separate typescript list.

John Milton Collection

500 items (dispersed).

The items available in first edition include [*Comus*], *A maske presented at Ludlow Castle* (1637); *Areopagitica: a Speech for the Liberty of Unlicenc'd Printing* (1644); *Eikonoklastes* (1649); and no less than six variant issues of the first edition of *Paradise Lost* (1667–69). The Library also holds a copy of the otherwise unremarkable *Obsequies to the Memorie of Mr Edward King* (1638), in which 'Lycidas', composed the previous year, made its first appearance under the initials 'J.M.'. Furthermore there is a collection of Milton's pamphlets on divorce.

Finding aids: recorded in general printed-book catalogue.

Minor Sixteenth-Century Italian Writers Collection

1,000 items (dispersed).

There are available 40 editions, dating from 1549 to 1804, of the poet Benedetto Varchi, together with significant collections for other poets including Olimpo degli Alessandri, Giovanni Agostino Cazza, Mazini Brocardo and Antonio Fregoso. Dramatists are represented by Sperone Speroni (24 items dating from 1542 to 1740) and Leonardo Salviati (27 editions published between 1564 and 1810). Examples of prose writers include the eminent jurist, Mantova Benavides (with twelve editions), the Florentine politician Matteo Palmieri (with six items) and the diplomat and humanist Gian Giorgio Trissino (with 29 editions published between 1524 and 1746). Of Alessandro Piccolomini's astronomical writings there are 26 editions and variants issued between 1516 and 1611.

See also the Bullock Collection (p. 18).

Finding aids: recorded in general printed-book catalogue.

Douglas Munro Dumas Collection

2,500 items.

Literature, Drama & Music

The collection relating to the novelist and dramatist Alexandre Dumas père (1802–70) was amassed by the late Douglas Munro of Cupar in Fife, compiler of three definitive Dumas bibliographies. Through his contacts with booksellers worldwide, Munro was able to amass an impressive array of Dumas first editions, including the first illustrated edition of *Le Compte de Monte Cristo* (Paris, 1846), *Antony*, apparently the most sought-after of Dumas's early dramas (Paris, 1831), and *Mademoiselle de Belle-Isle* (Paris, 1839). There are numerous English translations of Dumas's works, including first translations into English as well as later versions from the second half of the 20th century. Munro also collected adaptations of Dumas's works including abridgements for children; essays and prefaces penned by Dumas; and Dumas ephemera and memorabilia. There are albums and envelopes containing portraits of the author, press cuttings, stamps, theatre programmes and photographs. An enormous cinema poster advertises the Metro-Goldwyn-Mayer film *Le secret de Monte-Cristo* (1961). There is also much supporting secondary literature.

Finding aids: recorded in general printed-book catalogue. See also note in *John Rylands Research Institute Newsletter*, no. 10 (Summer 1995), pp. 10–12.

Music Collections

9,000 items.

Music was not actively collected by Mrs Rylands, and only in recent years has it begun to figure prominently among the Special Collections. Most of the printed music dates from after 1780. Unusually for an academic library, the printed music collection is strong in English popular songs from the 1880s through to the 1940s.

There are numerous musical manuscripts scattered among the Library's Special Collections. These fall into three main groups. Firstly, the mainly medieval Latin Manuscripts (p. 31) include liturgical texts containing musical notation, with a great deal of Gregorian chant. Secondly, there are over 30 musical manuscripts among the formerly uncatalogued University MSS, largely comprising scores of 18th- and 19th-century British music. Thirdly, the Methodist Archives (p. 59) contain a wealth of correspondence and other material relating to the Wesley family, among whom were three musicians, Samuel (1766–1837), his brother Charles (1757–1834), and Samuel's son Samuel Sebastian (1810–76). Other items include an English harpsichord manuscript of c.1754, and a lute book and song book, both of the 17th century, from Tabley House. There are also some exotic music manuscripts among the Coptic, Ethiopic and Turkish Manuscripts (pp. 37 and 44), and various other oriental collections.

The Arthur D. Walker Music Collection, presented in 1994 by the former Music Librarian of JRULM, contains full, study and rare miniature scores; collected editions, especially of Bach and Handel; miscellaneous printed works; and facsimiles and photocopies of manuscripts, archives and early printed editions, together with research notes compiled by Mr Walker in the course of his studies of the music of Handel and Mahler.

Michael Kennedy (b. 1926), the Manchester music critic and author, presented a collection of papers to the Library in the late 1970s. This collection consists primarily of manuscript and typescript copies of his published works, including authorized biographies of Ralph Vaughan Williams and John Barbirolli, books on Richard Strauss, Gustav Mahler and Edward Elgar, and books on Manchester and its musical tradition – notably histories of the Hallé and the Royal Manchester (later Northern) College of Music. In addition there are a number of letters from Elgar's daughter, Carice Elgar Blake, and a large bundle of correspondence generated during Kennedy's research for his book on Vaughan Williams. The latter includes notes and letters from various well-known composers, conductors, musicians and writers who were acquainted with the composer, such as Adrian Boult, John Barbirolli, Benjamin Britten and Bertrand Russell. There is also a large quantity of correspondence with the composer's wife, Ursula Vaughan Williams.

The Leonard Behrens Papers (p. 103) contain material on the Hallé Orchestra, 1952–72.

Finding aids: published catalogue of music manuscripts, Barry Cooper, 'Catalogue of Pre-1900 Music Manuscripts in the John Rylands University Library of Manchester', *Bulletin of the John Rylands University Library of Manchester*, vol. 79, no. 2 (1997), pp. 27–101; card catalogue of the Walker Collection; unpublished catalogue of the Michael Kennedy Papers. All the Special Collections printed music (except for the Walker Collection) is recorded in the Printed Music card catalogue in the Main Library; all the main entries are duplicated in the Printed Music card catalogue in the Music Department.

Norman Nicholson Book Collection

700 items.

See also the Norman Nicholson Archive (p. 141).

The Library holds approximately 700 books from the personal library of the Cumbrian poet Norman Nicholson (1914–87), who spent almost his entire life in the small town of Millom. These are mainly first editions, signed and containing enclosures from the authors, and annotated by Nicholson. The collection contains an almost complete set of 20th-century poets including T.S. Eliot, W.H. Auden, Ted Hughes, Thom Gunn, Sylvia Plath, John Betjeman, Dylan Thomas, R.S. Thomas and Philip Larkin, and the presses represented include Faber & Faber, Marvell, Carcanet, Asphodel, Bloodaxe and Enitharmon. A collection of some 35 first and early editions of Nicholson's own writings includes five volumes signed by the author.

Finding aids: recorded in general printed-book catalogue.

Allardyce Nicoll Drama Collection

1,100 items.

This collection of 19th-century plays was formed by (John Ramsay) Allardyce Nicoll (1894–1976), Professor of English Language and Literature at Birmingham University, 1945–61, when he was writing his *History of the English Drama*. Very much acting editions with full stage directions, plans of settings and notes on costumes, the texts range from burlesque to tragedy. Both major authors and minor farceurs are represented, but Dionysius Lardner Boucicault, Sir Francis Cowley Burnand, Henry James Byron, Douglas William Jerrold, Thomas Morton and Sir Arthur Wing Pinero are among the dramatists for whom a considerable number of items are available.

Finding aids: recorded in general printed-book catalogue. See also separate unpublished handlist.

Nineteenth-Century Fiction Collection

3,000 items (dispersed).

Over 600 authors are represented, of whom just under one half are pre-Victorian. There is a substantial collection of three-decker novels, many in fine examples of publishers' bindings. The Seydi Collection, acquired in 1975 from the London bookseller Sevin Seydi, has added a further 350 items, representing 130 authors, the majority dating from the first half of the century. Many derive from subscription libraries.

Attention should be drawn to the first edition of William Makepeace Thackeray's *Vanity Fair* (1848), in the original cloth with the author's portrait of Lord Steyne on p. 336, which was later suppressed. For Charles Dickens *Pickwick Papers* (1836–37), *Bleak House* (1853) and *Edwin Drood* (1870) are available in their original part wrappers. Of *Oliver Twist* (1837) there is a first issue of the first edition with the final Cruikshank illustration which Dickens later rejected. The principal women writers are well represented in first edition: Jane Austen with *Emma* (1816), and *Northanger Abbey* and *Persuasion* (published together posthumously in 1818); Charlotte Brontë with *Jane Eyre* (1847), *Shirley* (1849), and *Villette* (1853); and George Eliot with *Silas Marner* (1861) and *Agatha* (1869), and a first edition in book form of *Romola* (1863). Among the lesser-known authors are Edward Bulwer-Lytton, Lady Georgiana Fullerton, Mrs Catherine Gore, James Grant and Emily Lawless.

Finding aids: recorded in general printed-book catalogue.

Marie Riefstahl Nordlinger's Proust Collection

120 items.

Marie Nordlinger was a friend of Marcel Proust and has been considered to be a model for some episodes featuring Albertine in *À la Recherche du Temps Perdu* (1913–27). The collection, donated by Nordlinger in 1974, comprises editions of Proust's writings and many secondary works bearing the signature of Marie Nordlinger. The general stock of the Main University Library also contains more than 400 Proust editions and critical works.

Finding aids: uncatalogued.

Francesco Petrarch Collection

1,000 items (dispersed).

The Petrarch Collection contains sixteen incunable editions of the *Rime*. These range in date from the *editio princeps* of 1470, printed in Venice by Vindelinus de Spira, to the edition of 1486 with its fashionable large type for the verse and smaller type for the commentary. Attention can be drawn to the beautiful and accurate Lauer edition of 1471 and three different Venetian editions of 1473. Manchester also holds two editions not found in the incomparable Willard Fiske Collection at Cornell University Library: the 1477 Neapolitan edition by Arnold of Brussels, and a Venetian edition of 1480 by an unknown printer. 80 of the approximately 150 editions published in the 16th century are present including all the Aldine editions, the counterfeit Lyonese copies, and two of the ten vellum copies of the 1501 edition. One of the latter is beautifully illuminated and is in a fine embroidered binding.

The Library also holds numerous editions of Petrarch's Latin works, including the earliest complete edition, printed by Amerbach in Basel in 1496.

Finding aids: recorded in general printed-book catalogue.

Literature, Drama & Music

John Ruskin Book Collection

400 items (dispersed).

See also the John Ruskin Papers (p. 142).

To complement the Library's outstanding collection of the letters and other manuscripts of John Ruskin, there is a large collection of Ruskin's first editions and other material relating to his works. Some 340 separate 19th-century editions are available, including not only the many items issued from Orpington but also the possible suspect and unauthorized Wise editions, many of which are printed on vellum. It is interesting to note that much of this collection was bought by Mrs Rylands herself before the foundation of the Library. Special attention can also be drawn to the pamphlet literature and other Ruskin ephemera in the Dame Mabel Tylecote Printed Collection (p. 117).

Finding aids: recorded in general printed-book catalogue.

Satterthwaite Collection

1,000 items.

The collection comprises children's books of the period from the 1870s to the 1930s, with particular reference to girls' literature and including some notable illustrated works. There is a long run of the periodical *Little Folks*, and a good collection of Beatrix Potter books, including variant bindings.

Finding aids: recorded in general printed-book catalogue.

Location: JRULM (Main Library).

Seventeenth-Century Literary Publications Collection

15,000 items (dispersed).

The Library's holdings encompass most of the landmark publications of 17th-century English literature. The substantial collections of works by Bunyan, Milton and Shakespeare are described individually elsewhere in this *Guide* (pp. 148, 154 and 159), but many other distinguished authors are represented in first and significant editions.

See also the Lloyd Roberts (p. 23), Tabley House (p. 26), English Tract (p. 113), Ferguson (p. 113), and Sutherland (p. 116) collections.

The first edition of *The Workes of Benjamin Jonson* (1616) and the 1640 edition are both present; the former is a variant imprint with an engraved title-page. For John Donne there is a grangerized copy of the posthumously published *Poems* (1633). In the same year appeared the first edition of George Herbert's *The Temple*, although reference should also be made to the 1679 edition, which includes an engraved portrait frontispiece and architectural plates.

Mid-century literature is well represented, with three issues of the first edition of Thomas Hobbes's *Leviathan* (1651), and a first edition of Izaak Walton's classic discourse on fishing, *The Compleat Angler* (1653). Both the unauthorized and first authorized editions of Sir Thomas Browne's *Religio Medici* (1642–43) are available. The Library holds the first authorized editions of parts one and two of Samuel Butler's *Hudibras* (1663–64), and the first edition of part three (1678). For John Dryden there are first editions of *Absalom and*

Achitophel (1681) and *The Medall: a Satyre Against Sedition* (1682), while a collection of ten of his plays, bound into a single volume, includes four first editions (1669–78).

Finding aids: recorded in general printed-book catalogue.

Shakespeare Collection

1,400 items (dispersed).

The Library's collection of Shakespeariana is particularly rich. All four Shakespeare Folios are present, published in 1623, 1632, 1664 and 1685, together with many 19th- and 20th-century facsimiles of the First Folio including Wright's type facsimile of 1808 and Staunton's first photo-lithographic facsimile of 1866. The First Folio is interesting as being the actual copy used by Theobald in 1733 in preparation of his edition of Shakespeare's works. Of even greater interest is the copy of *Mr Shakespeare's Sonnets* (1609), with the variant imprint, and the contemporary price of 5d marked on the title page. Lord Spencer's grangerized copy of the plays of Shakespeare, edited by Samuel Johnson and George Steevens in 1793, was formerly Steevens's own copy which he enriched by the insertion of several thousand engravings of great rarity. The entire publishing history of Shakespeare is represented in the Library's collections, with deluxe and illustrated editions, modern texts and critical works.

Finding aids: recorded in general printed-book catalogue.

Sharpe Chapbook Collection

600 items.

The Sharpe Collection of Chapbooks was formed by Charles Kirkpatrick Sharpe (1781–1851), the antiquary, etcher and authority on Scottish ballad literature. About half the collection consists of early 19th-century items mainly printed in Stirling, Falkirk and Kilmarnock, the remainder being printed in Newcastle upon Tyne, the acknowledged capital of chapbook literature.

Finding aids: recorded in general printed-book catalogue. See also note in *Bulletin of the John Rylands Library*, vol. 37 (1954–55), pp. 9–10.

Upton Sinclair Collection

1,000 items.

Upton Beall Sinclair (1878–1968) began writing novels at the age of fifteen, in order to pay his way through college in New York. His early novels include *King Midas* (1901), *The Journal of Arthur Sterling* (1903) and *Manassas* (1904). In 1906 he published at his own expense the work for which he is best known today, *The Jungle*, a realistic study of the Chicago stockyards and meat-packing industry. In 1915 Sinclair moved to California where he wrote a series of pamphlets on various aspects of American life: *The Profits of Religion* (1918), *The Goose-step* (1923) and *The Goslings* (1924), which dealt with education, *Mammonart* (1925) and *Money Writes!* (1927). In 1934 Sinclair ran for the governorship of California under the banner of the EPIC (End Poverty in California) League. Later books include the *World's End* series of novels featuring Lanny Budd. In addition Sinclair also wrote on diet and health and on psychic phenomena, and he penned the popular children's book *The Gnomobile*.

The collection contains some 870 monographs, including first editions of virtually all of Sinclair's major works; numerous translations of works such as *Oil!*, *The Jungle* and *Mental Radio* into French, German, Spanish, Italian, Russian, Hebrew, Serbo-Croat, Norwegian, Dutch and Danish; and a wide range of critical literature. Many of the books contain autograph inscriptions from Sinclair. In addition there are periodicals relating to Sinclair; files of correspondence with figures such as Floyd Dell, Theodore Dreiser, Jack London, Frank Harris and H.L. Mencken; and much rare ephemera relating to the socialist novelist, including newspaper clippings, photographs, tape recordings and gramophone records, and a bound volume of issues of Upton Sinclair's campaigning newspaper *EPIC News* (1934–35). The collection was amassed over 30 years by Mr Edward Allatt of West Drayton, Middlesex, who was a personal friend of Sinclair; his arrangement of the collection has been preserved.

Finding aids: monographs recorded in general printed-book catalogue.

Edmund Spenser Collection

125 items (dispersed).

The Library has a particularly fine collection of 16th-century editions of Spenser's poetry. Works represented in first edition include *Complaints: Containing Sundrie Small Poemes of the Worlds Vanitie* (1591), *Colin Clouts Come Home Againe* (1595), *Amoretti* and *Epithalamion* (1595), *Fowre Hymnes* (1596), and Spenser's allegorical masterpiece, the *Faerie Queene* (1590–96). While the collection lacks the exceedingly scarce first edition of the *Shepheardes Calender*, of which only seven copies are recorded, the third edition (1586) is present. The Library also holds a first edition of the prose work *A View of the Present State of Ireland*, written in 1595–96, but not published until 1633. Among the many later editions and critical literature, a copy of the majestic Ashendene Press edition of the *Faerie Queene* (1923) merits special notice, being one of twelve printed on vellum.

Finding aids: recorded in general printed-book catalogue.

Torquato Tasso Collection

500 items (dispersed).

The Library has 45 editions of Torquato Tasso's great epic poem *Gerusalemme Liberata* published between 1580 and 1824 including eleven 16th-century examples. These include the lavishly-illustrated Castello edition with inferior text published in Genoa in 1590, as well as the third Malaspina edition of 1583 and both editions of 1585. Dialect versions include those in Bergamese, Calabrian, Genoese, Milanese, Neapolitan and Venetian ranging in date from 1670 to 1816. All English translations are present from 1600 to 1811. The Library has five editions of *Gerusalemme Conquistata* ranging in date from 1594 to 1628, together with 31 editions of Tasso's pastoral comedy *Aminta* published between 1581 and 1820.

Finding aids: recorded in general printed-book catalogue.

Francis Thompson Collection

400 items.

Francis Thompson (1859–1907), poet and prose writer, was born in Preston, Lancashire, and studied medicine unsuccessfully at Owens College from 1876 to 1882, three times failing his examinations. He moved to London, where he fell prey to opium addiction and suffered destitution. He published his first volume of poetry in 1893; this included his most famous work, 'The Hound of Heaven'. The collection comprises first editions of Thompson's poems and prose, with critical and biographical publications. Very few of the items described by Stonehill are wanting. There is an especially fine edition of *The Hound of Heaven* (Chatto and Windus, 1914), and an edition of the *Works* printed at Bernard Newdigate's Arden Press for Francis and Wilfrid Meynell (1913). The latter volume is handsomely bound in full vellum, with an autograph letter from Wilfred and two typescript notes from Francis tipped in. Wilfrid Meynell was Thompson's editor, friend and literary executor.

Literature, Drama & Music

Finding aids: recorded in general printed-book catalogue.

Eugène Vinaver Collection

400 items.

The book collection of Eugène Vinaver (1899–1979), Professor of French Language and Literature at Manchester University from 1933 to 1966, reflects his interest in Arthurian literature and medieval studies, together with his wider concern for European culture.

Finding aids: uncatalogued.

Walt Whitman Book Collection

400 items.

The Charles F. Sixsmith collection of the works of Walt Whitman includes 22 different editions of *Leaves of Grass* and over 100 works of criticism, many being presentation copies in limited editions. There is much material relating to the Bolton Whitman Circle of which Sixsmith was a member. Charles E. Feinberg of Detroit made important additions to the Whitman Collection. In all there are nearly 60 separate editions and issues of *Leaves of Grass* and some 70 editions of other works by Whitman. Save for the early temperance novel *Franklin Evans; or, The Inebriate* (1842), virtually every item described by Wells and Goldsmith is available.

See also the Walt Whitman Manuscript Collections (p. 145).

The Sixsmith collection also contains works of, or relating to, the English socialist, writer and friend of Whitman, Edward Carpenter.

Finding aids: recorded in general printed-book catalogue. See notes in *Bulletin of the John Rylands Library*, vol. 37 (1954–55), pp. 10–11; vol. 40 (1957–58), pp. 266–7.

Thomas J. Wise Collection

100 items (dispersed).

The collection of privately-printed pamphlets by John Ruskin, Elizabeth Barrett Browning and Robert Browning, George Borrow, Alfred Lord Tennyson, Algernon Swinburne and other authors is of importance in the history of bibliography as since 1934 many of the items have been recognized as forgeries by Wise.

Finding aids: recorded in general printed-book catalogue.

TRIVMPHVS

Sopra de queſto ſuperbo & Triumphale uectabulo, uidi uno bianchiſſimo Cycno, negli amoroſi amplexi duna inclyta Nympha filiola
de Theſeo, dincredibile bellecia formata, & cum el diuino roſtro obſcu
lantiſe, demiſſe le ale, tegeua le parte denudate della ígenua Hera, Et cũ
diuini & uoluptici oblectamenti iſtauano delectabilmente iucundiſſi-
mi ambi connexi, Et el diuino Olore tra le delicate & niuee coxe collo-
cato. Laquale commodamente ſedeua ſopra dui Puluini di panno doro, exquiſitamente di mollicula lanugine tomentati, cum tutti gli ſum-
ptuoſi & ornanti correlarii opportuni. Et ella induta de ueſta Nympha
le ſubtile, de ſerico bianchiſſimo cum trama doro texto præluccente
Agli loci competenti elegante ornato de petre pretioſe.
Sencia defecto de qualunque coſa che ad incremen-
to di dilecto uenuſtamente concorre. Summa
mente agli intuenti conſpicuo & dele
ctabile. Cum tutte le parte che
al primo fue deſcripto
di laude & plau
ſo.

*

HISTORY OF ART & ARCHITECTURE

Manuscript Resources

Aside from the abundance of richly-illuminated Western medieval, Near Eastern and Far Eastern Manuscripts, the Library holds outstanding collections relating to 19th-century art history, and especially to the Pre-Raphaelite circle, with papers of the artist William Holman Hunt, the artist and collector Charles Fairfax Murray, the writer and critic John Ruskin, the critic and connoisseur Marion Harry Spielmann, and the Manchester artist Robert Crozier. 20th-century material includes the papers of the artist Frank O. Salisbury, who specialized in portraiture and in historical and religious subjects, Margaret Pilkington, wood-engraver and Honorary Director of the Whitworth Art Gallery, and Stephen Raw, contemporary letter artist.

Other material of potential interest to art historians occurs in drama- and film-related collections such as the Basil Dean, Robert Donat and Stephen Joseph papers (which contain original artwork, photographs, and set and costume designs), in the Carcanet Press Archive, and in the papers of the concrete poet dom silvester houédard and the children's writer Alison Uttley. The papers of Dorothy Richardson comprise detailed accounts of travel in England during the late 18th century, illustrated with drawings, and offer extensive scope for cultural, social, gender and art historical studies.

Architectural holdings comprise the archives of the Manchester Society of Architects and the Society of Architectural Historians of Great Britain, the papers of the distinguished architect Sir Hubert Worthington, and the Edward Freeman Papers, which include thousands of drawings of churches and correspondence with Sir George Gilbert Scott and other architects. The archives of the John Rylands Library contain information on the design and construction of this internationally-important, Grade 1 listed building. Students of country-house architecture, landscape design and garden history will also find useful material among the Muniment and Charter Collections.

Printed Resources

The Library's holdings of printed materials relating to the history of art are outstanding, and range chronologically from early 15th-century block-books to finely illustrated books and designer bookbindings of the late 20th century. The Incunabula Collection contains block-books and pre-1500 publications which combine woodcuts with movable type. However, the Library's holdings of Illustrated Books range through the whole history of printing, representing the work of hundreds of artists and illustrators, from Dürer to Raw, and featuring almost every technique ever employed in book illustration.

The Library holds a wide range of other printed materials of interest to students of art history, in addition to illustrated books:

❧ a complete set of the engravings of Piranesi;
❧ a set of Turner's *Liber Studiorum* in the best states;
❧ a large collection of loose cartoons and caricatures by Hogarth, Gillray, Rowlandson, Cruikshank and others;
❧ a copy of William Fox Talbot's pioneering photographic work, *The Pencil of Nature* (1844);
❧ the John Ruskin Book Collection;

❧ within the dom silvester houédard Book Collection numerous poster poems, concrete poems, artists' books and three-dimensional works of art;

❧ bookplates by Charles William Sherborn and John Paul Rylands within the Viner Bookplate Collection;

❧ historic and contemporary bookbindings and book jackets.

Secondary sources include facsimile editions and standard reference works on antiquities, fine art, engravings, numismatics, furniture, stained glass, ceramics, textiles and costume.

Students of architecture will find a large collection of historic surveys and treatises, both English and Continental, including works on the Classical, Medieval, Renaissance, Baroque, Georgian and Victorian periods. Authors include Vitruvius, Alberti, Palladio, Adam, Soane and Repton. In addition to works on 'bricks and mortar' architecture, there are texts of interest for studies in landscape history and land use, garden history, death and the afterlife, the functioning of cities and concepts of space and ritual.

Bibliography

Campbell Dodgson, *Woodcuts of the Fifteenth Century in the John Rylands Library* (Manchester, 1915).

H. Guppy and G. Vine, *A Classified Catalogue of the Works on Architecture and the Allied Arts in the Principal Libraries of Manchester and Salford* (Manchester, 1909).

John Rylands Library, *The Beginnings of Printed Book Illustration: Catalogue of an Exhibition of Printed Book Illustrations in the Fifteenth Century with Sixteen Facsimiles* (Manchester, 1933).

For information on English garden books see note on an exhibition in *Bulletin of the John Rylands University Library of Manchester*, vol. 59 (1976–77), pp. 253–5.

Select alphabetical list of resources: (MS: Manuscript/Archive; PR: Printed)

MANUSCRIPT RESOURCES

Robert Crozier Collection

Date range: 1783–1910.

A small collection of letters relating to the Manchester artist Robert Crozier (1815–91). Crozier first exhibited at the Royal Manchester Institution in 1841, and at the Royal Academy in 1854, but it was the success of an exhibition at Peel Park, Salford, in 1857 that encouraged Crozier and other local artists to set up the Manchester Academy of Fine Arts in 1859. Shortly after its foundation Crozier was appointed Literary Secretary of the Academy, a position which he held until he was elected Treasurer in 1868, and from 1878 until a month before his death he was President of the Academy.

The collection comprises letters addressed to Crozier, and others collected by him. These include autograph letters of Dante Gabriel Rossetti, Sir Edwin Landseer, William Cowper, Edward Jenner, Florence Nightingale, George Frederic Watts, Sir Charles Lock Eastlake, Sir Coutts Lindsay and Frederic J. Shields. Several letters relate to the fund set up to support the widow and children of William Bradley (1801–57), the Manchester portrait painter.

Finding aids: unpublished detailed catalogue.

Holman Hunt Papers

Date range: 1843–1911.

Papers of William Holman Hunt (1827–1910), Pre-Raphaelite painter, comprising diaries recording his visits to Egypt and Palestine, and over 300 letters. They are of great value to art historians, as they contain comments on the progress of works such as *The Hireling Shepherd, The Light of the World, The Awakening Conscience, The Scapegoat, The Shadow of Death, The Triumph of the Innocents* and *May Morning on Magdalen Tower*. The letters also contain references to important contemporaries such as Augustus Egg, Michael Frederick Halliday, Sir John Everett Millais, Coventry Patmore, Dante Gabriel Rossetti and Alfred Lord Tennyson. There are 49 letters to his close friend Edward Lear, 35 to Thomas Combe, director of the Clarendon Press, and a further 24 to the painter Frederic James Shields.

See also the John Ruskin Papers (p. 142), the Fairfax Murray Papers (p. 166) and the Spielmann Collection (p. 168).

History of Art & Architecture

Finding aids: recorded in published handlist of English Manuscripts (English MSS 1210–1216, 1239, 1268, 1275). Alternative form: published microfilm: *John Ruskin, the Pre-Raphaelite Brotherhood, and Arts and Crafts Movement: the Ruskin, Holman Hunt, Fairfax Murray, Spielmann and Related Collections from the John Rylands University Library, Manchester* (Woodbridge: Research Publications, 1990).

Manchester Society of Architects Archive

See also the papers of Sir Hubert Worthington, sometime president of the Society (p. 169).

Date range: 1865–1995.

Records of the Manchester Society of Architects, which was founded in 1865 and amalgamated with the Manchester Architectural Association in 1891. In 1969 the Society was reconstituted as a branch of the Royal Institute of British Architects. Records include annual reports, minute books, membership data, and correspondence files relating to the administration of the Society, professional standards, education, training and exhibitions.

Finding aids: published handlist: A. Kenney, 'Catalogue of the Archives of the Manchester Society of Architects', *Bulletin of the John Rylands University Library of Manchester*, vol. 74, no. 2 (1992), pp. 37–63. Unpublished handlist of additional material deposited in 1994.

Fairfax Murray Papers

Date range: 1849–1919.

Letters and papers of Charles Fairfax Murray (1849–1919), Pre-Raphaelite painter and art collector. Fairfax Murray worked as a copyist for John Ruskin and was assistant to Dante Gabriel Rossetti and Edward Burne-Jones. He later worked as a buying agent for the National Gallery and a consultant for Messrs Agnew, but is best known as a collector of art.

See also the John Ruskin Papers (p. 142), the Holman Hunt Papers (p. 165) and the Spielmann Collection (p. 168).

The collection numbers over 1,500 items. There are important groupings of material relating to Sir Edward Burne-Jones, including letters from his wife Georgiana and photographs of the Burne-Jones and Morris children; letters and photographs relating to Charles Augustus Howell, who was for many years Ruskin's secretary and later close companion of Rossetti, Whistler and Swinburne; and letters and papers of the sculptors and brothers William, Henry and Charles Behnes. In addition there are over 700 letters to Fairfax Murray from a wide range of correspondents and 200 letters exchanged between other correspondents. These include many of the leading figures of the contemporary art world, such as Sir Charles Lock Eastlake, George Cruikshank, Myles Birket Foster, William Holman Hunt, Frederic Lord Leighton, William Morris, Dante Gabriel Rossetti, John Ruskin and Frederick Sandys.

Finding aids: recorded in published handlist of English Manuscripts (English MSS 1278–1283). Alternative form: published microfilm: *John Ruskin, the Pre-Raphaelite Brotherhood, and Arts and Crafts Movement: the Ruskin, Holman Hunt, Fairfax Murray, Spielmann and Related Collections from the John Rylands University Library, Manchester* (Woodbridge: Research Publications, 1990).

Margaret Pilkington Papers

Date range: 20th century.

Papers of Margaret Pilkington (1891–1974), Deputy Chairman and Honorary Director of the Whitworth Art Gallery in the University of Manchester, 1935–59. She trained at the

Slade School of Art and was an artist of some importance in her own right, particularly in the medium of wood-engraving. She was Chairman of the Society of Wood Engravers from 1952 to 1967.

The papers comprise correspondence, lecture notes, detailed diaries and personal sketchbooks and material relating to the Red Rose Guild of Craftsmen.

Finding aids: unlisted. See Margaret Pilkington, *A Victorian Venture: the Manchester Whitworth Art Gallery* (Manchester, 1953); David Blamires, *Margaret Pilkington* (Buxton, 1995).

Stephen Raw Papers

Date range: 1985 to present.

Papers of Stephen Raw, letter artist. Raw trained and then taught at Manchester Polytechnic in the 1970s, before moving to Papua New Guinea to lecture in typography and lettering at the National Arts School, Port Moresby. For the past eighteen years he has been a freelance letter artist, while continuing to teach at Manchester Metropolitan University and Glasgow School of Art.

The archive consists exclusively of material relating to Raw's work for the Carcanet Press (*q.v.*), for whom he has been the book-jacket designer since 1985. There are two classes of material: artist's files containing visual and written letters relating to particular book covers; and artist's roughs of book covers. These provide an excellent representation of the process of letter art, book-jacket design and book production.

Finding aids: catalogue in course of preparation.

Dorothy Richardson Papers

Date range: 1761–1802.

Dorothy Richardson was born in 1748, the daughter of the Rev. Henry Richardson, Rector of Thornton in Craven, Yorkshire. Between 1761 and 1801 she undertook a series of tours of England in the company of members of her family, visiting Yorkshire, Lancashire, Derbyshire, Nottinghamshire, Oxford, Bath and London. An unmarried, highly-educated and leisured women, Richardson undertook her journeys with a high degree of seriousness and in a quest for knowledge. She described her travels in a series of accounts, recording details of antiquarian sites, country houses, museums, manufactures, geological features and landscapes – traditionally viewed as masculine preoccupations. The accounts are illustrated with numerous pen-and-ink drawings.

In a recent study they have been described as "a series of writings which are neither confession nor fable, but which lie somewhere between autobiography and chronicle, history and inventory", constituting "a paradigmatic case of disciplined recording that challenges received notions of travel, pleasure, gender, and knowledge in England in the second half of the eighteenth century" (Pointon, pp. 102, 124). They provide extensive scope for cultural, social, gender, art historical, antiquarian and topographical studies.

Finding aids: recorded in published handlist of English Manuscripts (English MSS 1122–1129). See also Marcia Pointon, *Strategies for Showing: Women, Possession, and Representation in English Visual Culture 1665–1800* (Oxford, 1997), pp. 89–130.

Frank O. Salisbury Papers (Methodist Archives)

Date range: 1910–60.

Papers of Francis Owen Salisbury (1874–1962), artist. He was born at Harpenden, Hertfordshire, one of eleven children of Henry Salisbury and Susan Hawes. At the age of fifteen he was apprenticed to his brother, (H.) James Salisbury, in his stained-glass works at St Albans. Frank's interest in painting was fostered by attendance at a London drawing academy, and at the age of eighteen he won a five-year scholarship at the Royal Academy Schools, where he won several medals and later became a regular exhibitor. He was an artist of very great stature; his interests included portraiture (he painted several official portraits of statesmen), heraldry and pageantry, religious subjects, and the depiction of historical and ceremonial events.

All of these interests are represented in the collection, which includes Frank O. Salisbury's personal and business correspondence with friends and distinguished sitters at home and abroad. Additional papers relating to individual paintings and memorials are also included, together with autobiographical writings and material concerning his publications and exhibitions. A substantial amount of visual material is included within the collection, in the form of preliminary sketches, photographs and other reproductions.

Finding aids: unpublished handlist.

Society of Architectural Historians of Great Britain Archive

Date range: 1956–83.

Archive of the Society of Architectural Historians of Great Britain, founded in 1956. Papers comprise Executive Committee minutes and correspondence, general correspondence, correspondence of individual officers, correspondence and papers relating to membership, proceedings of annual general meetings and annual conferences, papers relating to study tours and lectures, press cuttings, newsletters, and miscellaneous printed and promotional material.

Finding aids: unpublished handlist.

Spielmann Collection

*See also the John Ruskin
Papers (p. 142), the
Holman Hunt Papers
(p. 165) and the Fairfax
Murray Papers (p. 166).*

Date range: 1885–1914.

Papers of Marion Harry Spielmann (1858–1948), the well-known critic and connoisseur of the fine arts. Spielmann was a friend of many of the leading British artists of the late 19th and early 20th centuries and author of several works on artistic and literary subjects. In 1883 he joined the *Pall Mall Gazette* and from 1886 to 1904 was editor of the *Magazine of Art*.

The papers date chiefly from this period and include correspondence with Edwin Austin Abbey, Sir Lawrence Alma-Tadema, Sir Frank Brangwyn, Ford Madox Brown, Walter Crane, William Powell Frith, Sir Hubert von Herkomer, William Holman Hunt, Frederic Lord Leighton, Sir Edward Poynter, Val Prinsep, Sir William Blake Richmond, William Michael Rossetti, Sir (William) Hamo Thornycroft and George Frederic Watts. Miscellaneous papers include holograph articles from notable artists and critics submitted to Spielmann for publication in the *Magazine of Art*, many containing the author's and editor's emendations, as well as notes by Spielmann himself on his editorship.

Finding aids: recorded in published handlist of English Manuscripts (English MSS 1288–1303). Alternative form: published microfilm: *John Ruskin, the Pre-Raphaelite Brotherhood, and Arts and Crafts Movement: the Ruskin, Holman Hunt, Fairfax Murray, Spielmann and Related Collections from the John Rylands University Library, Manchester* (Woodbridge: Research Publications, 1990).

Sir Hubert Worthington Papers

Date range: 1913–64.

Papers of Sir Hubert Worthington (1886–1963), architect. After training with Sir Edwin Lutyens in Rome, and war service with the Manchester Regiment, in 1923 Worthington was appointed Professor of Architecture at the Royal College of Art. He resigned in 1928 to return to the well-known family practice of Thomas Worthington & Son, and in 1929 he took up the Slade lectureship in architecture at Oxford. Worthington designed numerous buildings in Oxford and restored war damage at Manchester Cathedral, the Inner Temple, London, and Westminster School. He was a vice-president of the Royal Institute of British Architects and president of the Manchester Society of Architects (*q.v.*).

The archive comprises architectural plans of Imperial College, the Inner Temple and elsewhere; photographs of buildings in Cheshire, Lancashire, Oxfordshire and other counties, and photographs of war memorials and gravestones; specifications, estimates and quotations for commissions; minutes and reports relating to commissions; correspondence relating to commissions; fees for architectural work undertaken by Worthington; manuscript lecture notes on the history of architecture; miscellaneous printed matter; and items relating to Worthington's family.

Finding aids: unpublished handlist.

PRINTED RESOURCES

Illustrated Books

Almost every technique ever employed in book illustration is represented in the Library's holdings: woodcuts, engravings on wood, copper and steel, mezzotints, etchings on copper and steel, aquatints, lithographs, tipped-in photographs, chemitypes, heliotypes, collotypes, line-blocks, half-tones and chromolithographs.

The Incunabula Collection (p. 21) comprises fifteen block-books and a number of block-prints, including the *St Christopher Woodcut* of 1423, the earliest surviving example of European printing to bear a date, and the only surviving wood block used to print a block-book, an as yet unidentified variant edition of the *Apocalypse*. Albrecht Pfister in Bamberg was the first printer to introduce woodcuts into books printed with movable type. The Library holds the only examples in Britain of Pfister's output – four complete works and part of a fifth, including his *Historie von Joseph, Daniel, Judith und Esther* and the *Biblia Pauperum* of 1462. The woodcuts in both works are hand-coloured.

Among the other numerous illustrated incunabula are a copy (again unique in Britain) of Ulrich Han's 1467 edition of the *Meditationes* of Cardinal Turrecremata, the first Italian illustrated book; a copy of the first book to contain illustrations of a technical nature, Roberto Valturio's *De Re Militari*, which was printed by Johannes de Verona in 1472; a Florentine edition of Dante printed in 1481 with images engraved by Bandinelli after

Botticelli; and a copy of the most famous of Venetian illustrated books, the *Hypneroto-machia Poliphili*, printed by Aldus Manutius in 1499. Noteworthy among German illustrated incunables are a copy of Johann Zainer's edition of Boccaccio's *De Claris Mulieribus* (Ulm, 1473), whose woodcuts so impressed Emery Walker and William Morris, and copies of the German and Latin versions of Hartmann Schedel's *Nürnberg Chronicle*, ornamented with some 1,800 illustrations by Michael Wolgemut (Nürnberg, Anton Koberger, 1493). Many of the incunables are illuminated or hand-coloured. The Hiero von Holtorp Collection (p. 21) also includes two portfolios of early engravings and etchings, and eight portfolios of woodcuts.

Among the many artists and illustrators who feature in the Library's printed holdings the following are worthy of note:

Michael Wolgemut (1434–1519), Albrecht Dürer (1471–1528), Lucas Cranach (1472–1553), Hans Holbein the Younger (1497–1543), Jan Calcar (c.1499–1546), Hans Schaüfelein (fl. 1505–38), Geofroy Tory (1480–1533), Jost Amman (1539–91), Wenceslaus Hollar (1607–77), Sebastien Leclerc (1637–1714), John Sturt (1658–1730), William Kent (1684–1748), George Vertue (1684–1756), William Hogarth (1697–1764);

George Powle (fl. 1764–71), Moses Griffith (fl. 1769–1809), Samuel Grimm (1734–94), Edward Edwards (1738–1806), Francis Jukes (1745–1812), Thomas Daniell (1749–1840), Thomas Bewick (1753–1828), Thomas Stothard (1755–1834), Thomas Rowlandson (1756–1827), James Gillray (1757–1815), William Blake (1757–1827) (including a copy of Young's *Night Thoughts* hand-coloured by Blake himself), William Daniell (1769–1837), J.M.W. Turner (1775–1851), John James Audubon (1785–1851), John Martin (1789–1854), George Cruikshank (1792–1878), David Roberts (1796–1864);

John Gould (1804–81), Edward Lear (1812–88), Hablot Knight Browne ('Phiz') (1815–82), John Ruskin (1819–1900), Edward Dalziel (1817–1905), John Tenniel (1820–1914), Thomas Dalziel (1823–1906), Myles Birket Foster (1825–99), William Holman Hunt (1827–1910), Dante Gabriel Rossetti (1828–82), John Everett Millais (1829–96), Gustav Doré (1832–83), Edward Burne-Jones (1833–98), William Morris (1834–96), George du Maurier (1834–96), Walter Crane (1845–1915), Randolph Caldecott (1846–86), Kate Greenaway (1846–1901), Herbert Railton (1858–1911), Lucien Pissarro (1863–1944), Charles Ricketts (1866–1931), Beatrix Potter (1866–1943), Arthur Rackham (1867–1939), Edmund J. Sullivan (1869–1933), Charles Robinson (1870–1937), Jack Butler Yeats (1871–1957), Aubrey Beardsley (1872–98) (the Library has a complete run of *The Yellow Book*, 1894–97), William Nicholson (1872–1949), Edmund Dulac (1882–1953), Eric Gill (1882–1940), Gwen Raverat (1885–1957), Robert Gibbings (1889–1958), Paul Nash (1889–1946), John Nash (1893–1977), Agnes Miller Parker (1895–1980), Clare Leighton (1899–1989);

Barnett Freedman (1901–58), Charles Tunnicliffe (1901–79), Eric Ravilious (1903–42), Edward Bawden (1903–89) and Stephen Raw (1952–).

The Natural History and Ornithological Collection (p. 182) comprises most of the great 18th- and 19th-century illustrated botanical and ornithological books. The Private Press Collection (p. 22) and Casdagli Collection (p. 19) contain a particularly fine selection of books illustrated or decorated by Burne-Jones, Morris, Pissarro, Ricketts, Jack B. Yeats, Raverat, Gill, Gibbings, Agnes Miller Parker and other members of the British school of wood-engraving.

Finding aids: recorded in general printed-book catalogue.

Location: JRULM (Deansgate, dispersed).

Among the Library's large collection of historic architectural surveys and treatises the following works are particularly noteworthy: at least nine editions of Vitruvius's *De Architectura*, the earliest printed in Rome in 1486; Sebastiano Serlio's *Regole Generali di Architettura* (1540); Leon Battista Alberti's *I Dieci Libri de l'Architettura* (1546); Andrea Palladio's *De Re Aedificatoria* (1485) and *I Quattro Libri dell' Architettura* (1570); Jan Vredeman de Vries' *Variae Architecturae Formae* (1601); Colin Campbell's *Vitruvius Britannicus; or the British Architect* (1715–71); J. Kip's *Nouveau Théâtre de la Grande Bretagne* (1724–28); Robert Adam's *Ruins of the Palace of the Emperor Diocletian at Spalatro in Dalmatia* (1764); Sir John Soane's *Designs in Architecture* (1778) and *Plans, Elevations and Sections of Buildings Executed in the Counties of Norfolk, Suffolk, Yorkshire...* (1788); Humphry Repton's *Sketches and Hints on Landscape Gardening* (1794), *Observations on the Theory and Practice of Landscape Gardening* (1803), and facsimiles of several of his *Red Books*; and Joseph Nash's *The Mansions of England* (1839–49).

There are also works which are of interest for studies of landscape history, land use, gardens of the Renaissance and later periods, the development of cities and town planning, public health and sanitation, civic and religious rituals, sepulchral inscriptions and the architecture of death, and concepts of space.

Finding aids: recorded in general printed-book catalogue. See also H. Guppy and G. Vine, *A Classified Catalogue of the Works on Architecture and the Allied Arts in the Principal Libraries of Manchester and Salford* (Manchester, 1909).

Location: JRULM (Deansgate, dispersed).

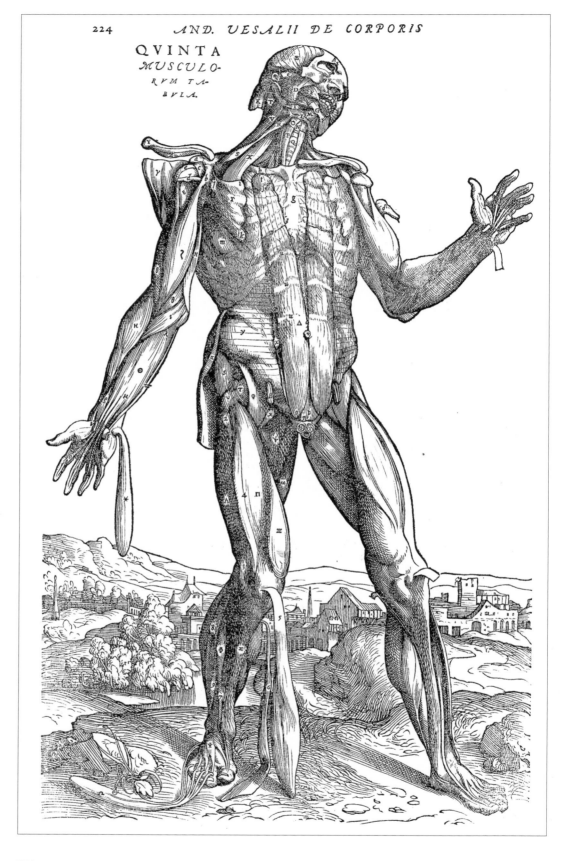

HISTORY OF SCIENCE & MEDICINE

Manuscript Resources

The Library houses significant scientific and medical archive collections. They include the archives from Jodrell Bank Radio Telescope (including papers of Sir Bernard Lovell) and papers of the optical astronomer Zdenek Kopal, as well as records relating to Joseph Black, John Dalton, Sir Henry Roscoe and George Burkhardt (Chemistry); Henry Baker (Biology); Sir William Boyd Dawkins (Geology); Sir Arthur Schuster (Physics); Robert Salmon Hutton (Metallurgy); and Arthur Marshall and Claude Wilson Wardlaw (Zoology and Botany).

The University of Manchester played a critical role in the early development of computing: the world's first stored-program computer, built by a team led by Tom Kilburn and Professor F.C. Williams, ran on 21 June 1948. Collaboration with Ferranti Ltd led to the production of the first commercially-available computer, the Ferranti Mark 1, in 1951. Manchester also pioneered the teaching of computer science in British universities. The National Archive for the History of Computing, which was established in 1987 under the auspices of the University's Centre for the History of Science, Technology and Medicine, is one of the foremost repositories in this field. It holds archives of many companies, organizations and individuals involved in the early development of computing, such as English Electric, Ferranti, International Computers Ltd (ICL), the Meteorological Office, the National Research Development Corporation, Alan Turing and F.C. Williams.

The Manchester Medical Society collection contains a large number of 18th- and 19th-century medical manuscripts. Elsewhere, there are 19th- and 20th-century medical records among the Hibbert-Ware Papers and the Heald Family Papers, while earlier material is to be found within the Greek, Irish, Arabic, Persian and Turkish manuscript collections and the Genizah fragments among the Hebrew Manuscripts. Finally, the Records of Henshaw's Society for the Blind document the history of a charity involved in the education and welfare of the blind and partially-sighted.

Printed Resources

There are notable printed holdings for the study of the history of science and medicine in the John Rylands University Library, from the earliest editions of Plato, Aristotle, Euclid, Hippocrates and Galen, through to works of the early 20th century by such scientific luminaries as Wilhelm Roentgen, J.J. Thomson and Marie Curie. The humanist philosophers, mathematicians, theoreticians, astronomers, natural scientists and physicians of the 16th and 17th centuries are particularly well represented, with important editions of Nicolaus Copernicus, Girolamo Cardano, Charles Estienne, Michael Servetus, Andreas Vesalius, Pierre de la Ramée (Petrus Ramus), Francis Bacon, Galileo Galilei, Johann Kepler, René Descartes, John Wilkins, Robert Boyle, Christiaan Huygens and Robert Hooke.

The Mathematical Printed Collection contains many first and notable editions which chart the history of the discipline, from Pythagoras through to Carl Friedrich Gauss (1777–1855), the last man to be called the Prince of Mathematics. The Medical Printed Collections include some 3,000 medical books printed before 1701, among them 200 incunables, while the Bullock Collection contains Italian medical texts from the 16th century onwards. The Deaf Education Collection is the most important collection on surdo-mutism in the

British Isles. The Partington Collection is a major resource for the history of chemistry, while the Smith Memorial Collection and Schunck Library contain works on physics, chemistry and dyes. There is also an important Natural History and Ornithological Collection comprising most of the great 18th- and 19th-century illustrated botanical and ornithological books. The Marie Stopes and Birth Control Collection deals extensively with issues of birth control and eugenics in the first half of the 20th century.

Bibliography

An Exhibition of Notable Books on Science and Medicine Held in the Arts Library of the University (Manchester, 1962).

Ethel M. Parkinson and Audrey E. Lumb, *Catalogue of Medical Books in Manchester University Library, 1480–1700* (Manchester, 1972).

John V. Pickstone, 'Some Manchester Sources for the History of Science, Technology and Medicine, with Special Reference to the John Rylands University Library of Manchester', *Bulletin of the John Rylands University Library of Manchester*, vol. 71, no. 2 (1989), pp. 159–80.

Select alphabetical list of resources: (MS: Manuscript/Archive; PR: Printed)

JOHN RYLANDS UNIVERSITY LIBRARY
OF MANCHESTER

A guide to special collections of the John Rylands University
Library of Manchester.   Manchester, John Rylands
University Library of Manchester, 1999.

272 p.   illus.   30 x 21 cm
ISBN 0 86373 138 4

Henry Baker Papers

History of Science & Medicine

Date range: 1722–70.

Eight substantial volumes contain notes and letters of Henry Baker (1698–1774), naturalist, poet and pioneer of education for the deaf and dumb (English MS 19). These cover his microscopical work, including experiments on the regeneration of Hydra (the Polyp). They also include extensive notes on his practice as a tutor for children with speech impediments.

Additional unlisted material comprises four volumes of Baker's *Exercises for the Deaf and Dumb*, and manuscript legal agreements between Baker and people with speech impediments.

See also the Deaf Education Collection (p. 20).

Finding aids: partially recorded in published handlist of English Manuscripts (English MS 19).

Joseph Black Papers

Date range: 1768–96.

Joseph Black (1728–99) is credited with several major contributions to chemical science, in particular the rediscovery of "fixed air" (carbon dioxide), the discovery of the bicarbonates, and the concepts of latent and specific heat. He thus laid the foundations of modern thermal science, and influenced James Watt in the development of the steam engine. He held chairs in medicine and chemistry at Glasgow (1756–66) and Edinburgh (1766–97), and was the first physician to George III in Scotland. The Library holds some fifteen volumes containing notes of chemistry lectures delivered by Black. Two volumes were compiled by William Henry (1774–1836), the Manchester physician and chemist, some of whose own lecture notes are also preserved.

Finding aids: recorded in unpublished card catalogue of University MSS.

George Burkhardt Papers

Date range: c.1924–67.

Papers of George Norman Burkhardt, Senior Lecturer in Chemistry at Manchester University, 1934–67. Burkhardt was for many years devoted to the cause of scientific education in Manchester and his papers illuminate the teaching of science in universities. They comprise typescript copies of Manchester University chemistry theses, typescript and manuscript copies of works on chemistry by Burkhardt and others, correspondence, notes on chemistry by Burkhardt, copies of Burkhardt's publications, papers of the Manchester Joint Research Council which promoted liaison between science and industry, 1944–67, printed materials relating to chemistry, and material on several other aspects of education and the study of science in general.

Finding aids: unpublished handlist.

Location: JRULM (Main Library).

John Dalton Papers

Date range: 1788–1845.

Papers of John Dalton (1766–1844), pioneer of chemical science. Dalton was born near Cockermouth, Cumbria, but spent most of his life in Manchester. For many years he used a room at the house of the Manchester Literary and Philosophical Society as a study and laboratory. Dalton made contributions to meteorology and the study of gases, but his reputation rests on his development of the atomic theory and the publication of the first table of atomic weights, 'the great foundation stone in chemical science'.

The collection consists of over 200 items. There are 40 scientific manuscripts, including lecture notes and papers relating to Dalton's discoveries, laboratory notes and meteorological observations. Non-scientific items include 11 letters written by Dalton to various correspondents, 1788–1842; 14 volumes of personal accounts; papers relating to the Manchester Literary and Philosophical Society; 54 letters to Dalton, 1812–44; accounts of his executors, 1844–45; and papers relating to the Dalton Testimonial Committee, 1833–42. The collection is of fundamental importance for studies of the history of science, and in particular the development of chemistry in the early 19th century.

Finding aids: the papers are not separately listed but are included in A.L. Smyth, *John Dalton 1766–1844: a Bibliography of Works By and About Him*, revised edition (Manchester, 1997). See also note in *Bulletin of the John Rylands University Library of Manchester*, vol. 62 (1979–80), pp. 259–60; Diana Leitch and Alfred Williamson, *The Dalton Tradition* (Manchester, 1991).

Sir William Boyd Dawkins Papers

Date range: 1850–1929.

Papers of Sir William Boyd Dawkins (1837–1929), geologist, palaeontologist and antiquary, Professor of Geology at the University of Manchester (formerly Owens College) from 1872 to 1908. The collection relates largely to his career as a consultant engineering geologist involved in the coal industry, water supply projects and the construction of reservoirs, and the abortive Channel Tunnel project of the 1880s. It contains personal letters, consultancy reports, geological sections and notes, printed evidence to official committees, company prospectuses, maps and press cuttings. The collection is important for the history of geology, economic and business history, hydrogeology, civil engineering, the mining industry and industrial pollution.

Finding aids: published handlist, G. Tweedale & T. Procter, 'Catalogue of the Papers of Professor Sir William Boyd Dawkins in the John Rylands University Library of Manchester', *Bulletin of the John Rylands University Library of Manchester*, vol. 74, no. 2 (1992), pp. 3–36.

R.S. Hutton Papers

Date range: 1897–1970.

Papers of Professor Robert Salmon Hutton (1876–1970), lecturer in electro-chemistry at Manchester University, 1900–08, and Goldsmiths' Professor of Metallurgy at Cambridge University, 1931–44. Between 1908 and 1921 Hutton worked in the family firm of silversmiths in Sheffield, and in 1921 he became the director of the British Non-Ferrous Metals

Research Association. He was a pioneer of electric furnace technology, championed industrial research and development, and sought to foster links between universities and industry.

Hutton's papers include scientific correspondence with Sir Arthur Schuster (*q.v.*), Lord Rutherford and others, working papers and reports, newspaper cuttings, photographs of staff and equipment in Manchester University Physics Department, and copies of Hutton's numerous published papers.

Finding aids: unpublished handlist.

Jodrell Bank Archive

Date range: c.1924–90.

Papers relating to the Jodrell Bank Radio Telescope, deposited by Sir Bernard Lovell (b. 1913), Professor of Radio Astronomy at Manchester University and Director of Jodrell Bank, 1951–80.

The first radar transmitter and receiver was installed by Lovell at Jodrell Bank, Cheshire, in December 1945. In the late 1940s he conceived the idea of a steerable telescope with a paraboloid or reflecting bowl of 250-feet diameter. Construction began in October 1952 and the telescope entered service in August 1957. In October of that year it was involved in tracking the Soviet Sputnik satellite. Since then it has been involved in many astronomical and space research projects. Formerly known as the Mark IA, in July 1987 it was renamed the Lovell Telescope. It remains one of the largest steerable radio telescopes in the world.

The archive contains extensive files of correspondence, telexes, papers relating to the funding and construction of the telescope, papers relating to the history of computing and early computers developed at Manchester, accounting records, scientific reports, telescope log-books, research notebooks and copies of papers and articles published by Lovell and others. There is correspondence with international organizations, national funding bodies and research institutes, and individual scientists in Britain, the United States and the Soviet Union. There is also a quantity of pre-war material including Lovell's school reports, and papers and notes for Lovell's research into thin films and cosmic-ray showers.

The archive constitutes a key source for the history of radio astronomy and science in general, and for studies of the funding and organization of scientific research and higher education.

Finding aids: on-line catalogue available at: http://www.man.ac.uk/Science_Engineering/CHSTM/jba/jbacat.htm. See also Dudley Saward, *Bernard Lovell: a Biography* (London, 1984).

Zdenek Kopal Papers

Date range: 1950s–80s.

Zdenek Kopal (1914–93) was Professor of Astronomy at Manchester University from 1951 until 1981, during the era of the 'Space Race', the development of satellites and lunar exploration. Kopal was born in Litomysl in eastern Bohemia (now the Czech Republic) and his interest in astronomy developed during adolescence (he published his first paper at the age of sixteen). He taught at Harvard and the Massachusetts Institute of Technology during and after the Second World War, before moving to Manchester in 1951 to take up the new Chair of Astronomy. Kopal developed the Astronomy Department to achieve international status, and was instrumental in establishing the Manchester Lunar Programme, the lunar mapping project which paved the way for the Apollo missions. He is credited with producing 396 papers on optical astronomy.

The papers include a very large quantity of correspondence, including letters from fellow astronomers in the United States and the Soviet Union, early lunar charts and glass-plate photographs of the moon, numerous drafts of papers by Kopal, and a large collection of offprints and copies of articles by other scientists on satellite programmes, lunar exploration, and co-operation between British, American and Russian astronomers.

Finding aids: unlisted. See Zdenek Kopal, *Of Stars and Men: Reminiscences of an Astronomer* (Bristol, 1986).

Manchester Medical Society Manuscripts

Date range: 18th–19th centuries.

The Manchester Medical Society was founded, in part, to supply local medical men with a library. From its foundation in 1834 to 1845 the library was housed in Faulkner Street, close to Manchester Infirmary, and in 1845 it moved to the Royal Manchester Institution. In 1873 the library was transferred to Owens College after it had incorporated the local medical school.

*See also the Medical
Printed Collections
(p. 182).*

The collection contains surgeons' and physicians' notebooks, *materia medica*, pharmacopoeia, lecture notes and treatises on surgery, anatomy, physiology, paediatrics, obstetrics and gynaecology. The majority of texts are in English, but some are in Latin and German, and there are English translations of Continental treatises. Authors include Alexander Monro II (1733–1817), the great Dutch physician Hermann Boerhaave (1668–1738), William Cullen (1710–90), Sir Astley Paton Cooper (1768–1841), John Hunter (1728–93) and Thomas Young. In addition there is a 19th-century receipt book for Manchester Medical Society.

Finding aids: unlisted.

Arthur Marshall Papers

Date range: 1884–93.

A small collection of papers of Arthur Milnes Marshall (1852–93), naturalist, Professor of Zoology at Owens College (later the University of Manchester), 1879–93, Secretary and subsequently Chairman of the Board of Studies of the Victoria University. He published a number of important papers on the origin and development of nervous systems in higher animals, before his death in a climbing accident. There is material relating to the academic disciplines of zoology and botany: Marshall is acknowledged as a pioneer in the teaching of both subjects. There are also papers concerning the foundation and early years of the Athletic Union, in which Marshall was closely involved.

Finding aids: unpublished handlist.

Location: JRULM (Main Library).

Date range: 1930s–90s.

Computers have shaped many aspects of the economy and society of the industrialized world during the second half of the 20th century. The computer industry itself has been characterized by intense technological development, rapid growth, massive structural change, and hence short-term corporate memory. By the 1980s it was becoming recognized that many of the artefacts, historical records and personal recollections from the early decades of computing, in which Britain played a major role, were fast disappearing. The National Archive for the History of Computing was therefore established in 1987 under the auspices of the University of Manchester's Centre for the History of Science, Technology and Medicine, to provide a repository for the artefacts, archives and oral testimonies of computer history. The aims of the NAHC are: to produce a comprehensive listing of records relating to the history of computing in Britain and to encourage their preservation; to preserve records that are at risk; to conduct and record interviews with leading figures in the history of computing in order to establish an oral history archive; and to undertake research into computer history and to stimulate research by organizing conferences and postgraduate teaching and supervision.

The NAHC holds archives of many companies and public bodies which have been prominent in the history of computing, such as the Admiralty Computing Service; the Atomic Research Establishment, Fort Halstead, Kent; Cambridge University Computer Laboratory; English Electric Company Ltd; Ferranti Ltd; International Computers Ltd (ICL); LEO Computers Ltd; Manchester University Department of Computer Science; Marconi Wireless Telegraph Company Ltd; the Meteorological Office; the National Physical Laboratory; the National Research Development Corporation (NRDC); the Royal Aircraft Establishment, Farnborough; the Royal Radar Establishment; Scientific Computing Service Ltd; and the United Kingdom Atomic Energy Authority.

There are also papers of several individuals involved in the development of computing, most notably Douglas R. Hartree (1897–1958), Alan Turing (1912–54) and Professor Sir F.C. Williams (1911–77).

Items include photographs of machines, components and production facilities; technical drawings and specifications; hardware and software manuals; trade catalogues, price lists, technical information sheets and promotional literature; working papers and reports; published reports, articles and monographs; correspondence; and audio-visual material.

Finding aids: on-line catalogue available at: http://www.man.ac.uk/Science_Engineering/CHSTM/nahc.htm. See also Geoffrey Tweedale, 'The National Archive for the History of Computing', *Journal of the Society of Archivists*, vol. 10, no. 1 (1989), pp. 1-8. For further information contact the National Archive for the History of Computing, Centre for the History of Science, Technology and Medicine, Mathematics Tower, Manchester University, Manchester, M13 9PL; email: nahc@fs4.ma.man.ac.uk; telephone: 0161 275 5845; fax: 0161 275 5699.

Location: JRULM (Main Library) and CHSTM.

Henry Roscoe Papers

Date range: 1857–1906.

Papers of Sir Henry Enfield Roscoe (1833–1915), Professor of Chemistry at Owens College (which later became the University of Manchester) from 1857 to 1885, when he was elected Liberal MP for South Manchester. The collection comprises letter-books containing drafts of Roscoe's publications and copies of letters and reports concerning Roscoe's work as a consultant for local authorities in the analysis of industrial pollution. There are also newspaper cuttings, lecture notes and offprints of Roscoe's publications.

In addition to the collection above, English MSS 963–964 comprise two volumes containing a collection of letters to Roscoe, and miscellaneous papers, printed cuttings and photographs relating to Roscoe, to his fields of activity and to other eminent scientists. Correspondents include Robert Wilhelm Bunsen, Leo Königsberger, Richard Meyer, Louis Pasteur, Georg Quincke and Sir Ronald Ross.

Finding aids: unpublished handlist of main collection, and published handlist of English Manuscripts (English MSS 963–964). See also H.R. Roscoe, *The Life and Experiences of Sir Henry Enfield Roscoe, Written by Himself* (1906); T.E. Thorpe, *The Right Honourable Sir Henry Roscoe: a Biographical Sketch* (London, 1916).

Arthur Schuster Papers

Date range: 1851–1934.

Papers of Sir Arthur Schuster (1851–1934), Langworthy Professor of Physics at the University of Manchester (formerly Owens College) from 1888 to 1907, and pioneer in several areas of scientific study at Manchester. Schuster's interests were wide-ranging: terrestrial magnetism, optics, solar physics, and the mathematical theory of periodicities. He introduced meteorology as a subject studied in British universities. After his retirement in 1907 he devoted himself to the administration of the Royal Society, and to the organization of international co-operation in science.

The collection contains correspondence between Schuster and many of the leading scientists of the period, such as Lord Rutherford. Correspondence with Sir Robert Falcon Scott and the meteorologist Sir George Clarke Simpson concerns Scott's last, ill-fated Antarctic Expedition. There are also copies of working papers, lecture notes and reports, and copies of Schuster's numerous published papers reflecting his diverse interests. The collection has major significance for studies of the history of physics teaching and research.

Finding aids: unpublished handlist.

Claude Wilson Wardlaw Papers

Date range: 1935–65.

Papers of Claude Wilson Wardlaw, Barker Professor of Cryptogamic Botany (1940–60) and George Harrison Professor of Botany (1958–66) at the University of Manchester. Wardlaw was an international authority on diseases of the banana and one of the foremost researchers in the world on plant morphogenesis, the study of plant form. He acted as a consultant on tropical crop diseases to several companies. His papers comprise typescripts and proofs of the monographs *Banana Diseases* (1935, revised 1961), *Reflections on some Diseases and Pests of the Oil Palm* (1965) and *Organization and Evolution in Plants* (1965);

typescripts and proofs of several articles on morphogenesis; and an album of cytological illustrations.

Finding aids: recorded in unpublished card catalogue of University MSS.

Location: JRULM (Main Library).

PRINTED RESOURCES

Mathematical Printed Collection

1,000 items (dispersed).

The Library has a wide range of printed works which chart the history of mathematics, from ancient times to the 19th century. All the eminent Greek mathematicians are represented in early or significant editions: Pythagoras, with two editions of Hierocles' commentary on his *Carmina Aurea*, printed by Bartholomaeus de Valdezoccho (Padua, 1474) and Arnold Pannartz (Rome, 1475); Aristotle, with the first edition of the complete works in Greek (Aldus, Venice, 1495–98); Euclid, with copies of the first edition of the *Elements*, printed by Ratdolt in a Latin translation (Venice, 1482), the first edition of the Greek text printed by Hervagius (Basel, 1533), and the first English translation by Sir Henry Billingsley (1570); and Archimedes, with the first edition by Hervagius (Basel, 1544). Boethius made Latin redactions of a number of Greek scientific writings in around 500 AD. The Library has over fifty editions of his works, the earliest being the *De Consolatione Philosophiae* (Savigliano, 1470).

Medieval and Renaissance writers in the collection include the 13th-century redactor Johannes Campanus, with editions from 1490 onwards; the Aristotelian scholar Nicole d'Oresme, Bishop of Lisieux; the German astronomer and mathematician Johann Müller, known as Regiomontanus, represented by three editions from 1474–76; the French logician Pierre de la Ramée (Petrus Ramus), several copies of whose *Arithmeticae Libri Duo* are to be found within the Christie Collection (p. 19); and the Italians Girolamo Cardano and Niccolò Tartaglia. Among the former's works is *De Subtilitate Libri XXI* (Nürnberg, 1550), while Tartaglia is represented by *Quesiti et Inventioni Diverse* (Venice, 1546).

The great expansion of mathematical studies in the 17th century is reflected in the number of editions of Galileo Galilei, Marin Mersenne, René Descartes, Blaise Pascal and Gottfried Leibniz. For Galileo the Library holds first editions of *Il Saggiatore* (Rome, 1623), *Dialogo… sopra i Due Massimi Sistemi del Mondo* (Florence, 1632), and *Discorsi e Dimonstrazioni Matematiche* (Leiden, 1638). British mathematicians include Robert Recorde, Leonard Digges, John Napier (who published the first table of logarithms in 1614), John Wallis (who made important contributions to calculus) and, of course, Sir Isaac Newton, who is represented by first editions of *Philosophiae Naturalis Principia Mathematica* (1687), *Opticks* (1704) and *The Method of Fluxions and Infinite Series* (1736).

Among later mathematicians, attention should be drawn to the works of Leonhard Euler (with some eighteen editions between 1736 and 1812); Jean Le Rond d'Alembert (represented by sixteen editions between 1743 and 1805); Gaspard Monge, whose *Feuilles d'Analyse Appliquée à la Géométrie* (1800) established the algebraic methods of three-dimensional geometry; Carl Friedrich Gauss, arguably the most important figure in 19th-century mathematics; and Augustin-Louis Cauchy (1789–1857).

Finding aids: recorded in general printed-book catalogue.

30,000 items.

The Library's holdings of historical medical material are among the most important in Britain. The Manchester Medical Society, founded in 1834, deposited its collection in the Library in 1875, a decision which was fully confirmed in 1930. The Society's library consisted of just over 1,000 volumes in 1835, but growth was rapid after 1858 when Thomas Windsor became honorary librarian, the catalogue issued in 1890 listing some 29,000 volumes. There are now in the Library some 3,000 medical books printed before 1701 including about 200 incunables; there are also around 4,000 18th-century items.

Particularly noteworthy are first and second editions of Andreas Vesalius's *De Humani Corporis Fabrica* (Basel, 1543 & 1555), with magnificent engraved plates by Titian's pupil, Jan Calcar. Mention should also be made of the first Latin edition of Hippocrates (Basel, 1526); the Aldine edition of Galen's complete works in Greek (Venice, 1525), and Thomas Linacre's translations of individual works into Latin, printed by Richard Pynson (London, 1522–24); the first edition of Charles Estienne's celebrated *De Dissectione Partium Corporis Humani* (Paris, 1545); Gaspar Tagliocozzo's pioneering work on plastic surgery, *De Curtorum Chirurgia Per Insitionem* (Venice, 1597); the first English editions of William Harvey's *Anatomical Exercises* on the circulation of the blood and on the generation of living creatures (London, 1653); works on obstetrics and midwifery such as Jakob Ruff's *De Conceptu et Generatione Hominis* (Frankfurt, 1587), translated into English as *The Expert Midwife* (London, 1637), and François Mauriceau's *Traité des Maladies des Femme... Grosses et... Accouchées* (Paris, 1681); and the first editions of Robert Boyle's *Memoirs for the Natural History of Humane Blood* (London, 1684), Edward Jenner's *Inquiry into the Causes and Effects of the Variolae Vaccinae* (London, 1798), and Richard Bright's two-volume *Reports of Medical Cases* (London, 1827–31), in which various diseases are examined in the light of morbid anatomy.

See also the Bullock Collection (p. 18), the Deaf Education Collection (p. 20) and the Manchester Medical Society Manuscripts (p. 178).

Finding aids: pre-1701 books are catalogued in Ethel M. Parkinson and Audrey E. Lumb, *Catalogue of Medical Books in Manchester University Library, 1480–1700* (Manchester, 1972); all material acquired up to 1890 is recorded in *Catalogue of the Library of the Manchester Medical Society* (Manchester, 1890); material acquired subsequently is recorded in the medical card catalogue at the Main Library.

Location: JRULM (Deansgate and Main Library); most pre-1801 books are at Deansgate, more modern material at the Main Library and stores.

Natural History and Ornithological Collection

2,000 items (dispersed).

The Library has a particularly fine collection of 18th- and 19th-century bird books. These include the works of Thomas Bewick, George Edwards, Georges-Louis Leclerc Compte de Buffon, François Le Vaillant and Daniel Giraud Elliot; a complete and uniformly-bound set of the publications of John Gould; and John James Audubon's massive elephant-folio *Birds of America*. Earlier works on natural history include Conrad Gesner's *Historiae Animalium* (Zurich, 1587), and Marcello Malpighi's pioneering monograph on the silkworm (London, 1669). Among books on fish, Markus Elieser Bloch's beautifully illustrated *Ichtyologie, ou Histoire Naturelle des Poissons* (Berlin, 1785–97) merits particular notice.

The Library also has a substantial collection of the great Herbals, ranging from the Latin and German editions of the Herbarius of 1484 and 1485, and Leonhard Fuchs's *New Kreüterbuch* (1543), to Frederick Sander's *Reichenbachia* of 1888–94, including fine editions of John Gerard, John Parkinson, William Curtis, James Sowerby, Nicolaas Jacquin, Rembert Dodoens and Nicholas Culpeper. Mention must also be made of the sets of Pierre Joseph Redouté's *Les Roses* (1817–24) and *Les Liliacées* (1802–10). The recently-purchased copy of Robert Thornton's magnificent *Temple of Flora* (1799–1807) is considered to be one of the most perfect and complete in existence.

The study of natural history along modern, scientific lines began in the 18th century, with the classification of genera and species by Linnaeus. The Library holds the tenth edition of his *Systema Naturae* (1758–59), which is recognized as the foundation of all subsequent taxonomy. The Library also possesses the first and numerous subsequent editions of the ever-popular *The Natural History and Antiquities of Selborne* (1789) by the Reverend Gilbert White, who was much influenced by Linnaeus. These complement a small collection of Gilbert White manuscripts and letters (p. 79).

The works of Charles Darwin, who revolutionized the understanding and study of natural history in the next century, are particularly well represented. The Library possesses three copies of the first edition of *Narrative of the Surveying Voyages of His Majesty's Ships Adventure and Beagle* (1839), a first edition of *The Zoology of the Voyage of HMS Beagle* (1839–43), and copies of the first four editions of *On the Origin of Species by Means of Natural Selection* (1859–66), all in original cloth.

Finding aids: recorded in general printed-book catalogue.

Partington Collection

1,500 items.

This collection of books on the history of science was bequeathed in 1966 by James Riddick Partington (1886–1965), formerly lecturer and demonstrator in chemistry at Manchester University, and Professor of Chemistry at London University from 1919 to 1951. Partington was a leading scholar in the field of inorganic, physical and historical chemistry, and his *A History of Chemistry* (1964) remains a seminal text.

The collection is particularly rich in books on chemistry, embracing every aspect of the science from the early Greek and Arabic treatises, through the chemical revolution of the 18th and 19th centuries, to modern researches into atomic chemistry. It contains 16th-century books of secrets and alchemical and metallurgical works, many illustrated; 17th-century editions of such writers as Jan Baptista van Helmont, Andreas Libavius, Johann Rudolf Glauber and Robert Boyle; 18th-century texts by Joseph Black (*q.v.*), Carl Wilhelm Scheele, Joseph Priestley, Antoine Laurent Lavoisier and Claude Louis Berthollet; and works by chemists of the 19th century such as Humphry Davy, Michael Faraday and Jöns Jacob Berzelius. Particularly noteworthy are a copy of Robert Hooke's *Micrographia* (1665); a rare collection of Greek treatises by Demokritos and others, *De arte magna* (1573); a 1533 edition of Georgius Agricola, dealing with medicinal substances; and a very scarce German collection, *Alchimia vera*, published in the early 17th century.

In addition to printed books, the collection contains manuscript notebooks, lantern slides, theses supervised by Partington, and many hundreds of offprints and pamphlets, all as yet uncatalogued.

Finding aids: books recorded in general printed-book catalogue; other material uncatalogued.

Smith Memorial Collection and Schunck Library

4,000 items.

The Smith Memorial Collection of books on chemistry and physics was formed by Robert Angus Smith (1817–84), who was appointed the first Alkali Acts inspector in 1862 and is known as the 'father of acid rain'. The collection was donated in 1885.

The separate Schunck Library consists of 19th-century books on chemistry with special emphasis on colour and dyes. It was amassed by (Henry) Edward Schunck (1820–1903), the industrialist and dye expert, who undertook significant research into the properties of indigo, chlorophyll and alizarin. 170 items from the collection are at Deansgate, the remainder at the Main Library.

Finding aids: Deansgate items recorded in general printed-book catalogue; also separate handwritten catalogue of the Schunck Library.

Location: JRULM (Deansgate and Main Library).

Marie Stopes and Birth Control Collection

600 items.

Marie Stopes (1880–1958) was the first woman to join the scientific staff of the University of Manchester, being appointed assistant lecturer and demonstrator in botany in 1904. In 1921 she founded the Mothers' Clinic for Birth Control in London, and she devoted herself to sex education and family planning. The collection includes approximately 160 early editions of books and pamphlets written by Marie Stopes, the remainder of the collection consisting of books from the library of the Society for Constructive Birth Control.

Finding aids: recorded in general printed-book catalogue.

MANCHESTER UNIVERSITY & ACADEMICS' PAPERS

THE ARCHIVES of Manchester University and its predecessor institution, Owens College, are important resources for the history of higher education and research. As well as the institutional archives of the University itself, there are papers of numerous former professors and lecturers, notably William Stanley Jevons (Philosophy and Political Economy); Samuel Alexander and Robert Adamson (Philosophy); Sir Lewis Namier, James Tait and T.F. Tout (History); John Strachan (Greek); C.B. Cox (English); Eve Reymond (Egyptology); and Samuel Finer (History of Government). There are also papers of the former Professor of Industrial and Commercial Law and later Vice-Chancellor, Sir William Mansfield Cooper, and of Sir Philip Hartog, secretary to the Victoria University extension scheme. Outside the University, there are papers of the freelance historian Edward Freeman, and a small collection of Sigmund Freud letters. The John Rylands Library Archive is itself a significant resource for studies of book-collecting and bibliography.

See also the History of Science and Medicine (p. 173).

Select alphabetical list of resources:

Robert Adamson Papers

Date range: 1870s–90s.

Papers of Robert Adamson (1852–1902), philosopher, Professor of Logic and Mental and Moral Philosophy, 1876–93, and Professor of Political Economy, 1876–82, at Owens College (later the University of Manchester). Adamson took a prominent role in the administration of the Victoria University, serving as secretary, and later treasurer, of the Board of Studies, and he was an advocate of the admission of women on equal terms with men.

Although unlisted, the papers are sufficiently compact to be readily accessible. They include notebooks and manuscripts on logic and philosophy, and also on the working class and other contemporary social themes. There are also transcriptions of writings by the logician and philosopher, Rudolf Hermann Lotze. Adamson was an innovative thinker and his papers are an important source for studies of the development of philosophy.

Finding aids: unlisted.

Location: JRULM (Main Library).

Samuel Alexander Papers

Date range: 1877–1938.

Papers of Samuel Alexander (1859–1938), Professor of Philosophy at Owens College and later Manchester University, 1893–1924. Manchester's most distinguished philosopher, he was a pioneer in modernizing the discipline by recognizing the philosophical significance of contemporary developments in psychology, biology and evolutionary theory. Alexander is best known for his theory of 'emergent evolution', expounded in his major work, *Space, Time and Deity* (1920), in which he argued that existence is hierarchically ordered, and that through a process of evolution ever higher levels of existence emerge. In later life Alexander broadened his interests to include aesthetics and literature. He was active in the life and politics of the University, and was a keen advocate of women's suffrage.

Alexander's papers include large numbers of letters, numerous accounts, receipts and business letters from publishers, research notebooks, pamphlets and offprints, and biographical and obituary material. Correspondents include the philosophers Bertrand Russell and Alfred North Whitehead, the writers A.N. Monkhouse and C.E. Montague (*q.v.*), the physicist Ernest Rutherford, and the Zionist pioneer Chaim Weizmann (Alexander supported the campaign for a Jewish homeland in Palestine).

Finding aids: unpublished handlist of main correspondence sequence. See also B.D. Brettschneider, *The Philosophy of Samuel Alexander: Idealism in 'Space, Time and Deity'* (New York, 1964); M.R. Konvitz, *On the Nature of Value: the Philosophy of Samuel Alexander* (New York, 1967); J.W. McCarthy, *The Naturalism of Samuel Alexander* (New York, 1948); A.P. Stiernotte, *God and Space-time: Deity in the Philosophy of Samuel Alexander* (New York, 1954).

William Mansfield Cooper Papers

Date range: 1948–70.

Papers of Sir William Mansfield Cooper (1903–92), Professor of Industrial and Commercial Law at Manchester University, 1949–70, and Vice-Chancellor of the University, 1956–70. His papers relate not only to his distinguished University career, but also to a wide range of external interests, such as the setting up of schools television services by the Independent Television Authority, the Fulbright Commission for fostering Anglo-American academic contacts, and above all the promotion of co-operation on higher education in Europe. There are minutes, reports and other printed matter recording the activities of the Western European Union European Universities Committee, the Standing Conference of Rectors and Vice-Chancellors of the European Universities, and various sections of the Council of Europe, especially the Committee for Higher Education and Research.

Finding aids: partial unpublished handlist.

Location: JRULM (Main Library).

Samuel Finer Papers

Date range: 1948–93.

Papers of Samuel Finer (1915–93), Professor of Government at Manchester University, 1966–74, and Gladstone Professor of Government and Public Administration at Oxford, 1974–82. The collection comprises research notes, background material and drafts for Professor Finer's monumental *The History of Government from the Earliest Times* (Oxford University Press, 1997); and typescript and manuscript drafts and notes of earlier publications; lecture notes; files of research notes and articles on various aspects of the history of government; and offprints and copies of articles and papers by Finer and others. The collection is highly significant for studies of the history of government and historiography.

Finding aids: unpublished accession list.

Manchester University & Academics' Papers

Edward Freeman Papers

Date range: 1843–95.

Papers of Edward Augustus Freeman (1823–92), freelance historian and journalist. Freeman is best remembered as one of the leading Victorian writers on English medieval history, and his most enduring monument is his six-volume *The History of the Norman Conquest of England* (1867–79). He was also an authority on the ancient world, especially the development of Greek civilization, and was a passionate supporter of modern Greece and the struggle of Orthodox Christians in the Balkans for independence from the Turkish Empire. He had a further interest in architecture, and particularly in ecclesiastical buildings, and his first book was *A History of Architecture* (1849). Freeman made three attempts to obtain a professorship at Oxford before his very belated appointment in 1884 to the Regius Professorship of Modern History.

The archive comprises correspondence, much of which reflects Freeman's interests in architecture, High Anglicanism, the Orthodox Church, classical and modern Greece, and the Balkans; proof and published copies of Freeman's printed works; manuscript writings by Freeman, including a virtually complete original manuscript of *The History of the Norman Conquest of England*; scrapbooks containing cuttings, reviews and correspondence; diplomas, honours and decorations awarded to Freeman. There is also a collection of over 6,200 pen-and-ink sketches by Freeman of churches in England, Wales, France, Germany, Italy and Switzerland, many of which are no longer standing. These are an invaluable resource for architectural and art historians.

See also the Edward Freeman Printed Collection (p. 114).

The correspondence includes 79 letters from the architect Sir George Gilbert Scott; and other letters from Walter Bagehot, economist, political analyst and journalist; Richard William Church, Dean of St Paul's and friend of Newman; Alexander Fraser, Scottish philosopher and editor of the *North British Review*; Sir Stephen Glynne, MP and antiquary; Walter Farquhar Hook, Dean of Chichester and church historian; Richard Holt Hutton, theologian and journalist; Sir Henry James Sumner Maine, prominent jurist and contributor to the *Saturday Review*; Sir Clements Robert Markham, geographer; Friedrich Max Müller, Sanskrit scholar and student of Eastern religions; Viscount Strangford, eccentric traveller and orientalist; the Rev. Henry Thompson, religious author and classical scholar; and John Byrne Leicester Warren, 3rd Baron de Tabley (*q.v.*), poet, botanist, numismatist and man of letters.

Finding aids: published handlist, P. McNiven, 'Handlist of the Papers of Edward Augustus Freeman in the John Rylands University Library of Manchester', *Bulletin of the John Rylands University Library of Manchester*, vol. 72, no. 2 (1990), pp. 27–71. See also M.E. Bratchel, *Edward Augustus Freeman and the Victorian Interpretation of the Norman Conquest* (Ilfracombe, 1969); H.A. Cronne, 'Edward Augustus Freeman, 1823–1892', *History*, vol. 28 (1943), pp. 78–82.

Sigmund Freud Papers

Date range: c.1911–38.

Collection of correspondence in English between Sigmund Freud and his nephew Sam, the son of his elder half-brother Emanuel who emigrated to England and settled in Manchester. The collection consists of 69 letters from Freud to Sam, 1911–38, and 61 copies of replies by Sam, 1914–31, plus 4 letters from Freud to his niece Pauline, 1931–38, and 3 letters from Freud's daughter Anna to her cousin Sam, 1920. The correspondence almost entirely concerns family matters and includes accounts of the difficult conditions in Austria after the First World War.

Finding aids: outline list.

Philip Hartog Papers

Date range: 1899–1904.

Small collection of correspondence and papers of Sir Philip(pe) Joseph Hartog (1864–1947), Assistant Lecturer in Chemistry at Owens College, who was better known for his role as secretary to the Victoria University extension scheme before he was appointed Registrar of the University of London in 1903. Papers include correspondence with William Haldane Gee, C.P. Scott, Alfred Waterhouse and others; printed matter relating to the debate concerning the creation of the Victoria University of Manchester, including articles, reports, newspaper cuttings, minutes, draft charters and a copy of the Owens College Act 1899; and reviews of Hartog's book, *The Owens College, Manchester* (Manchester, 1900).

Finding aids: unpublished handlist. See also Mabel H. Hartog, *P.J. Hartog: a Memoir* (London, 1949).

Location: JRULM (Main Library).

Jevons Family Papers

Date range: 1799–1959.

Papers of the Jevons family, especially William Stanley Jevons (1835–82), Professor of Logic, Mental and Moral Philosophy, and Political Economy at Owens College, Manchester, 1866–76, and Professor of Political Economy at University College, London, 1876–80. William Stanley Jevons was a true polymath, whose research spanned many disciplines. His outstanding contributions were in the fields of economics and logic (he has been described as the founder of mathematical economics), but his published writings also encompassed chemistry, meteorology, geology, astronomy, geometry, physiology, sociology and the philosophy of science.

W.S. Jevons's papers comprise over 600 letters from family, relations, colleagues and academic associates, including Charles Babbage, mathematician and inventor of the

Difference Engine calculating machine; Walter Bagehot, economist, political analyst and journalist; George Bentham, botanist; George Boole, mathematician and logician; John Bright, reforming orator and statesman; William Ewart Gladstone; Robert Harley, mathematician; Sir John Herschel, astronomer and chemist; Alfred Marshall, economist; James Martineau, the Unitarian divine; the philosopher and economist John Stuart Mill; Henry Enfield Roscoe (q.v.), Professor of Chemistry at Owens College, 1857–86; and Alfred Lord Tennyson. There are also diaries, notebooks and photograph albums recording Jevons's activities and career in Australia, when he was employed as assayer at the Sydney mint and also carried out detailed social surveys of the city's slums, 1854–59; research notes; and manuscript drafts and copies of his many printed works.

Manchester University & Academics' Papers

There are papers relating to about 40 other members of the Jevons family, including material relating to William Stanley Jevons's father, Thomas Jevons (1791–1855), a businessman and inventor; the latter's eldest daughter Lucy Ann (1830–1910); Harriet Ann (1838–1910), wife of William Stanley Jevons; and their son Herbert Stanley Jevons (1875–1955); and to another twenty members of the related Roscoe, Taylor, Boyce and Scott families.

Finding aids: published handlist, P. McNiven, 'Handlist of the Jevons Archives in the John Rylands University Library of Manchester', *Bulletin of the John Rylands University Library of Manchester*, vol. 66 (1983–84), pp. 213–55. Alternative form: published microfilm: *The Papers of William Stanley Jevons, 1835–1882, from the John Rylands University Library of Manchester* (Marlborough: Adam Matthew Publications, 1991).

Lewis Namier Papers

Date range: c.1920–62.

Papers of Sir Lewis Bernstein Namier (1888–1960), prominent historian and Professor of History at Manchester University, 1931–53. Namier was born in Poland to non-practising Jewish parents, and moved to England in his late teens, entering Balliol College, Oxford, in 1908. He took British nationality in 1913. After spending several years in the business and diplomatic worlds, he settled down to a full-time academic career in the mid-1920s, with a particular interest in British parliamentary history. Two major works, *The Structure of Politics at the Accession of George III* (1929) and *England in the Age of the American Revolution* (1930), established him in the front rank of British historians.

Namier also features in the Manchester Guardian *Archive (p. 104).*

The archive contains notes and drafts of *The Structure of Politics*, but it chiefly consists of post-war material relating to the *History of Parliament* series (Namier was responsible for the period 1754–90) and his biography of Charles Townshend. There is also some correspondence, and there are items connected with Lady Julia Namier's biography of her husband, including appreciations and obituaries.

Finding aids: unpublished handlist.

John Strachan Papers

Date range: c.1885–1907.

Papers of John Strachan (1862–1907), Hulme Professor of Greek, 1885–1907, and Professor of Sanskrit and Comparative Religion, 1890–1907, in Owens College and later the University of Manchester. Strachan is best remembered as a leading figure in the revival of Celtic studies. His collection of manuscript notebooks contains information on philosophy, the classics, and the Irish Gaelic language.

See also the Strachan Book Collection (p. 25).

Finding aids: unlisted.
Location: JRULM (Main Library).

James Tait Papers

Date range: c.1881–1944.

Papers of James Tait (1863–1944), Professor of Ancient and Medieval History at the University of Manchester, 1902–19. Like T.F. Tout, James Tait was a prominent member of the 'Manchester History School'. Indeed, after gaining a first in modern history at Oxford, he spent his entire academic career in Manchester. His publications included *Medieval Manchester and the Beginnings of Lancashire* (1904) and *The Medieval English Borough* (1936), and he also edited several important medieval texts. He served as the first president of the English Place-Name Society from 1923 until 1932. Tait's papers include correspondence, original manuscripts, notebooks and printed matter.

Finding aids: provisional list of correspondence only.

Location: JRULM (Main Library).

T.F. Tout Papers

Date range: c.1890–1935.

Papers of Thomas Frederick Tout (1855–1929), Professor of Medieval and Modern History at Owens College and later the University of Manchester, 1890–1925. Tout was, with James Tait, one of the two leading figures of the 'Manchester History School' and is best known for his *Chapters in the Administrative History of Medieval England* (6 vols, 1920–31), *The Political History of England, 1216–1377* (1905), and *The Place of the Reign of Edward II in English History* (1914). He was actively involved in the life and running of the University and his papers contain a wealth of information on general academic affairs as well as his own historical research.

Tout's papers include notebooks, drafts of many historical works, newspaper cuttings, photographs, and a large quantity of correspondence. Correspondents include the historians V.H. Galbraith, R.L. Poole, F.M. Powicke and James Tait, the philosopher Samuel Alexander (*q.v.*), Winston Churchill and C.P. Scott, editor of the *Manchester Guardian*. There are many letters from Tout's former pupils serving in the First World War, recording their experiences. There is also considerable family correspondence, including over 120 letters to Tout from his wife Mary.

The collection also contains several hundred letters and papers preserved by Mary Tout, who was herself an historian and a campaigner for the development of women's education. Her role in the University Women's Federation is well documented. Altogether the collection has significance for the history of higher education, the history of historical research and teaching, women's studies, particularly in relation to education, and military history.

Additional material was generously donated in 1998 by Mr Tom Sharp, grandson of T.F. Tout and Mary Tout. This comprises further papers of his grandparents, and papers of Herbert Tout (1904–97), their son, who worked on the Bristol Social Survey during the late 1930s. This study recorded in minute detail social conditions, housing standards and the cost of living in the city.

Finding aids: partial outline list; see also F.M. Powicke, *T.F. Tout, 1855–1929* (London, 1931).

Location: JRULM (Main Library).

Moses Tyson Papers

Date range: 1897–1969.

A small collection of papers of Moses Tyson (1897–1969), Keeper of Western Manuscripts at the John Rylands Library, 1927–35, Librarian of Manchester University, 1935–65, and subsequently Librarian Emeritus. There is material relating to his career as librarian and historian, as well as personal correspondence and a number of documents and photographs concerning his family and his wartime service.

Finding aids: provisional outline list.

Location: JRULM (Main Library).

University of Manchester Archives

Date range: 1851 to present.

The origins of Manchester University can be traced back to 1845 when the Manchester merchant John Owens (1790–1846) bequeathed almost £100,000 for the foundation of "an institution for providing or aiding the means of instructing and improving young persons of the male sex (and being of an age not less than fourteen years) in such branches of learning and science as were then and might be… taught in the English Universities". Thus Owens College was established in 1851 in Richard Cobden's house on Quay Street. The College was affiliated to the University of London, and students who successfully completed a two-year course at Manchester had the opportunity to take external London degrees. Owens College moved to its present site on Oxford Road in 1873. A separate college for women was opened in Brunswick Street in 1877 and in 1883 the Department for Women was established as part of Owens College. The success of the College led to a campaign, from about 1876 onwards, for it to be accorded university status. However, conservative suspicions within the established universities, and misgivings among similar colleges about the elevation of Owens College, led to the compromise which became the Victoria University. From 1880 to 1884 Owens College was the sole constituent of this federal university of northern England, to be joined in 1884 and 1887 by Liverpool and Leeds respectively. By the turn of the century there was pressure again for the establishment of an independent University of Manchester. In 1903 the federal university was disbanded and Owens College became the Victoria University of Manchester. The Faculty of Technology was established in 1905 as the University of Manchester Institute of Science and Technology (UMIST). UMIST became a fully independent institution in 1994.

The archives largely derive from the central administration of the University; comparatively little material from academic departments has survived. One of the most accessible sources for the history of the University is the set of printed Calendars, from 1862 onwards, which include lists of staff, graduates and students, syllabuses, details of fees, prizes and fellowships, and examination results.

Other records include the printed Reports of the Council to the Court of Governors, 1872 to the present, containing financial data and information on teaching and research; minutes and working papers of the Council and Senate, and of Council committees; records of the Vice-Chancellor's Department (correspondence, papers relating to university funding, newscuttings, VCs' engagement diaries, texts of articles and speeches by VCs); Registrar's Department correspondence; printed material relating to the history of Owens College and the University; printed material relating to individual departments and institutions of the University; general University publications; copies of articles and lectures by staff; declaration books containing personal details of newly-enrolled students; student registers; sets of examination papers (incorporated in the Calendar from 1862 to 1911); minute books of the students' union; student newspapers, magazines and other publications and ephemera concerning student politics; photographs and newscuttings.

The archives are important in charting the development of one of the earliest 'red-brick' universities. They are an invaluable source for studies of the history of higher education generally, issues such as the campaign to achieve equal access for women to higher education, trends in academic research and teaching, and student militancy.

Finding aids: outline handlists.

Location: JRULM (Main Library).

John Rylands Library Archive

Date range: 1890 to present.

The John Rylands Library was founded by Mrs Enriqueta Augustina Rylands as a memorial to her husband, who died in December 1888 leaving a fortune of some £2.5 million. John Rylands had developed the family firm of Rylands & Sons (see p. 96) into one of the largest and most profitable cotton manufacturing concerns in Britain. Mrs Rylands employed the architect Basil Champneys to design a building in the neo-Gothic style. Construction began in 1890 and the Library opened to the public on January 1st 1900. Mrs Rylands's original intention had been to create a primarily theological library, but her purchases of the Spencer Collection of printed books in 1892, and the Crawford Collection of Western, Near Eastern and Far Eastern manuscripts in 1901, transformed the Library into a scholarly institution of international status. The Library was administered as an independent institution by a Council of Governors and a Board of Trustees. In 1972 the John Rylands Library merged with the Library of Manchester University to form the John Rylands University Library of Manchester, the third largest academic library in the United Kingdom. The original John Rylands Library building now houses the Special Collections Division of the JRULM.

The archives of the John Rylands Library are substantial and comprehensive. They include specifications, plans, accounts and correspondence concerning the original construction of the library (including correspondence between Mrs Rylands and Basil Champneys) and subsequent alterations and enlargements to the building; minute books of the Trustees, Governors, Book Committee and other committees; annual reports and statements of account; ledgers, cash books, petty cash books, wages books, invoices and other financial records; book and manuscript accession registers; letter-books; correspondence with readers, scholars, other institutions and suppliers; applications for readers' tickets; visitors' books; material relating to publications and exhibitions; newspaper cuttings books; and legal papers. As well as illuminating the history of the Library, the archive contains material of interest for wider studies in art history, architectural history, bibliography and 19th-century book-collecting.

Access: by prior permission only. Finding aids: unpublished shelf-list. See also Henry Guppy, *The John Rylands Library, Manchester, 1899–1935: a Brief Record of its History* (Manchester, 1935).

10th-century ivory panel from the covers of a Gospel-book attributed to Trier, Germany. The three panels depict (from the top) the Annunciation, the Nativity and the Baptism of Christ.

MML/4/12

CHURCH LEAGUE FOR WOMEN'S SUFFRAGE
MANCHESTER BRANCH

•

INVITES ALL MEMBERS, SUFFRAGISTS & FRIENDS TO UNITE IN A SPECIAL

SERVICE OF THANKSGIVING

FOR THE NEW POWERS AND RESPONSIBILITIES CONFERRED ON WOMEN AND

THE DEDICATION

OF THESE TO THE

SERVICE OF GOD

AND THE

WELFARE OF MANKIND.

Service will be held in the Cathedral, Manchester on Saturday, February 23rd. at 5 p.m.

Preacher: Rev. CANON GREEN

On the same day there will be Special Celebrations of the Holy Communion at Sacred Trinity Church, Salford, at 7-30 a.m., and in the Cathedral (Derby Chapel,) at 9-30 a.m.

RICHARD BATES, Art Printer, 9-11, Stockton St., Clarendon St., Oxford Rd., Manchester.

INDEX OF COLLECTIONS

GENERAL INDEX

AN ATTEMPT has been made to index all persons, corporate bodies, places and subjects mentioned in the text of the *Guide*. While the index is therefore comprehensive (if not exhaustive) in this respect, researchers are advised that this is not an index to the entire holdings of the Library. Absence from the index does not necessarily imply that a person, place or subject is not represented in the Library's holdings.

Personal, corporate and place names have been constructed in accordance with the National Council on Archives *Rules for the Construction of Personal, Place and Corporate Names* (1997). Dates of birth and death and additional qualifiers are largely derived from the *Dictionary of National Biography*, as well as *Who's Who, Who Was Who*, and other standard reference sources. Sovereigns and members of royal families are indexed under their forenames. Titled persons are indexed under their family name, with a cross reference from the title. Popes are indexed under their papal names. Compound surnames, whether hyphenated or not, are indexed under their final elements. This accords with the practice adopted in the *New Dictionary of National Biography*, and in the NCA *Rules*.

Ordnance Survey National Grid references are given for places within the United Kingdom. Specific places overseas are identified by co-ordinates of latitude and longitude, to the nearest five minutes. The forms of place-names which were contemporary with the original sources have generally been preferred to present-day forms; thus Southern Rhodesia, not Zimbabwe.

Library of Congress Subject Headings, 21st edition (1998), has been used as the basis for the construction of subject index entries, with modifications to take account of local conditions and the primary nature of the materials. Cross references are used extensively to guide the reader from general terms to the more specific, and to navigate between related subjects.

Word-order alphabetization has been used, in this order of predecence: commas, spaces, hyphens, alphanumeric characters. The prefixes Sir, Dame etc. have been ignored in alphabetizing personal names. Thus: *Black, Joseph*; *Black Papers*; *Black-letter*; *Blackburn*.

Grey, Edward (1862–1933), Viscount Grey of
Fallodon, statesman
correspondence with, 105
Grey, George Harry (1737–1819), 5th Earl of
Stamford
papers of, 79
Grey, George Harry (1765–1845), 6th Earl of
Stamford
papers of, 79
Grey, Mary (1704–1772), Countess of Stamford
papers of, 79
Grey, William (1819–1872), Rev.
papers of, 79
Grey family, Earls of Stamford
archives of, 78–9, 84
Grieve, Christopher Murray (1892–1978), Scottish
poet and critic, pseudonym Hugh MacDiarmid
editions of works by, 149
Griffith, Moses (fl 1769–1809), draughtsman and
engraver
books illustrated by, 170
Grimaldi, Giovanni Battista (c 1524–c 1612), Italian
bibliophile
bindings for, 23
Grimm, Samuel Hieronymus (1734–1794), watercolour painter
books illustrated by, 170
Grimond, Joseph (1913–1993), Baron Grimond,
politician
correspondence with, 105
Grimshaw, William (1708–1763), Anglican clergyman
and evangelist
papers of, 55
Grolier de Servieres, Jean (1479–1565), Vicomte
D'Agiusy, French bibliophile
bindings for, 23
Grosmont, Monmouthshire, so 4024
churches and chapels in, 52
Grosvenor, Richard (1795–1869), 2nd Marquis of
Westminster
correspondence with, 76
Gryphius, Sebastian (1491–1556), German printer
books printed by, 20
Guardian newspaper
archive of, 104
cuttings from, 115
editions of, 105
staff, 103, 105, 109, 140, 143, 190
Guarini, Giovanni Battista (1538–1612), Italian
poet
editions of works by, 18, 151
Guicciardini, Piero (1808–1886), member of
Christian Brethren
papers of, 52
Guild of St George
papers re, 142
Guiney, Louise Imogen (d 1920), Anglo-American
writer
correspondence with, 144

Gulliver's Travels
editions of, 151
Gunn, Thomson William (b 1929), Anglo-American
poet
editions of works by, 156
Gusford Hall, Suffolk. *See* St Mary Stoke parish,
Suffolk
Gutenberg, Johann (? 1400–1468), printer
books printed by, 21
Guthrie, Sir William Tyrone (1900–1971), director
and theatre designer
correspondence with, 135
Guttinguer, Ulric (1785–1866), French poet and
man of letters
correspondence with, 138
Gwasg Gregynog
books from, 22
Gwynne family, of Garth, Brecknockshire
papers of, 64
Gynaecology
manuscripts on, 178

Hackney, London, TQ 3484
schools and colleges in, 63
Haddon, Derbyshire. *See* Over Haddon, Derbyshire
Hadfield, Derbyshire, SK 0296
property in, 83
Hadfield family, of Hadfield, Derbyshire
archives of, 83
Hadrian IV (c 1100–1159), Pope
Papal bull from, 82
Haggadah, 39
Hainault, Philippa of. *See* Philippa (c 1314–1369),
consort of Edward III
Hakluyt, Richard (? 1552–1616), geographer
editions of works by, 127
Haldane, Richard Burdon (1856–1928), Viscount
Haldane, statesman
correspondence with, 105
Hale, Bowdon parish, Cheshire, SJ 7786
property in, 79, 86
Hale family
papers of, 75
Halifax, 1st Earl of. *See* Wood, Edward Frederick
Lindley (1881–1959)
Hall, Martha (? 1707–1791), wife of Westley
papers of, 64
Hall family
archives of, 77
papers of, 106
Hallé Orchestra
papers re, 103
Halliday, Michael Frederick (1822–1869), artist
papers re, 165
Hamburger, Michael Peter Leopold (b 1924), poet
and translator
editions of works by, 149
Hamilton, G.W. (1807–1868), Colonel
library of, 33

Padeloup, Antoine Michel (1685–1758), French
    bookbinder
    bindings by, 20
Padiham, Whalley parish, Lancashire, SD 7933
    churches and chapels in, 50
    textile industry in, 109
Padua, Italy, 45°25'N 11°55'E
    printing in, 181
Paediatrics
    manuscripts on, 178
Pakistan
    foundation of, 121
Palestine. *See also* Israel
    description and travel, 127, 165
    history, 107, 186
    views of, 127
Pali literature, 41
Pali manuscripts, 41
Palladio, Andrea (1508–1580), Italian architect and
    writer
    editions of works by, 25, 171
Pallas, Peter Simon (1741–1811), naturalist
    editions of works by, 127
Palm-leaf
    works written on, 40–3
Palmieri, Matteo (1406–1475), Florentine politician
    and author
    editions of works by, 154
Pamphlets, 56, 65, 67–70, 98, 110, 113, 115, 117, 125,
    151, 154, 159, 161, 184, 186. *See also* Tracts
Pandupratapa, 40
Pankhurst, Emmeline (1858–1928), suffragette
    correspondence with, 105, 137
Pannartz, Arnold (fl 1465–1473), printer
    books printed by, 22, 149, 181
Pannington Hall, Suffolk. *See* Wherstead, Suffolk
Paolozzi, Sir Eduardo (b 1924), Scottish sculptor
    sculptural maquette by, 152
Papyri
    Arabic, 36
    Coptic, 37
    Egyptian, 37
    Greek, 30
    Latin, 31
Paramount Famous Lasky Corporation
    papers re, 135
Paris, France, 48°50'N 2°20'E
    Commune, 1871, 138
    documents re, 116
    printing in, 20, 22, 24–5, 153, 155, 182
    trade with Britain, 97
Parker, Agnes Miller (1895–1980), wood-engraver
    books illustrated by, 170
Parker, Louis Napoleon (1852–1944), musician and
    playwright
    correspondence with, 134
Parker, Matthew (1504–1575), Archbishop of
    Canterbury
    editions of works by, 24

Parker family, of Chelford, Cheshire
    archives of, 74
Parkinson, John (1567–1650), apothecary and herbalist
    editions of works by, 183
Parkinson, Roger (b 1939), military historian,
    pseudonym Matthew Holden
    papers of, 124
Parliament. *See under* England *and* Great Britain
Parliamentary Bills and Acts, 78, 86, 90, 98, 188
Parliamentary Committee for Women's Suffrage
    archive of, 110
Parma, Italy, 44°50'N 10°20'E
    printing in, 18, 152
Parsi literature, 41
Parsi manuscripts, 41
Partington, Bowdon parish, Cheshire, SJ 7191
    property in, 79
Partington, James Riddick (1886–1965), chemist and
    historian of science
    book collection of, 183
Pascal, Blaise (1623–1662), French mathematician,
    physicist and philosopher
    editions of works by, 181
Pashto literature, 40
Pashto manuscripts, 40
Passivism, 56. *See also* Conscientious objection
Pasteur, Louis (1822–1895), French chemist and
    microbiologist
    correspondence with, 180
Patents, 92
Patmore, Coventry Kersey Dighton (1823–1896),
    poet
    papers re, 165
Paton College, Nottingham
    archive of, 54
Paul IV (1476–1559), Pope
    Papal bull from, 82
Paul V (1552–1621), Pope
    brief of, 82
Payne, Roger (1738–1797), bookbinder
    bills of, 16
    bindings by, 16, 20
Paz, Octavio (1914–1998), Mexican poet
    editions of works by, 149
    papers re, 142
Peacock, J., Mr
    theatre programmes donated by, 137
Peake, Arthur Samuel (1865–1929), theologian and
    biblical scholar
    papers of, 60
Pearce, A. Preston, of Plymouth, Devon
    book collection of, 116
Pearl Harbour (Hawaii), attack on, 1941, 124
Pearson, J. Arthur (1870–1947), Unitarian minister
    papers of, 60
Pedigrees. *See under* Genealogy
Péladan, Joséphin Aimé (1859–1918), French play-
    wright and novelist
    editions of works by, 154

Pinero, Sir Arthur Wing (1855–1934), playwright
  editions of works by, 156
Pink, W. Duncombe, of Leigh, Lancashire
  papers of, 108
Pinter, Harold (b 1930), playwright
  correspondence with, 136
Piozzi, Hester Lynch (1741–1821), friend of Dr Johnson
  papers of, 144
Piranesi, Giovanni Battista (1720–1778), Italian artist
  engravings by, 163
Pissarro, Lucien (1863–1944), painter, wood-engraver
    and printer
  books illustrated by, 170
Pit Prop Theatre Company, Leigh, Lancashire
  archive of, 141
Pitt-Rivers, Augustus Henry Lane Fox (1827–1900).
    See Rivers, Augustus Henry Lane Fox Pitt-
Pius II (1405–1465), Pope
  Papal bull from, 81
Piyyûtîm, 38–9
Planning
  inquiries, 94
  works on, 171
Plans. *See* Maps and plans
Plant morphogenesis
  papers re, 180
Plassey, Battle of, 1757, 122
Plath, Sylvia (1932–1963), American poet
  editions of works by, 156
  papers of, 133
Plato, Greek philosopher
  editions of works by, 150, 173
Plays. *See* Drama
Plumley, Great Budworth parish, Cheshire, SJ 7175
  Holford in, 76
  property in, 76, 80
Pluscarden Priory, Morayshire, NJ 1457
  charters re, 82
PN Review periodical
  papers re, 133, 142
Poetry
  American, 133–4, 137, 143, 145, 149, 152, 156, 161
  Australian, 149
  Brazilian, 137
  Buginese, 43
  concrete, 137, 152
  English, 61
    14th century, 22
    15th century, 28
    16th century, 160
    17th century, 26, 152, 154, 158–9
    18th century, 18, 64, 75, 129, 144, 151, 153, 170
    19th century, 19, 23, 85, 129, 139, 144, 148,
      160–1, 187, 189
    20th century, 19, 105, 132–4, 136–7, 139, 141–2,
      144–5, 149, 152, 156
    epic, 149, 151, 154, 160
    French, 138, 144, 153
    German, 152

  Greek, 21, 150
  Hindu, 40
  Indian, 133
  Irish, 19, 105, 133, 137, 144, 149
  Italian, 18–19, 23, 31, 146–7, 150–1, 154, 157, 160,
    169
  Japanese, 46
  Javanese, 43
  Kannada, 40
  Latin, 18, 20, 23, 149
  metaphysical, 158
  Mexican, 142, 149
  Parsi, 41
  Pashto, 40
  pastoral, 18, 150–1, 154, 160
  performances, 135
  Persian, 42
  poets' papers, 75, 85, 105, 132–4, 137–9, 141–5, 187,
    189
  poster poems, 137
  Punjabi, 40
  Scottish, 133, 137, 149
  Sinhalese, 40
  Swiss, 137
  Turkish, 44
  Welsh, 133–4, 156
  women poets, 18, 133
Poland
  history, 108
  Jewish community in, 39
  languages, 26
  social life and customs, 39, 108
Police, 105
  parish and township constables, 78, 84
Political history
  China, 103
  Czechoslovakia, 103
  England, 26, 32, 81, 113, 116, 158
  France, 29, 114–15, 123
  Germany, 103, 105
  Great Britain, 26, 28, 56–7, 74, 76, 80, 84–5,
    99–117, 121, 123, 150, 187–9
  India, 103, 121–3, 126
  Ireland, 84, 144, 160
  Italy, 31, 81, 123
  Russia, 103, 105
  Scotland, 113, 117
  Spain, 123
  United States, 103, 159
  USSR, 110
Political science
  papers re, 187, 189
  printed works on, 112–13, 153, 158
  study and teaching, 187
Poll books, 83, 116
  transcripts of, 108
Pollution, 94
  industrial, 176, 180, 184
  smoke nuisance, 56

Taylor, John Edward (1791–1844), founder of the *Manchester Guardian*, 104

Taylor family
papers of, 189

Taylor family, of Shropshire
archives of, 81

Tea trade
papers re, 122

Tealdi, Pietro Ascagno, of Manchester, merchant
business papers of, 97

Tearle, Sir Godfrey Seymour (1884–1953), actor
correspondence with, 134

Technical manuals, 179

Telescopes, 177

Television in education
papers re, 186

Telugu language, 26

Telugu literature, 40

Telugu manuscripts, 40

Tempest, Margaret (d 1982), author and illustrator
books illustrated by, 145

Tenniel, Sir John (1820–1914), artist and cartoonist
books illustrated by, 170

Tennyson, Alfred (1809–1892), 1st Baron Tennyson, poet
correspondence with, 189
editions of works by, 129
forged editions of, 161
papers re, 165

Terence, Roman playwright. *See* Terentius Afer, Publius

Terentius Afer, Publius, Roman playwright
editions of works by, 18

Thackeray, William Makepeace (1811–1863), novelist
editions of works by, 129, 157
letters of, 136

Thai manuscripts, 43

Thailand
languages, 26, 43
literature, 43
religion, 43
social life and customs, 43

Theatre. *See also* Actors and actresses; *and* Drama *for references to the literary aspects of drama*
Australia, 138
children's, 143
design, 139
finance, 134, 136, 141
France, 154
Great Britain, 134–6, 138–41, 143–4, 147, 156
history, 134–6, 138–41, 143–4, 147, 156
in education, 141, 143
Ireland, 136, 138
lighting, 134, 139
photographs, 135, 138–40, 142–3
popular, 141
production and direction, 134–6, 138–9, 141, 154, 156
programmes, 135, 137–8, 140–2, 155

radical, 141
repertory, 134–6, 139–40
reviews, 135, 137, 140
stage-setting and scenery, 134–6, 138–9, 141, 156
theatre-in-the-round, 139
United States, 139

Thebes, Egypt, 25°40'N 32°40'E
papyri from, 37

Thelwall, Runcorn parish, Cheshire, SJ 6587
property in, 76, 78, 86

Theocritus, Greek poet
editions of works by, 150

Theological colleges, 50, 54, 56, 60, 62–5, 67, 70

Theology, 19, 47–71, 137. *See also* Christianity; Devotional literature; Ecumenism; Nonconformity; Protestantism; Puritanism; Reformation; Sermons and sermon notes
controversial literature, 69–70, 113, 116, 148
feminist, 65
printed works on, 24, 26, 112–13, 116, 152
socialist, 57, 65

Thera, Mayurapada
manuscript of work by, 40

Thermodynamics
research, 175

Therunnanse, Karatota
manuscript of work by, 40

Theses, 175, 184

Thin films
study and teaching, 177

Thomas, Dylan Marlais (1914–1953), poet
editions of works by, 156

Thomas, Ronald Stuart (b 1913), Welsh poet
editions of works by, 156
papers of, 133

Thomas Botfield & Co., coal and iron company
archive of, 91

Thompson, Francis (1859–1907), poet and prose writer
editions of works by, 160

Thompson, George (1804–1878), anti-slavery campaigner
papers of, 104

Thompson, Henry (1797–1878), clergyman and writer
correspondence with, 187

Thompson, William (1775–1833), political economist
editions of works by, 112

Thomson, James (1700–1748), poet
editions of works by, 151

Thomson, Sir Joseph John (1856–1940), physicist
editions of works by, 173

Thomson, W.T., artist
portrait miniature by, 136

Thomson Byrom Collection, 86

Thorndike, Dame Agnes Sybil (1882–1976), actress
correspondence with, 134, 137, 140

Thornton, Robert John (? 1768–1837), botanical and medical writer
editions of works by, 183

William Caxton's
printer's device, from
Guy de Roye,
Doctrinal of Sapyence
(Westminster: 1489).
(*See page 22*)